△△△△△△

DAHCOTAH

or, *Life and Legends of the Sioux*

DAHCOTAH

or, Life and Legends of the Sioux

around Fort Snelling

BY MARY HENDERSON EASTMAN

PREFACE BY RENA NEUMANN COEN

ILLUSTRATED FROM DRAWINGS BY CAPTAIN SETH EASTMAN

AFTON HISTORICAL SOCIETY PRESS

AFTON, MINNESOTA

DAHCOTAH; OR,
LIFE AND LEGENDS OF THE SIOUX
was first published by John Wiley,
New York, in 1849.

New material © 1995 Afton Historical Society Press

Library of Congress Catalog Number 95-077777
ISBN 0-9639338-5-X

Sarah P. Rubinstein edited
Rena Neumann Coen's Preface.
Clerical support for this book project was
provided by Mary Susan Englund.

FRONTISPIECE:
The St. Peters River near its Confluence with the Mississippi,
watercolor on paper, 1848.

PUBLISHER'S NOTE

"MY BOOK IS OUT at last," Mary Eastman wrote on April 30, 1849, to her friend Henry Sibley in Mendota (a fur trading settlement at the junction of the St. Peter's and the Mississippi rivers, across from Fort Snelling). "I believe father has sent you a copy from New York where he is at present on a medical board."

There were two mistakes in the book, Mrs. Eastman informed Sibley (who would become the first governor of the state of Minnesota). "On the eighth page [p. 6 this edition], *captain* of the post should read *chaplain* of the post." This was bad enough, but the second error embarrassed her even more.

> On the 12th page [p. 10] . . . the expression "my piano and singing" should read "my singing." We suppose this ludicrous error must have occurred in this way. Father copied the manuscript for me, I being occupied with the care of my little Frank, and he knowing we sent a piano west and not remembering it was sunk in the Ohio River, must have introduced "the piano" himself. . . . I write you this, knowing that you will make these remarks to persons who may read it at Fort Snelling and the neighbourhood—and it will prevent their thinking I wished to make any pretensions."

Having finally vindicated Mary by pointing out these small flaws in the original book, we will go on to say that, in an attempt to preserve the flavor of this frontier classic, except for obvious typos, we have not attempted to correct or update the spelling or punctuation contained in it.

Dahcotah; or, Life and Legends of the Sioux presents an unparalleled glimpse into Sioux (Dakota) customs and manners by a writer who had the advantage of long-term residency among the Indians. The wife of army officer and illustrator Captain Seth Eastman, Mary Eastman gathered the material for this book during their seven years in the 1840s at Fort Snelling in what became Minnesota Territory.

The new Preface is a biographical essay about Mary Eastman by Rena Neumann Coen, Professor Emerita of art history at St. Cloud State University, who brought to this project a longtime interest in Mary Eastman. Dr. Coen's many books include *Painting and Sculpture in Minnesota, 1820-1914* and *In the Mainstream: The Art of Alexis Jean Fournier (1865-1948)*.

The watercolor illustrations are by Seth Eastman (see *Seth Eastman: A Portfolio of North American Indians*, Afton Historical Society Press, 1995). The two plates illustrating Dr. Coen's Preface (*Indians Courting* and *Wenona's Leap*) are used courtesy of W. Duncan MacMillan. Transparencies for the balance of the Seth Eastman illustrations were furnished by the Minnesota Historical Society.

The latter illustrations are all small watercolor paintings, each only approximately 4 $^1/_2$ inches by 7 inches. They are part of a once-lost portfolio of miniature landscapes that Seth Eastman painted of the unspoiled Mississippi River between 1846 and 1848. Concerning their quality, art historian John Francis McDermott wrote (in *Seth Eastman's Mississippi: A Lost Portfolio Recovered*, University of Illinois Press, 1973):

> So small that they might have been painted with the aid of a jeweler's glass, so sharply distinct that the artist might have been viewing the scenes through a telescope, so sensitive in the use of atmosphere, so delicate in their tints, these pictures are a glowing triumph [for Eastman].

PUBLICATION OF this beautiful new edition of *Dahcotah; or, Life and Legends of the Sioux* was made possible by the generosity of W. Duncan MacMillan of Wayzata, Minnesota. It is dedicated to the memory of his wife of forty-two years, Sarah Stevens MacMillan, a longtime friend of the arts in Minnesota, who died while the book was in production.

Patricia Condon Johnston
June 1995

PREFACE

MARY HENDERSON EASTMAN
A Biographical Essay

ᴀᴀᴀᴀᴀ

RENA NEUMANN COEN

WHEN MARY HENDERSON EASTMAN arrived at
Fort Snelling (near present-day Minneapolis) on September 30, 1841, she was
about to embark on the defining experience of her life. At the age of twenty-
three she was already a wife and the mother of three children. The family was
accompanying Captain Seth Eastman of Company D, First United States
Infantry, who was beginning his second tour of duty at the fort and assuming
command of the post.

Mary's first reaction to the Indians she saw around Fort Snelling was one
of fear. "Their tall, unbending forms," she wrote, "their savage hauteur, the
piercing black eye, the quiet indifference of manner . . . how different were
they from the eastern Indians." Although the yells she heard outside the
high walls of the fort initially filled her with apprehension, she soon grew
accustomed to them and "to all other occasional Indian excitements, that
served to vary the monotony of garrison life" (p. 5). In fact, she discovered in
herself an abiding and sympathetic interest in the Indians, so that she
attempted to learn their language and especially the songs they sang at their
dances. Unfortunately, Little Hill, the Dakota leader who undertook to teach
her, was "a famous singer, but with little perseverance as a teacher of music.
He soon lost all patience with me," Mary admitted, and "refused to continue
the lesson, declaring that he could never make me sing like a Sioux squaw"
(p. 10). In spite of her failure, the Indians readily answered the many
questions she put to them about their laws, their religious beliefs, and their
legends. As they sat by the fire and smoked their pipes, they recounted to

her the stories of the Great Spirit, of Haokah the giant, and the power of the sacred medicine. These stories and others she gathered and retold in her published writings. Indeed, Mary Eastman, who would probably not have known the term had she heard it, was an early ethnologist who deserves recognition for her perceptive curiosity about Indian life and for the sympathy and diligence with which she recorded it.

As is the case with many nineteenth-century women, not much is known about Mary's early life, or even much that is personal in her later life. Women's lives were seen within the context of the destinies of men. As historian Carolyn Heilbrun has observed, to be a woman meant "putting a man at the center of one's life and to allow to occur only what honors his prime position."[1] The result was that the subject's own desires and quests were secondary. Biographers of these women must not only choose one interpretation of their subjects over another but, far more difficult, reinvent the lives their subjects led, discovering from what evidence they can find the processes and decisions, the choices, and the unique experiences that lay within the life stories. In Mary Eastman's case, the absence of dates, and even of documented events, forces one to glean what one can from her writings, both about her own life as well as about her attitudes toward herself and others. Fortunately Mary was never one to keep her opinions to herself, and a careful reading of what she wrote reveals much about her personality and history. What emerges is a person who was in some ways almost paradigmatic for her time and social position but in crucial other instances far ahead of it, particularly in her acute observations about the Indians she met and the white men who interacted with them.

Mary even disclosed, occasionally and with some degree of ambivalence, early feminist thoughts, remarking disapprovingly on women's subservient position in a male-dominated Indian society. Although she compared that society unfavorably with her own in this respect, she was well aware of the dominant position of men in her own society, too. "I have sometimes thought that if, when a warrior, be he chief or commoner throws a stick of wood at his wife's head, she were to cast it back at his, he might, perhaps, be taught better behaviour." But Mary was a sensible person and, although she may have been tempted to do so, she refrained from instilling "such insubordinate notions into the heads of my Sioux female friends, lest some ultra 'brave,' in a desperate rage, might substitute the tomahawk for the log." She was also cognizant that "these opinions, too, might have made me unpopular with Sioux and Turks—and, perchance, with some of my more enlightened friends, who are self-constituted 'lords of creation'" (p. 9).

Such a readiness to speak her mind forthrightly was characteristic of Mary, and it astonished the Indian men who were accustomed to a different manner in their women. Mary wrote that, although surprised "at the boldness with which I reproved them," it nevertheless "raised me much in their estimation." In fact, on one occasion one of the Dakota leaders, whom she had taken to task rather frequently, expressed an interest in having her for a wife. She commented "that I did not fancy having my head split open every few days with a stick of wood" (p. 9).

In addition to speaking her mind, another of Mary's attributes was an abundance of physical and mental energy. Besides the care of her children and her writing, she helped her husband sell his paintings. Moreover, she was instrumental in, if not mainly responsible for, his receiving the commission from the United States government to illustrate Henry Rowe Schoolcraft's monumental work, *The History, Condition and Prospects of the Indian Tribes of the United States,* published under the direction of the secretary of war and the commissioner of Indian affairs.

MARY HENDERSON was born at Warrenton, Fauquier County, Virginia, in 1818. She was the fifth daughter and sixth of the nine children of Dr. Thomas Henderson (1787-1854) and Anna Maria Truxton Henderson (1792-1857). Her early childhood, "that calm and pleasant period of my life,"[2] was spent in Virginia where her father, a graduate in medicine from the University of Pennsylvania (1809), practiced before moving with his family to Washington, D.C., to become a professor in the medical department of Columbian College. Her mother came from a prominent Philadelphia family. She was the daughter of Commodore Thomas Truxton, a well-known naval officer whose own forebears had fought in the American Revolutionary War.[3] It was probably in Washington that Mary received her schooling, a good education as shown by the literary facility she subsequently demonstrated.

On December 31, 1832, Dr. Henderson was appointed assistant surgeon of the United States Army, and the Henderson family moved to the Military Academy at West Point. It was there that Mary met Seth Eastman, a native of

Maine, who had graduated from West Point in 1829 and had returned there in 1833 as assistant teacher of drawing. He was already an experienced military man, having served several tours of duty at Fort Crawford (near present-day Prairie du Chien, Wisconsin), at Fort Snelling, and briefer tours in the Seminole Wars in Florida and in Louisiana and Connecticut.

In 1835 Mary Henderson and Seth Eastman married at West Point. The exact date of the wedding is unknown.[4] As a later writer observed in a memorial following Eastman's death, from Eastman's alliance with Mary Henderson "to the end of his life, he reaped the fruits of sympathy with a cultivated mind, in full accord with his own in all his most cherished studies."[5]

Six children were born of the marriage. The three eldest, Robert Langdon, Thomas Henderson, and Virginia Henderson, accompanied their parents to Fort Snelling. Two more sons, Frank Smith and Mac Henderson, were born at the fort. A sixth child and fifth son was born several years later.

Seth Eastman was not only a military man but also a gifted artist, who recorded the life of the Dakota Indians. The drawing pad and pencil were never far from his hand, and his formidable body of work shows a dispassionate eye and a skillful hand. But if her husband accurately portrayed the appearance of the Dakota, their dress, their council meetings, their buffalo hunts and ceremonial dances, it was Mary who sympathetically preserved the colorful and profoundly revealing stories and legends that were so much a part of the Dakota way of life.

Mary was much impressed by the scenic beauty of the site, which is at the confluence of the Mississippi and Minnesota (then called the St. Peters) rivers. Because of the fort's stone construction and its position on a commanding bluff above the rivers, she thought it had "somewhat the appearance of an old German castle, or one of the strongholds on the Rhine" (p. 1).

Her new home was a small but comfortable house in the southeast corner of the fort. Built on the slope of the bluff, it commanded a view of the surrounding plains and the two rivers below. The main floor had a central hall dividing four rooms, two on each side, each with its own large fireplace. An attic, or loft, provided sleeping accommodations for the children, servants, and frequent visitors. The kitchen and a room apparently used as an office were below the main floor but were light and airy because of the house being built into the bluff.[6] The structure seems to have been the work of a master mason. Unlike the other more primitive fort buildings, it had well-cut and finished stonework, and the facade made an effort to bow to the prevailing architectural styles. Sometime after 1835 but before the Eastmans' arrival, a one-story portico with four simple rectangular Doric columns was added. Four flat pilaster strips, echoing the columns, were placed where the portico met the stone wall of the building, giving it a vaguely Federal appearance. This style was further invoked in the graceful fanlight over the double entry doors, even though the pointed arched panes in the fan window were in the gothic manner that was more common in the 1830s and 1840s. A stepped gable over the entry porch gave it further emphasis and recalled the Dutch or Flemish style of the mansions of the Hudson River Valley.

Much less is known about the interior of the house. Some years after Mary left Fort Snelling, however, she described in her book, *Aunt Phillis's Cabin,* a military station in the north, "in the season when there is three feet of snow and winter's bleakest winds,"[7] without a doubt referring to the winter she knew at Fort Snelling. But in Mary's novel, the bleakness of the out-of-doors "did not inconvenience the company assembled in the comfortable parlor" of the captain's quarters, "with a coal grate almost as large as the room and the curtains closely drawn over the windows." Mrs. Moore, the captain's fictional wife, was "reduced to the utmost extremity of her wits to make the room look modern, but it is astonishing, the genius of army ladies for putting the best foot forward."[8] Whether modern or not, the captain's wife was successful in making the parlor cozy and attractive, indeed, "the very realization of home comfort. The lounge by the three windows was covered with a small figured French chintz and it was a delightful seat or bed as the occasion required. She had the legs of several of the chairs sawed off, and made cushions for them, covered with pieces of the chintz left over from the lounge. The arm chairs that looked at each other from either side of the fireplace, not being of velvet, were made it sit in," proving that Mrs. Moore (or Mary) was a practical home decorator with an eye toward comfort rather than display. One amenity that Mrs. Moore's parlor contained and Mary's did not was a piano. Mary liked to sing and accompany herself on the piano, and the Eastmans had shipped a piano west when they moved to Fort Snelling. On the way, however, it was lost in the Ohio River.[9]

The description of Mrs. Moore's parlor somehow rings true for Mary Eastman's parlor, especially as she identifies Mrs. Moore as an "industrious, intelligent southern woman." A further clue can be deduced from the comment that the captain's wife had an aversion to dogs. Mary was afraid of dogs and disliked them, as she later admitted. Furthermore, Mrs. Moore also had an antipathy to Yankees, as Mary's Virginia birth would have predisposed her to do. But Mrs. Moore's (and Mary's) dislike of dogs and Yankees suddenly disappeared when "she fell desperately in love with the Captain (a Yankee)" and allowed "his great Newfoundland dog . . . to lick her hand and rest his cold black nose on her lap." There were other objects of comfort and decoration in the parlor, too, including a rug, which the dog "thought had been purchased for him," nice china candlesticks on the mantelpiece, a silver urn that had been Mrs. Moore's great-grandmother's and "a lard lamp which lit up everything astonishingly."

Nor were the meals served in the captain's quarters of a Spartan sort either. The company Mary described "had just returned from the dining room where they had dined on cold turkey and mince pies . . . [and they] were in an exceedingly high state of health and spirits." Mary, by this account, was hardly condemned to an austere and comfortless domestic life in the frontier post. Neither was she entirely cut off from white civilization, for by 1841 steamboats were plying the Mississippi, bringing travelers from the east and regularly delivering mail.

When Mary Eastman settled down to her life at Fort Snelling she found another child of her husband's there. This situation was far from unique. The officers and men at the frontier posts who came out before they were married or before their wives joined them were hardly celibate. Many of them formed relationships with Indian women who bore them children. Although Seth Eastman's first tour of duty at Fort Snelling was of relatively short duration, it was long enough for him to form a relationship with Stands Like a Spirit, daughter of Cloud Man, a leader of the Mdewakanton Dakota village at Lake Calhoun. The result of the liaison was a daughter, Mary Nancy, who was also known as Wenona, in accordance with the Dakota custom of giving a first-born daughter that name. Mary Nancy, or Nancy as she was called, was born in 1831. Her son Charles later confirmed this year for her birth, saying that "not long after" his mother's birth, Eastman was ordered to the Seminole War in Florida, and he left in November 1831.

How much Mary knew of her husband's eldest daughter and whether she learned of the girl's existence before or after arriving at the fort are matters of speculation. Although the men made no secret of their children—after all, everyone at the fort knew who they were and who their fathers were—one can be curious about their reception by the white wives of their fathers and how the children were treated by these women.

The only record of any sort of the relationship between Mary and Nancy occurs in a puzzling reference to Mary in a letter from George Turner, the army surgeon at Fort Snelling, to William C. Baker, dated January 16, 1848. Turner mentioned that when scarlet fever struck Mary and the Eastman children—Virginia was seriously ill—that "Mrs. Eastman sent for Mary [Nancy?] to come quick to take charge of the sick child and seemed willing to resign herself totally to an enemy's care and Mary [Nancy] has not neglected her charge. It was a strange scene and one which I hope will teach Mrs. E. a salutary lesson."[10] It is conceivable that the older woman and the young girl had exchanged some heated words or Mary may have been jealous of the affection that, according to a tradition in Cloud Man's family, Seth Eastman continued to show toward his eldest daughter.[11] It is even possible that George Turner bore some animosity toward Mary. Whatever the case, Mary and Nancy Eastman were apparently well acquainted and, in the crisis of her daughter's illness, it was Nancy to whom Mary turned for help, which seems to have been willingly given.

Mary's relationship with the Dakota was warm. From the first, those who had known Eastman a decade earlier were eager to shake hands with "Eastman's squaw." They brought their wives and children to see her, and there was a good deal of visiting back and forth with the Dakota in their villages. The Indians seemed to view the fact that Mary was writing about them in a positive light. Her task was made easier by the strong friendships she formed with many of them, particularly the women. During the bout with scarlet fever, a number of Dakota women crept noiselessly into Virginia's room and watched and wept beside her. "They leaned over the foot of the bed; their expressive and subdued countenances full of sorrow." Later they told Mary that "much water fell from their eyes, day and night, while they thought she would die" (p. 8). One Dakota woman in particular, Old Harper or Harpstinah, who wore a necklace made of the hands and feet of Ojibwa children (the Ojibwa were the Dakotas' implacable enemies), was especially devoted to the child, and when everyone else was exhausted from the constant care she needed, Harpstinah offered to sit up with her and tend the fire. Mary agreed, and while she lay down near her daughter to rest, she watched the Dakota woman. She later wrote, "I was far away from the home of my childhood, and a Sioux woman, with her knife in her belt, was assisting me in the care of my only daughter" (p. 8). (It is interesting that Mary made no mention here of Nancy Eastman as a care giver for the critically ill Virginia.)

After the family recovered from the fever, Mary returned to collecting and writing down the legends of the Dakota. In her descriptions, she tried to be both realistic and compassionate. On the one hand, she viewed them as ignorant, idolatrous, and savage and unflinchingly portrayed the violence of their lives, but she also saw a noble and dignified people, degenerating and losing its proud spirit as a result of white encroachment. She wanted to memorialize what she perceived as a people sadly doomed to perish from the earth. Mary observed of the Dakota men that they were handsome and intelligent until they were corrupted by contact with the whites (p. 3-4). While the Indians' had a reputation for violence, Mary pointed out that the history of Euro–Americans was replete with instances of bloodshed (p. 71).

Mary closely identified with the Dakota women, whose role in Indian society she particularly deplored. Describing the hard life of the Indian woman who was nevertheless welcoming and hospitable, she pitied the burdens of life that made her look old before her time. "Labor and privation," she observed, "are not preservative of beauty" (p. 4).

Mary's particular friend among the Dakota, the one who told her many of the stories and legends of her people, was Chequered Cloud, a medicine woman and legend teller. Mary called her a "prophetess of the forest" and promised her readers to be true to her informant's words (p. 30). This medicine woman was a remarkable person—tall and still possessed of a graceful dignity. More than "seventy winters had passed over her" when Mary first met her and became her friend, "but the brightness of her eye is undimmed by time, and her brow speaks of intellect." Although all of

Chequered Cloud's loved ones, including her children, had died, she still went from tepee to tepee, seeking to cure her friends (p. 27). She came often to visit Mary, smoke her pipe, and tell her the stories of her people so that she, in turn, would tell her friends about the Dakota and their legends (p. 30).

By 1848 Mary had a publisher for the legends of the Dakota. She also had illustrations, four lithographs after her husband's paintings, to offer with them. In a letter to Henry Lewis, their good friend and a painter of some note, she wrote that "Mr. Wiley is to publish my book and on better terms than I had any reason to expect, since I was 'all unknown to fame' . . . I should, I acknowledge, be gratified to gain a little reputation and I am sincere in the hope that more will be taught of doing good to the sufferers in our country than formerly. I feel a strong attachment to my old Indian friends for their own sakes as well as for their beautiful country. I aim at describing nature and her children who have truly been guided by her light."[12] Mary also remarked that she could now get constant employment by writing for papers or magazines but that she had in mind another volume about the Indians.

Mary's literary career was launched with the April 1849 publication of *Dahcotah; Life and Legends of the Sioux Around Fort Snelling*. The event brought Mary the kind of invitation she was hoping for. She was immediately asked to contribute to *The Iris, An Illuminated Souvenir* for 1852. This magazine, edited by John S. Hart and published by Lippincott, Grambo and Company in Philadelphia, was a widely circulated women's journal containing essays, stories, poems, and some illustrations. For Mary's contribution of eighteen stories and poems (some of the stories retold legends that had already appeared in *Dahcotah*), her husband supplied eight illuminations in the form of chromolithographs based on his paintings. Perhaps the most interesting of these were *Indian Courting* (fig. 1) and *Marriage Customs of the Indians*. There was also a landscape of *Wenona's Leap* (fig. 2), sometimes called *Maiden Rock*, a steep and rocky promontory on the Wisconsin side of the Mississippi River, a few miles below the widening of the river at Lake Pepin.

Meanwhile, the Eastmans' residence at Fort Snelling had ended. At the end of the summer of 1848, Captain Eastman received orders reassigning him to duty in Texas. Quite reluctantly, the family packed their belongings, bid

farewell to their friends, both white and Indian, and embarked on the steamboat, *Dr. Franklin*, for St. Louis. There they parted company, the captain to proceed to Texas and Mary to head east to New England with their five children, her head still filled with memories of the time she had spent at Fort Snelling, listening to and writing down the legends and stories of the Dakota.

1. *Indian Courting*, watercolor on paper, ca. 1852.

Although Mary was "quite distraught" at the prospect of "parting with my old man"[13] in St. Louis, she had little time to grieve. The children needed her attention, and she had other matters to attend to as well. Henry Lewis was in St. Louis, painting his panorama of the Mississippi River from the Falls of St. Anthony to New Orleans. Mary may have wanted to discuss a partnership that he had earlier proposed to Eastman to collaborate on the panorama, which was a large, continuous painting, many yards in length that was wound on two rollers, to be unrolled, for a fee, before an audience. This type of "moving picture" was a popular form of entertainment in the mid-nineteenth

2. Wenona's Leap: Lake Pepin, Miss. River, watercolor on paper, ca. 1852.

century, and many artists used it to make money on their art. Lewis had proposed that he paint the landscape background of the panorama and Eastman contribute the Indian figures to the work. In the end, Eastman decided against such a collaboration and stayed with his Indian paintings, but the proposal may still have been open when Mary was in St. Louis.

Lewis also had in his St. Louis studio several Eastman canvases that he was attempting to sell for his friend. The paintings had been there for some time, and it is possible that Mary intended to pick up some of the pictures and drop them off at the Western Art Union in Cincinnati on her way east. She was now following still another career, for, however informal it may have been, she was acting as her husband's business agent for the sale of his paintings. Eastman did not intend to live by his art or use his paintings "to accumulate gold" since he considered himself essentially a soldier.[14] Nevertheless he needed income from his paintings because his officer's pay was far from lavish, and he had five children to support and educate. Mary carried on a lengthy business correspondence with Colonel Warner, head of the Art Union branch in Cincinnati, where she succeeded in selling a number of paintings.

The American Art Union, which also had branches in Philadelphia and Boston, was in essence a lottery open to all who paid an annual membership fee, and the prizes were original works of art. The annual drawing for the lottery was held with some ceremony, and the winner received one of a number of oil paintings purchased by the Art Union for that purpose. The Art Union was immensely successful, and at one point had sixteen thousand subscribers. Before it went out of existence in 1852, it had distributed some 2,400 paintings and also 150,000 engravings of paintings of popular interest that went to all the subscribers who had not won the grand prize of an original painting. No wonder then that Mary was eager to take her husband's paintings there.

After dropping her husband's pictures off in Cincinnati, Mary and the children continued on their journey east.   By the time they reached New York, Mary was "half dead," as she wrote to Henry Lewis.[15] Mac Henderson, her youngest child, had caught the mumps on leaving Cincinnati and was seriously ill.   Frank, too, came down with the disease and was quite sick when they arrived in New Hampshire. By January, however, when she was writing to Lewis, both boys were convalescing. Mac was staying with his grandfather, Dr. Henderson, who was then stationed in Portsmouth, and Mary, Frank, and Virginia were with Captain Eastman's father near Concord. The two older boys, Robert Langdon and Thomas Henderson, were boarding in the town of Concord and going to school.

Mary was still busy, trying to sell more of her husband's paintings through correspondence with Colonel Warner, to whom she occasionally conveyed some personal information as well. She wrote him from New London, Connecticut, on June 27, 1849, of a disastrous fire in St. Louis the previous May 17 that involved heavy losses for the Eastmans. But she did not go into any detail about what was lost, so it is impossible to know whether the fire destroyed their furniture and household effects that were warehoused in St. Louis or some of Seth Eastman's paintings.

During the years that Mary was negotiating with the Art Union, she was also deeply involved in obtaining for her husband the prize she was convinced would crown his achievement as the premier painter of the Indians of the United

States. For that effort she felt she had to be where she could exert the most influence in the pursuit of that goal—Washington, D.C.

It is not known exactly when the Eastmans established residence in Washington. The city directories do not list them until 1853, although Mary indicated in a letter dated March 16, 1856, to Benjamin Pringle, member of Congress from New York and chairman of the Committee on Indian Affairs, that they had been living in Washington for five years. Even before that, however, they had been intermittently resident in the nation's capital since the end of 1849 or the beginning of 1850. Their sixth child, a boy, was born in Washington in 1851.[16]

Mary's goal was to have her husband reassigned to duty in the Office of Indian Affairs to work on Schoolcraft's *Indian Tribes of the United States,* which was published in Philadelphia by Lippincott, Grambo and Company in 1851-57. Congress authorized the work on March 3, 1847, and directed the Office of Indian Affairs to collect information on the Indian tribes. Schoolcraft, known as an explorer and prolific writer about the Indians and their myths and legends as well as the namer of Lake Itasca (headwaters of the Mississippi River), was chosen to gather the material and write the report. The task of illustrating the work, however, remained unassigned. John S. Robb, a reporter for the *St. Louis Reveille* who had admired Eastman's Indian paintings at Fort Snelling, was sure that Eastman would be the best choice for that job. Eastman, himself, thought so, ever since he had received a circular from Schoolcraft requesting information on the Indians of the Upper Mississippi.

Eastman's initial request to the Office of Indian Affairs to be transferred to Washington "to the duty of painting, if the work being compiled on the North American Indians is to be illustrated with engravings" was, after a good deal of bureaucratic shuffling, denied. But Mary, if not Seth, was not willing to take no for an answer. While her husband was fulfilling his duties in Texas, she took up his cause with all the determination and perseverance of which she was capable. Although her husband was refused a transfer, he could still apply for a furlough, and she turned to their friend, Henry H. Sibley, delegate to Congress from Minnesota Territory, for help. She sent him letter after letter, alternately badgering him and pleading with him to use his influence in getting her husband transferred or furloughed. "I know political influence does everything now-a-days," she wrote, "and I expect you to succeed at least in getting the furlough—my organ of hope, you see, is very large."[17] Sibley eventually acted on Mary's request, writing on February 5, 1849, to the secretary of war (who then had jurisdiction over the Office of Indian Affairs), urging that Eastman be granted a leave of absence to work on Indian subjects for the government. Although this application, too, was turned down, Eastman was nevertheless granted five month's leave. How this came about is not quite clear, but Mary thought that Sibley was responsible for obtaining the leave, and she promptly thanked him on April 30, 1849, "for the kind interest" he took in Captain Eastman's affairs. She wrote him that "it was through you, I know, that he was so handsomely spoken of in the house and Senate also."[18] Indeed, Mary was so grateful that she dedicated *Dahcotah* not only to her parents but also to Sibley for "his many acts of friendship."

A number of crises, including a cholera epidemic that was raging in Texas and that took the life of Eastman's second in command, delayed the captain's departure for the east until September. He went first to Washington to report and then was free to join Mary, probably at New London, where she was staying with her father, who was then stationed there. The lengthy family visits also included Concord, New Hampshire, to see the Eastman family and then to Lexington, Virginia, to see Mary's sister, Sarah, and her husband, Colonel Francis Henney Smith. Two sketches drawn by Eastman of Virginia Military Institute and the town of Lexington are dated December 1 and December 5, 1849.

At the end of December 1849 or the beginning of January 1850, Captain Eastman reported to the Office of Indian Affairs to start work on the Schoolcraft project. At the beginning of their relationship, the Eastmans and the Schoolcrafts seem to have been on good terms with each other, and for a while they were even next door neighbors on E Street. Eastman, in fact, did much more for Schoolcraft than simply illustrate his work. Schoolcraft, crippled by lameness and also frequently absent for extended periods when he went to Philadelphia to oversee Lippincott and Grambo's production of what he was pleased to call "his great national work," left the job of running the office, handling routine correspondence, and in general "minding the shop" to a willing and cooperative Eastman, who still found the time to turn out suitable illustrations. And Mary, too, was initially pleased with the situation and arranged several social events. On one occasion she invited a visiting delegation of Dakota men to evening tea where she surprised and delighted them with conversation in Dakota.[19]

Schoolcraft's impossible ego and his wife's imperious and slightly ridiculous self-aggrandizement eventually led to a coolness between the two couples, which became a definite chill when Schoolcraft attempted to take all the credit for the project, according Eastman only grudging recognition for his work. Mary's jealousy was fanned by her awareness that Schoolcraft's government funding was quite generous (even though he believed he deserved more) while Eastman's work was being done for his regular army pay, barely adequate for the high cost of living in Washington. But the last straw was Schoolcraft's assumption that Eastman's plates for the engravings belonged to him to use as he saw fit, without regard to Eastman's claims as the artist. Eventually, without Eastman's knowledge or consent, Congress issued the copyright for Schoolcraft's work, together with the plates made for it, to Mrs. Schoolcraft, and although Mary later tried to press the Eastmans' claim to them, Congress took no action and let the matter stand.

While she was busy defending her husband's claims and also pressing for his permanent reassignment to Washington, Mary was continuing her career as a writer. As she wrote to Benjamin Pringle on March 16, 1856, "However one may love art . . . one must eat and be clothed, and so must one's children—and wife. . . . During the whole time of our residence in Washington, I have had, by excessive application, to apply to their utmost use, such slight abilities as I may possess, in order that we may live here."[20]

She contributed stories and poems to *The Iris* and other magazines and published some novels through Lippincott and Grambo. Mary's most immediately successful book commercially was written in 1852. From June 1851 to April 1852, Harriet Beecher Stowe's antislavery novel, *Uncle Tom's Cabin*, had been running in serial form in the *Washington National Era*, and in March 1852 it came out as a book. Only five months later, her sentiments as a Virginia-born lady outraged by Stowe's abolitionist novel, Mary interrupted her Indian writings to rush into print *Aunt Phillis's Cabin; or Southern Life as It Really Is*. It contained a few illustrations, but they were not by her husband. Mary's book enjoyed immediate popularity in spite of the thinness of its plot and its unpersuasive arguments. Three thousand copies were sold on the day of its publication and ten thousand more within two weeks.[21] *Aunt Phillis's Cabin* was widely reviewed, both in the North and in the South, and although some critics found it "truthful in its portrayal of southern characters and manners" and claimed that "it represented many delightful pictures of society," even the friendliest reviewers noted that it bore "the evident marks of haste."[22] None felt that it ranked very high as a novel. Mary's novel lacks the passion, excitement, and sustainable plot that characterize Stowe's work. It failed even to keep up with Mary's earlier books.

Although *Aunt Phillis's Cabin* defended slavery as an institution sanctioned by both the Bible and the Constitution of the United States, Mary herself had doubts about it. She termed it "necessary; though an evil, it cannot be dispensed with."[23] This ambivalence occurs throughout the book as, for example, in the appalling story of Aunt Peggy. A slave and a bitter old woman, Aunt Peggy tells of the time when, as a young woman, she was kidnapped from her home in Africa by a black man and endured the fearsome voyage across the Atlantic Ocean.[24] Elsewhere Mary had her hero, Mr. Weston, state that "I have thought a great deal on the condition of the negroes in our country. . . . I would like to see every man and woman that God has made free. . . . Slavery is a curse on the master as well as the slave,"[25] a sentiment he repeats several times through the course of the book.[26] Nevertheless Mr. Weston is a slave owner, rationalizing that slavery is an economic necessity in the South. "In the North," he observes, "slavery was useless; nay more, it was a drawback to this section of the Union—therefore it was dispensed with. . . . The secret of Northern emancipation: they were relieved of the necessity of slavery."[27] Mr. Weston is well aware of the cruelty of slavery. When Lucy, his niece and ward, protests that slave children are sometimes sold away from their mothers and that she cannot imagine anyone so inhuman as to separate mother and child, he replies that although "it is the worst feature in slavery, and the state should provide laws to prevent it . . . such a circumstance is very uncommon."[28]

As she had already indicated in *Dahcotah*, Mary revealed herself as an incipient feminist and advocate for women's rights. In a passage that compared women with slaves, she wrote that St. Paul exhorted wives to be obedient to their husbands and servants to be obedient to their masters. But, she observed, "St. Paul did not take into consideration . . . women's rights. This is the era of mental and bodily emancipation. Take advantage of it, wives and negroes! But alas for the former: there is no society formed for their benefit; their day of deliverance has not yet formed and until its first gleamings arise in the east they must wear their chains."[29] One wonders how much Mary had heard of the fledgling Women's Rights Movement led by Elizabeth Cady Stanton, Lucretia

Mott, and Susan B. Anthony that had held its first convention in Seneca Falls, New York, on July 19, 1848. The Women's Rights Movement was closely tied to the abolitionist societies and held views diametrically opposed to Mary's as expressed in *Aunt Phillis's Cabin*. Mary was ambivalent about women's rights altogether because she still advocated a degree of obedience and submission for both slave and woman as "necessary for all order and good arrangement in the minor relations of life and [for] the comfort of society."[30]

Some years after the publication of *Aunt Phillis's Cabin*, Mary Eastman must have looked on with some degree of satisfaction at the discomfiture of her rival in literary ambition, Mary Howard Schoolcraft. Southern-born Mary Schoolcraft wrote a proslavery novel in 1860, entitled *The Black Gauntlet; A Tale of Plantation Life in South Carolina*, and she asked Lippincott, Grambo and Company to publish it. Because it lacked any literary merit and was essentially a "shapeless, grotesquely self indulgent exercise in conceit [with] no plot, no point, no character,"[31] it is not surprising that Lippincott turned her down. She eventually paid for its publication herself.

Mary Eastman seems to have modified her proslavery views by the time she wrote her long, narrative poem, *Jenny Wade at Gettysburg*, published in 1864. Jenny Wade is loyal to the Union, for whose army she is baking bread. Her house is within range of the guns of both armies, so she is urged to flee, but she refuses. While attending to her patriotic baking, a bullet "pierced her heart and she fell, a holy sacrifice in her country's cause." The Yankee sentiments of her husband and his friends must have tempered Mary's southern enthusiasms. Besides, her husband, her sons, and her son-in-law were in the service of the North during the Civil War, and she could scarcely be a traitor to their cause or to them. If she had any lingering doubts about the emancipation of the slaves, a strong patriotic loyalty to the preservation of the Union overrode it.[32]

In the years before the war, Mary seems to have been something of a favorite in the Lippincott and Grambo stable of authors, and they readily published her work. In 1853 Lippincott reissued Mary's Indian stories from *The Iris* as a separate volume, *The Romance of Indian Life*. Since it was published before the Schoolcrafts obtained copyright over them, the publisher used twenty-six engravings of Indian life that Seth Eastman had prepared for the Schoolcraft work. Mary supplied accompanying texts that described the customs represented in the engravings. In the following year, Lippincott published *Chicora and Other*

Regions of the Conquerors and Conquered, in which Mary offered more vignettes of the early history of North America and "some features in the character of its original inhabitants." Here, too, the publisher used Eastman plates from the *Indian Tribes of the United States.* But Mary had a somewhat flawed historical perspective. It is only when she wrote about regions she personally knew and Indians that she had observed and befriended that one can trust her observations. She was better at recounting the legends and customs she had heard and seen than she was at placing them in a historical context.

Chicora expressed Mary's anger at the white man's treatment of the Indians most vividly of all her books. In *Dahcotah,* although she described the degradation of the original inhabitants who were conquered by the white man, her tone was milder and her manner more restrained. Here, however, her tone was sharper, even acerbic. She started excoriating the white invaders of North America in her very first sentence as she reflected on the barbarity of the conquerors toward the conquered. She accused the Europeans of viewing the Indians as "beasts of labor or wild animals. They began to root them out with cruel toil or drive them deep into the forests." "Even in the North," she wrote, "the more hardy [Indian] races came under hands [that also] wronged them . . . enslaved them and gave them maddening draughts, placed firearms in their hands . . . Gradually, their homes were taken from them, and they were compelled to view the desolation of all they most valued."[33]

It was not only the military conquerors that Mary blamed. Although she was a religious person who strongly believed in the power of Christianity to wean the Indian from his warlike ways toward a better life, she was aware of the abuses that frequently accompanied the missionary's zeal. She observed that "the pretense of converting the aborigines to Christianity was a cloak that covered the harshest injustice."[34] Mary was even aware of the economic and political injustice that had affected the Indian way of life. In the story of O-ko-Pee in *The Romance of Indian Life,* Mary observed that "O-ko-Pee was too ignorant of the economy of nations to realize that when a people loses the right to self-government it yields forever the power of advancing in strength and happiness."[35] Embittered and alone, O-ko-Pee died in his isolated wigwam on the shore of the river near the trading establishment of Mendota, a sacrifice to the white man's rule. In *Dahcotah,* Mary had already exhorted the intelligent citizens of the United States not to "forget the aborigines of

this country. Their wrongs cry to heaven; their souls will be required of us"
(p. 31). Admonitions of this nature to her white countrymen were sprinkled
throughout Mary's Indian books, revealing a sense of injustice at the fate of a
wronged and disadvantaged people.

The same sense of injustice ultimately addressed itself to another
disadvantaged group, contemporary white women. In *Dahcotah*, although
she compared the status of Indian women unfavorably with her own, she
nevertheless identified herself with the Indian women based on their shared
experiences as mothers. It must be said, however, that this empathy of
common femininity Mary never extended to black women. It is as though
she was unaware of them as human beings, in spite of the horror stories she
recounted in *Aunt Phillis's Cabin*. And though she spoke of the chains that
similarly bound both slave and woman, the sense of commonality, so evident
when she wrote about Indian women, was completely absent when she wrote
about black ones. Apparently Mary never overcame the strong prejudices
of her Virginia childhood, at least to the extent of her failure to identify with
black women.

As for the male dominance of her own society, Mary most explicitly
addressed herself to this aspect of nineteenth-century life in an 1856 series
of stories called *Tales of a Fashionable Life*. Most of the stories were concerned
with the dangers of a life dedicated to pleasure and the shallow goals white
society imposed on its female members. Mary especially criticized the partying
and frenzied round of social activities for which elegant and expensive gowns
were required and upon which so much attention was lavished. The purpose
of all this exhausting activity was the entrapment of an eligible male into
matrimony. The only young lady who escaped this superficial life was Addie,
who, in spite of the objections of her parents and seven unmarried (but still
desperately trying) sisters, makes an independent choice in life. She
therefore took herself out of the social whirl and off to the remote frontier
town of St. Paul to teach in a school with a mixed population of white and
mixed-blood children. She not only succeeded in her independent life as a
teacher, but also married an attractive young lawyer, whom she brought back
east, in quiet triumph, to show her parents and seven still unwed sisters. To
Mary, Addie was a heroic symbol of what white womanhood could be, for she
wrote, "When a woman breaks down the bars of conventionalism that society

has put up to shut her out from energy, from hope, from all that is good . . . when she does this she is a heroine."[36]

In another of *Fashionable Life*'s even more telling stories, Mary described an incident that was probably autobiographical. The heroine confronted a "woman hater" who, at a social gathering at her home, spoke of books and authors. In a patronizing manner, he assumes that man desires fame while woman must tend the hearth and children and make puddings. His conversant answers that a woman can write books and make puddings. She says that she can do both, but unfortunately the pudding she makes the next day burns, due to the carelessness of her Irish kitchen maid, and pleading a sudden indisposition, she cancels the invitation she had extended the night before.[37]

After *Fashionable Life* only one more book, *Faster Angels,* published by Globe Printing House of Washington, D.C., came from Mary's pen, but she continued to write stories, poems, and articles for magazines.

Although her writing was financially necessary and undoubtedly a source of satisfaction to her literary ambitions, the concern closest to Mary's heart was to get her husband back in Washington on a permanent basis and free from what she considered the capricious orders of the War Department. On May 13, 1855, Captain Eastman had been ordered to rejoin his regiment, his work in Washington being considered finished, and Mary was as determined as she had previously been to get him back. Again she used the considerable powers of her pen to petition congressmen, and even Congress itself, to assign Captain Eastman to Washington permanently. Although she was eventually successful, it took some time, for it was not until 1867 that Seth Eastman was assigned to permanent duty at the United States Capitol to decorate the committee rooms with his paintings.

They were together for just eight more years. Captain Eastman was at work on a large *View of West Point,* the scene of so many of his cherished memories including his marriage to Mary Henderson, when he died suddenly at his easel on August 31, 1875. After her husband died, Mary continued to live at the home they had established at 1221 K Street, and except for a brief move to another location in 1880, she remained there until her own death.

Most of Mary's children grew up to serve in the armed forces and can be traced to a limited extent. Robert Langdon, the eldest, went to West Point and graduated from the United States Military Academy in May 1861. In July of that year he fought in the Civil War in the Battle of Manassas, near the town of Bull

Run, and rose to the rank of captain. Subsequently he was with the Army of the Potomac and at the Battle of Malvern in July 1862. He became chronically ill through disease contracted in the service, but in spite of his poor health, he was appointed professor of drawing and ethics at West Point in September 1862. His illness worsened, forcing his resignation in March 1865. He died in Washington on November 9, 1865, leaving a wife, Mary Angela Dorsey Eastman, and a daughter, Mary Henderson Eastman, born in New York in 1857.

Thomas Henderson became a midshipman on April 29, 1859, and retired in June 1883 as a commander in the navy. He died on March 18, 1888. Virginia married William S. Moore, who attained the rank of engineer in the navy in 1893 and retired six years later with the rank of commander. Frank Smith also served in the navy as a mate and was acting ensign after July 12, 1864. He was discharged on February 12, 1868.[38] Nothing further is known of Mac Henderson or the boy born in Washington in 1851.

Mary herself lived until her late sixties and died following a stroke on February 24, 1887, in Washington and is buried there in Oak Hill Cemetery. Her lasting legacy is in her writings about the Indians whom she memorialized as a vanishing people whose history, legends, and religious beliefs had enduring value. She saw in them the embodiment of the "noble savage" who was dignified, brave, and at harmony with nature until his corruption by white civilization. Although her other writings reflect quite revealingly on her own time and place, they are marred by the flowery, romantic style common in her era. Her writings about the Indians, however, especially of the Dakota whom she knew best, are different, more straightforward, and less tinged by an overlay of sentimentality. Here her observations have the ring of truth, and it is here that her legacy most securely lies.

Notes

1. Carolyn G. Heilbrun, *Writing a Woman's Life* (New York: W. W. Norton, 1988), 21, 31.

2. Lisa Mainiero, ed., *American Women Writers: A Critical Guide from Colonial Times to the Present* (New York: Frederick Unger Pub. Co., 1979-80), 1:568-69.

3. Edward T. James, ed., *Notable American Women, 1607-1950: A Biographical Dictionary* (Cambridge: Harvard University Press, 1971), 1: 545-46.

4. John Francis McDermott, *Seth Eastman, Pictorial Historian of the Indian* (Norman: University of Oklahoma Press, 1961), 24. McDermott assumes a June 9 date for Mary and Seth's wedding because Mary's sister, Sarah, was married on that day to Francis Henney Smith, Seth Eastman's friend and colleague at West Point. Smith had graduated from West Point in 1833 and was a professor of geography, history, and ethics before his appointment in 1839 as commandant of the Virginia Military Institute, a post he held until his death. Although a double wedding ceremony may have been held, there is no documentary evidence to support this assumption.

5. Edward T. Townsend, Memorial of General Seth Eastman, U.S. Army, Washington (?), 1875, Minnesota Historical Society.

6. Lisa Nagle, "Preliminary Research, Commandant's Quarters, Fort Snelling," Minnesota Historical Society, 1975. See also Robert A. Clouse, "Reconstruction Recommendations, Commandant's Quarters," Minnesota Historical Society.

7. Mary Eastman, *Aunt Phillis's Cabin* (Philadelphia: Lippincott, Grambo and Co., 1852), 52-60.

8. Eastman, *Aunt Phillis's Cabin*, 51.

9. Mary Eastman to Henry Sibley, Apr. 30, 1849, Henry H. Sibley Papers, Minnesota Historical Society.

10. George Turner to William C. Baker, Jan. 16, 1846, George Turner Papers, Minnesota Historical Society.

11. Charles Eastman to Hiram M. Hitchcock, Sept. 8, 1927, Charles Eastman Papers, Minnesota Historical Society.

12. Mary Eastman to Henry Lewis, Jan. 4, 1849, Henry Lewis Papers, Minnesota Historical Society.

13. McDermott, *Seth Eastman*, 64.

14. McDermott, *Seth Eastman*, 40.

15. McDermott, *Seth Eastman*, 64.

16. This child, unnamed, is referred to in the Henry Schoolcraft Papers in correspondence between Mary Eastman and Mary Schoolcraft. See Brian W. Dippie, *Catlin and His Contemporaries: The Politics of Patronage* (Lincoln: University of Nebraska Press, 1990), 482.

17. McDermott, *Seth Eastman*, 77.

18. McDermott, *Seth Eastman*, 79.

19. Dippie, *Catlin*, 211.

20. McDermott, *Seth Eastman*, 93.

21. A note to this effect appeared in *Arthur's Home Journal*, one of the magazines to which Mary Eastman contributed, on Aug. 21, 1852, as quoted in McDermott, *Seth Eastman*, 93.

22. McDermott, *Seth Eastman*, 94.

23. Eastman, *Aunt Phillis's Cabin*, 21.

24. Eastman, *Aunt Phillis's Cabin*, 148.

25. Eastman, *Aunt Phillis's Cabin*, 233.

26. Eastman, *Aunt Phillis's Cabin*, 277.

27. Eastman, *Aunt Phillis's Cabin*, 21-22.

28. Eastman, *Aunt Phillis's Cabin*, 44.

29. Eastman, *Aunt Phillis's Cabin*, 111.

30. Eastman, *Aunt Phillis's Cabin*, 12.

31. Dippie, *Catlin*, 199.

32. Mary Eastman, *Jenny Wade of Gettysburg* (Philadelphia: J. B. Lippincott, 1864), 24.

33. Mary Eastman, *Chicora, and Other Regions of the Conquerors and Conquered* (Philadelphia: Lippincott, Grambo and Co., 1854), 1.

34. Eastman, *Chicora*, 1.

35. Mary Eastman, *The Romance of Indian Life* (Philadelphia: Lippincott, Grambo and Co., 1853), 15.

36. Mary Eastman, *Tales of a Fashionable Life* (Philadelphia: Lippincott, Grambo and Co., 1856), 179.

37. Eastman, *Tales of a Fashionable Life*, 216-19.

38. Information on the Eastman children comes from McDermott, *Seth Eastman*, 65n6; *Pennsylvania Genealogical Magazine*, 17, no. 13 (June 1949): 27; Appleton's *Cyclopedia of American Biography*, 2:292; George W. Cullum, *Biographical Register of the Officers and Graduates of the United States Military Academy at West Point*, vol. 1 (Boston: Houghton Mifflin and Co., 1891).

ΛΛΛ✹ΛΛΛ

CONTENTS

Fort Snelling 1848. Head of Navigation 1848, watercolor on paper.

INTRODUCTION

THE MATERIALS for the following pages were gathered during a residence of seven years in the immediate neighborhood—nay—in the very midst of the once powerful but now nearly extinct tribe of Sioux or Dahcotah Indians.

Fort Snelling is situated seven miles below the Falls of St. Anthony, at the confluence of the Mississippi and St. Peter's rivers—built in 1819, and named after the gallant Colonel Snelling, of the army, by whom the work was erected. It is constructed of stone; is one of the strongest Indian forts in the United States; and being placed on a commanding bluff, has somewhat the appearance of an old German castle, or one of the strongholds on the Rhine.

The then recent removal of the Winnebagoes was rendered troublesome by the interference of Wabashaw, the Sioux chief, whose village is on the Mississippi, 1800 miles from its mouth. The father of Wabashaw was a noted Indian; and during the past summer, the son has given some indications that he inherits the father's talents and courage. When the Winnebagoes arrived at Wabashaw's prairie, the chief induced them not to continue their journey of removal; offered them land to settle upon near him, and told them it was not really the wish of their Great Father, that they should remove. His bribes and eloquence induced the Winnebagoes to refuse to proceed; although there was a company of volunteer dragoons and infantry with them. This delay occasioning much expense and trouble, the government agents applied for assistance to the command at Fort Snelling. There was but one company there; and the commanding officer, with twenty men and some friendly Sioux, went down to assist the agent.

There was an Indian council held on the occasion. The Sioux who went from Fort Snelling promised to speak in favor of the removal. During the council, however, not one of them said a word—for which they afterwards gave a satisfactory reason. Wabashaw, though a young man, had such influence over his band, that his orders invariably received implicit obedience. When the council commenced, Wabashaw had placed a young warrior behind each of the friendly Sioux who he knew would speak in favor of the removal, with orders to shoot down the first one who rose for that purpose. This stratagem may be considered a characteristic specimen of the temper and habits of the Sioux chiefs, whose tribe we bring before the reader in their most conspicuous ceremonies and habits. The Winnebagoes were finally removed, but not until Wabashaw was taken prisoner and carried to Fort Snelling. Wabashaw's pike-bearer was a fine looking warrior, named "Many Lightnings."

The village of "Little Crow," another able and influential Sioux chief, is situated twenty miles below the Falls of St. Anthony. He has four wives, all sisters, and the youngest of them almost a child. There are other villages of the tribe, below and above Fort Snelling.

The scenery about Fort Snelling is rich in beauty. The falls of St. Anthony are familiar to travellers, and to readers of Indian sketches. Between the fort and these falls are the "Little Falls," forty feet in height, on a stream that empties into the Mississippi. The Indians call them Mine-hah-hah, or "laughing waters." In sight of Fort Snelling is a beautiful hill called Morgan's Bluff; the Indians call it "God's House." They have a tradition that it is the residence of their god of the waters, whom they call Unk-ta-he. Nothing can be more lovely than the situation and appearance of this hill; it commands on every side a magnificent view, and during the summer it is carpeted with long grass and prairie flowers. But, to those who have lived the last few years at Fort Snelling, this hill presents another source of interest. On its top are buried three young children, who were models of health and beauty until the scarlet fever found its way into regions hitherto shielded from its approach. They lived but long enough on earth to secure them an entrance into heaven. Life, which ought to be a blessing to all, was to them one of untold value; for it was a short journey to a better land—a translation from the yet unfelt cares of earth to the bright and endless joys of heaven.

Opposite the Fort is Pilot Knob, a high peak, used as a burial-place by the Indians; just below it is the village of Mendota, or the "Meeting of the Waters."

But to me, the greatest objects of interest and curiosity were the original owners of the country, whose teepees could be seen in every direction. One could soon know all that was to be known about Pilot Knob or St. Anthony's falls; but one is puzzled completely to comprehend the character of an Indian man, woman, or child. At one moment, you see an Indian chief raise himself to his full height, and say that the ground on which he stands is his own;

at the next, beg bread and pork from an enemy. An Indian woman will scornfully refuse to wash an article that might be needed by a white family—and the next moment, declare that she had not washed her face in fifteen years! An Indian child of three years old, will cling to its mother under the walls of the Fort, and then plunge into the Mississippi, and swim half way across, in hopes of finding an apple that has been thrown in. We may well feel much curiosity to look into the habits, manners, and motives of a race exhibiting such contradictions.

There is a great deal said of Indian warriors—and justly too of the Sioux. They are, as a race, tall fine-looking men; and many of those who have not been degraded by association with the frontier class of white people, nor had their intellects destroyed by the white man's fire-water, have minds of high order, and reason with a correctness that would put to the blush the powers of many an educated logician. Yet are these men called savages, and morally associated with the tomahawk and scalping knife. Few regard them as reasonable creatures, or as beings endowed by their creator with souls, that are here to be fitted for the responsibilities of the Indians hereafter.

Good men are sending the Bible to all parts of the world. Sermons are preached in behalf of fellow-creatures who are perishing in regions known only to us in name. And here, within reach of comparatively the slightest exertion; here, not many miles from churches and schools, and all the moral influences abounding in Christian society; here, in a country endowed with every advantage that God can bestow, are perishing, body and soul, our own countrymen: perishing too from disease, starvation and intemperance, and all the evils incident to their unhappy condition. White men, Christian men, are driving them back; rooting out their very names from the face of the earth. Ah! these men can seek the country of the Sioux when money is to be gained: but how few care for the sufferings of the Dahcotahs! how few would give a piece of money, a prayer, or even a thought, towards their present and eternal good.

Yet are they not altogether neglected. Doctor Williamson, one of the missionaries among the Sioux, lives near Fort Snelling. He is exerting himself to the utmost to promote the moral welfare of the unhappy people among whom he expects to pass his life. He has a school for the Indian children, and many of them read well. On the Sabbath, divine service is regularly held, and he has labored to promote the cause of temperance among the Sioux.

Christian exertion is unhappily too much influenced by the apprehension that little can be done for the savage. How is it with the man on his fire-water mission the Indian? Does he doubt? Does he fail?

As a great motive to improve the moral character of the Indians, I present the condition of the women in their tribes. A degraded state of woman is universally characteristic of savage life, as her elevated influence in civilized society is the conspicuous standard of moral and social virtue. The peculiar sorrows of the Sioux woman commence at her birth. Even as a child she is despised, in comparison with the brother beside her, who is one day to be a great warrior. As a maiden, she is valued while the young man, who wants her for a wife, may have a doubt of his success. But when she is a wife, there is little sympathy for her condition. How soon do the oppressive storms and contentions of life root out all that is kind or gentle in her heart. She must bear the burdens of the family. Should her husband wish it, she must travel all day with a heavy weight on her back; and at night when they stop, her hands must prepare the food for her family before she retires to rest.

Her work is never done. She makes the summer and the winter house. For the former she peels the bark from the trees in the spring; for the latter she sews the deer-skin together. She tans the skins of which coats, mocassins, and leggins are to be made for the family; she has to scrape it and prepare it while other cares are pressing upon her. When her child is born, she has no opportunities for rest or quiet. She must paddle the canoe for her husband—pain and feebleness must be forgotten. She is always hospitable. Visit her in her teepee, and she willingly gives you what you need, if in her power; and with alacrity does what she can to promote your comfort. In her looks there is little that is attractive. Time has not caused the wrinkles in her forehead, nor the furrows in her cheek. They are the traces of want, passion, sorrows and tears. Her bent form was once light and graceful. Labor and privations are not preservative of beauty.

Let it not be deemed impertinent if I venture to urge upon those who care for the wretched wherever their lot may be cast, the immense good that might be accomplished among these tribes by schools, which should open the minds of the young to the light of reason and Christianity. Even if the elder members are given up as hopeless, with the young there is always encouragement. Many a bright little creature among the Dahcotahs is as capable of receiving instruction as are the children of civilization. Why should they be neglected when the waters of benevolence are moving all around them?

It is not pretended that all the incidents related in these stories occurred exactly as they are stated. Most of them are entirely true; while in others the narrative is varied in order to show some prevalent custom, or to illustrate some sentiment to which these Indians are devoted. The Sioux are as firm believers in their religion as we are in ours; and they are far more particular in the discharge of what they conceive to be the obligations required by the objects of their faith and worship. There are many allusions to the belief and customs of the Dahcotahs that require explanation. For this purpose I have obtained from the Sioux themselves the information required. On matters of faith there is difference of opinion among them—but they do not make more points of difference on religion, or on any other subject, than white people do.

The day of the Dahcotah is far spent; to quote the language of a Chippeway chief, "The Indian's glory is passing away." They seem to be almost a God-forgotten race. Some few have give the missionary reason to hope that they have been made subjects of Christian faith—and the light, that has as yet broken in faint rays upon their darkness, may increase. He who takes account of the falling of a sparrow, will not altogether cast away so large a portion of his creatures. All Christian minds will wish success to the Indian missionary; and assuredly God will be true to his mercy, where man is found true to his duty.

The first impression created by the Sioux was the common one—fear. In their looks they were so different from the Indians I had occasionally seen. There was nothing in their aspect to indicate the success of efforts made to civilize them. Their tall, unbending forms, their savage hauteur, the piercing black eye, the quiet indifference of manner, the slow, stealthy step—how different were they from the eastern Indians, whose associations with the white people seem to have deprived them of all native dignity of bearing and of character. The yells heard outside the high wall of the fort at first filled me with alarm; but I soon became accustomed to them, and to all other occasional Indian excitements, that served to vary the monotony of garrison life. Before I felt much interest in the Sioux, they seemed to have great regard for me. My husband, before his marriage, had been stationed at Fort

Snelling and at Prairie du Chien. He was fond of hunting and roaming about the prairies; and left many friends among the Indians when he obeyed the order to return to an eastern station. On going back to the Indian country, he met with a warm welcome from his old acquaintances, who were eager to shake hands with "Eastman's squaw."

The old men laid their bony hands upon the heads of my little boys, admired their light hair, said their skins were very white; and, although I could not then understand their language, they told me many things, accompanied with earnest gesticulation. They brought their wives and young children to see me. I had been told that Indian women gossiped and stole; that they were filthy and troublesome. Yet I could not despise them: they were wives and mothers—God had implanted the same feelings in their hearts as in mine.

Some Indians visited us every day, and we frequently saw them at their villages. Captain E. spoke their language well; and without taking any pains to acquire it, I soon understood it so as to talk with them. The sufferings of the women and children, especially during the winter season, appealed to my heart. Their humility in asking for assistance contrasted strongly with the pompous begging of the men. Late in a winter's afternoon, Wenona, wife of a chief named the "Star," came to my room. Undoing a bundle that she took from under her blanket, she approached and showed it to me. It was an infant three days old, closely strapped to an Indian cradle. The wretched babe was shrivelled and already looking old from hunger. She warmed it by the fire, attempting to still its feeble cries.

"Do you nurse your baby well, Wenona?" I asked; "it looks so thin and small."

"How can I," was the reply, "when I have not eaten since it was born?"

Frequently we have heard of whole families perishing during severely cold weather. The father absent on a winter's hunt, the mother could not leave her children to apply to the fort for assistance, even had she strength left to reach there. The frozen bodies would be found in the lodges. The improvident character of the Indian is well known. Their annuities are soon spent; supplies received from government are used in feasting; and no provision is made for winters that are always long and severe. Though they receive frequent assistance from the public at the fort, the wants of all cannot be supplied. The captain of the post was generous towards them, as was always my friend Mrs. F., whom they highly esteemed. Yet some hearts are closed against appeals daily made to their humanity. An Indian woman may suffer from hunger or sickness, because her looks are repulsive and her garments unwashed: some will say they can bear the want of warm clothing, because they have been used to privation.

The women of the Sioux exhibit many striking peculiarities of character—the love of the marvellous, and a profound veneration for any and every thing connected with their religious faith; a willingness to labor and to learn; patience in submitting to insults from servants who consider them intruders in families; the evident recognition of the fact that they are a doomed race, and must submit to indignities that they dare not resent. They seem, too, so unused to sympathy, often comparing their lives of suffering and hardship with the ease and comfort enjoyed by the white women, it must be a hard heart, that could withhold sympathy from such poor creatures. Their home was mine—and such a home! The very sunsets, more bright and glorious than I had ever seen, seemed to loved to linger over the scenes amongst which we lived; the high bluffs of the "father of many waters" and the quiet shores of the "Mine sota;" the fairy rings on the prairie, and the "spirit lakes" that reposed beside them; the bold peak, Pilot Knob, on whose top the Indians bury their dead, with the small hills rising gradually around it—all were dear to the Sioux and to me. They believed that the rocks, and hills, and waters were peopled with fairies and spirits, whose power and anger they had ever been taught to fear. I knew that God, whose presence fills all nature, was there. In fancy they beheld their deities in the blackened cloud and fearful storm; I saw mine in the brightness of nature, the type of the unchanging light of Heaven.

They evinced the warmest gratitude to any who had ever displayed kind feelings towards them. When our little children were ill with scarlet fever, how grieved they were to witness their sufferings; especially as we watched Virginia, waiting, as we expected, to receive her parting breath. How strongly they were contrasted! that fair child, unconscious even of the presence of the many kind friends who had watched and wept beside her—and the aged Sioux women, who had crept noiselessly into the chamber. I remember them well, as they leaned over the foot of the bed; their expressive and subdued countenances full of sorrow. That small white hand, that lay so powerless, had ever been outstretched to welcome them when they came weary and hungry.

They told me afterwards, that "much water fell from their eyes day and night, while they thought she would die;" that the servants made them leave the sick room, and then turned them out of the house—but that they would not go home, waiting outside to hear of her.

During her convalescence, I found that they could "rejoice with those that rejoice" as well as "weep with those that wept." The fearful disease was abating in our family, and "Old Harper," as she is called in the Fort, offered to sit up and attend to the fire. We allowed her to do so, for the many who had so kindly assisted us were exhausted with fatigue. Joy had taken from me all inclination to sleep, and I lay down near my little girl, watching the old Sioux woman. She seemed to be reviewing the history of her life, so intently did she gaze at the bright coals on the hearth. Many strange thoughts apparently engaged her. She was, of her own accord, an inmate of the white man's house, waiting to do good to his sick child. She had wept bitterly for days, lest the child should be lost to her—and now she was full of happiness, at the prospect of her recovery.

How shall we reconcile this with the fact that Harper, or Harpstinah, was one of the Sioux women, who wore, as long as she could endure it, a necklace made of the hands and feet of Chippeway children? Here, in the silence of night, she turned often towards the bed, when the restless sleep of the child broke in on her meditation. She fancied I slept, but my mind was busy too. I was far away from the home of my childhood, and a Sioux woman, with her knife in her belt, was assisting me in the care of my only daughter. She thought Dr. T. was a "wonderful medicine man" to cure her; in which opinion we all cordially coincided.

I always listened with pleasure to the women, when allusion was made to their religion; but when they spoke of their tradition, I felt as a miser would, had he discovered a mine of gold. I had read the legends of the Maiden's Rock, and of St. Anthony's Falls. I asked Checkered Cloud to tell them to me. She did so—and how differently they were told! With my knowledge of the language, and the aid of my kind and excellent friend Mr. Prescott, all the dark passages in her narration were made clear. I thought the Indian tone of feeling was not rightly appreciated—their customs were not clearly stated, perhaps not fairly estimated. The red man, considered generally as a creature to be carried about and exhibited for money, was, in very truth, a being immortally endowed, though under a dispensation obscure to the more highly-favored white race. As they affirmed a belief in the traditions of their tribe, with what strength and beauty of diction they clothed their thoughts—how energetic in gesture! Alas! for the people who had no higher creed, no surer trust, for this and for another world.

However they may have been improved, no one could have had better opportunities than I, to acquire all information of interest respecting these Indians. I lived among them seven years. The chiefs from far and near were constantly visiting the Fort, and were always at our house. Not a sentiment is in the Legends that I did not hear from the lips of the Indian man or woman. They looked on my husband as their friend, and talked to him freely on all subjects, whether of religion, customs, or grievances. They were frequently told that I was writing about them, that every body might know what great warriors they were.

The men were sometimes astonished at the boldness with which I reproved them, though it raised me much in their estimation. I remember taking Bad Hail, one of their chiefs, to task, frequently; and on one occasion he told me, by way of showing his gratitude for the interest I took in his character, that he had three wives, all of whom he would give up if I would "leave Eastman, and come and live with him." I received his proposition, however, with Indian indifference, merely replying that I did not fancy having my head split open every few days with a stick of wood. He laughed heartily, after his fashion, conscious that the cap fitted, for he was in the habit of expending all his surplus bad temper upon his wives. I have sometimes thought, that if, when a warrior, be he chief or commoner, throws a stick of wood at his wife's head, she were to cast it back at his, he might, perhaps, be taught a better behaviour. But I never dared to instil such insubordinate notions into the heads of my Sioux female friends, lest some ultra "brave," in a desperate rage, might substitute the tomahawk for the log. These opinions, too, might have made me unpopular with Sioux and Turks—and, perhaps, with some of my more enlightened friends, who are self-constituted "lords of creation."

I noticed that Indians, like white people, instead of confessing and forsaking their sins, were apt to excuse themselves by telling how much worse their neighbors were. When told how wicked it was to have more than one wife, they defended themselves by declaring that the Winnebagoes had twice or thrice as many as the Sioux. The attempt to make one right of two wrongs seems to be instinctive.

I wished to learn correctly the Indian songs which they sing in celebrating their dances. I sent for a chief, Little Hill, who is a famous singer, but with little perseverance as a teacher of music. He soon lost all patience with me, refused to continue the lesson, declaring that he could never make me sing like a Sioux squaw. The low, guttural notes created the difficulty. He very quickly became tired of my piano and singing. The chiefs and medicine men always answered my questions readily, respecting their laws and religion; but, to insure good humor, they must first have something to eat. All the scraps of food collected in the kitchen; cold beef, cold buckwheat cakes; nothing went amiss, especially as to quantity. Pork is their delight—apples they are particularly fond of—and, in the absence of fire-water, molasses and water is a most acceptable beverage. Then they had to smoke and nod a little before the fire—and by and by I heard all about the Great Spirit, and Hookah the Giant, and the powers of the Sacred Medicine. All that is said in this book of their religion, laws, and sentiments, I learned from themselves, and most of the incidents occurred precisely as they are represented. Some few have been varied, but only where it might happily illustrate a peculiar custom or opinion.

Their medicine men, priests, and jugglers, are proverbially the greatest scamps of the tribe. My dear father must forgive me for reflecting so harshly on his brother practitioners, and be reconciled when he hears that they belong to the corps of quacks; for they doubt their own powers, and are constantly imposing on the credulity of others. On returning from an evening walk, we met, near the fort, a notable procession. First came an old medicine man, whose Indian name I cannot recall, but the children of the garrison called him "Old Sneak"—a most appropriate appellation, for he always looked as if he had just committed murder, and was afraid of being found out. On this occasion he looked particularly in character. What a representative of the learned faculty! After him, in Indian file, came his wife and children, a most cadaverous looking set. To use a western phrase, they all looked as if they were just "dug up." Their appearance was accounted for in the following ludicrous manner—the story is doubtless substantially true. There was a quantity of refuse medicine that had been collecting in the hospital at the fort, and Old Sneak happened to be present at a general clearing out. The medicine was given to him; and away he went to his home, hugging it up close to him like a veritable old miser. It was too precious to be shared with his neighbors; the medicine of the white man was "wahkun" (wonderful)—and, carrying out the principle that the more of a good thing the better, he, with his wife and children, took it all! I felt assured that the infant strapped to its mother's back was dying at that time.

The "dog dance" is held by the Sioux is great reverence; and the first time it has been celebrated near the fort for many years, was about five summers ago.

The Chippeways, with their chief, "Hole in the Day," were down on a visit, and the prairie outside the fort was covered with Indians of both tribes. The Chippeways sat on the grass at a little distance, watching the Sioux as they danced, "to show how brave they were, and how they could eat the hearts of their enemies." Most of the officers and ladies of the garrison were assembled on the hospital gallery to witness the dance.

The Sioux warriors formed a circle; in the centre was a pole fastened in the ground. One of the Indians killed a dog, and, taking out the heart and liver, held them for a few moments in a bucket of cold water, and then hung them up to the pole. After awhile, one of the warriors advanced towards it, barking. His attitude was irresistibly droll; he tried to make himself look as much as possible like a dog, and I thought he succeeded to admiration. He retreated, and another warrior advanced with a different sort of bark; more joined in, until there was a chorus of barking. Next, one becomes very courageous, jumps and barks towards the pole, biting off a piece of the flesh; another follows and does the same feat. One after another they all bark and bite. "Let dogs delight" would have been an appropriate melody for the occasion. They had to hold their heads back to swallow the morceau—it was evidently hard work. Several dogs were killed in succession, when, seeing some of the warriors looking pale and deadly sick, Captain E. determined to try how many of their enemies' hearts they could dispose of. He went down among the Indians and purchased another dog. They could not refuse to eat the heart. It made even the bravest of men sick to swallow the last mouthful—they were pale as death. I saw the last of it, and although John Gilpin's ride might be a desirable sight, yet when the Sioux celebrate another dog feast, "may I *not* be there to see."

Our intercourse with the Sioux was greatly facilitated, and our influence over them much increased, by the success attending my husband's efforts to paint their portraits. They though it supernatural (wahkun) to be represented on canvas. Some were prejudiced against sitting, others esteemed it a great compliment to be asked, but all expected to be paid for it. And if anything were wanting to complete our opportunities for gaining all information that was of interest, we found it in the daguerreotype. Captain E., knowing they were about to celebrate a feast he wished to paint in group, took his apparatus out, and, when they least expected it, transferred the group to his plate. The awe, consternation, astonishment and admiration, surpassed description. "Ho! Eastman is all wahkun!"

The Indians are fond of boasting and communicating their exploits and usages to those who have their confidence. While my husband has delineated their features with a pencil, I have occupied pleasantly many an hour in learning from them how to represent accurately the feelings and features of their hearts—feeble though my pen be. We never failed to gain a point by providing a good breakfast or dinner.

With the Rev. Mr. Pond and Dr. Williamson, both missionaries among the Sioux, I had many a pleasant interview and talk about the tribe. They kindly afforded me every assistance—and as they are perfectly acquainted with the language of the Sioux, and have studied their religion with the view to introduce the only true one, I could not have applied to more enlightened sources, or better authority.

The day we left Fort Snelling, I received from Mr. Pond the particulars of the fate of the Sioux woman who was taken prisoner by the Chippeways, and who is represented in the legend called The Wife. Soon after her return to her husband, he was killed by the Chippeways; and the difficulty was settled by the Chippeways paying to the Sioux what was considered the value of the murdered man, in goods, such as calico, tobacco &c.! After his death, the widow married a Sioux, named "Scarlet Face." They lived harmoniously for a while—but soon difficulties arose, and Scarlet Face, in a fit of savage rage, beat her to death. A most unromantic conclusion to her eventful life.

How vivid is our recollection of the grief the Sioux showed at parting with us. For although, at the time, it added to the pain naturally felt at leaving a place which had so long been our home; yet the sincere affection they evinced towards us and our children was most gratifying. They wished us to remember them, when far away, with kindness. The farewell of my friend Checkered Cloud can never be forgotten. She was my constant visitor for years; and, although a poor and despised Sioux woman, I learned to look upon her with respect and regard. Nor does my interest in her and her nation cease, because, in the chances of life, we may never meet again. It will still be my endeavor to depict all the customs, feasts and ceremonies of the Sioux, before it be too late. The account of them may be interesting, when the people who so long believed in them will be no more.

We can see they are passing away, but who can decide the interesting question of their origin? They told me that their nation had always lived in the valley of the Mississippi—that their wise men had asserted this for ages past. Some who have lived among them, think they crossed over from Persia in ships—and that they once possessed the knowledge of building large vessels, though they have now entirely lost it. This idea bears too little probability to command any confidence. The most general opinion is the often told one, that they are a remnant of God's ancient and chosen people. Be this as it may, they are "as the setting sun, or as the autumn leaves trampled upon by powerful riders."

They are receding rapidly, and with feeble resistance, before the giant strides of civilization. The hunting grounds of a few savages will soon become the haunts of densely peopled, civilized settlements. We should be better reconciled to this manifest destiny of the aborigines, if the inroads of civilization were worthy of it; if the last years of these, in some respects, noble people, were lit up with the hope-inspiring rays of Christianity. We are not to judge the Heathen; yet universal evidence gives the melancholy fact, that the light of nature does not lead the soul to God: and without judging of their destiny, we are bound to enlighten their minds. We know the great Being of whom they are ignorant; and well will it be for them and for us, in a day that awaits us all, if yet, though late, sadly late—yet not too late, we so give countenance and aid to the missionary, that the light of revealed truth may cheer the remaining period of their national and individual existence.

Will it be said that I am regarding, with partial eye and sentimental romance, but one side of the Sioux character? Have they no faults, as a people and individually? They are savages—and that goes far to answer the question. Perhaps the best answer is, the women have faults enough, and the men twice as many as the women. But if to be a savage is to be cruel, vindictive, ferocious—dare we say that to be a civilized man necessarily implies freedom from these traits?

Want of truth, and habitual dishonesty in little things, are prevalent traits among the Sioux. Most of them will take a kitchen spoon or fork, if they have a chance—and they think it fair thus to return the peculations of the whites. They probably have an idea of making up for the low price at which their lands have been valued, but maintaining a constant system of petty thefts—or perhaps they consider kitchen utensils as curiosities, just as the whites do their mocassins and necklaces of bear's claws. Yes—it must be confessed, however unsentimental, they almost all steal.

The men think it undignified for them to steal, so they send their wives thus unlawfully to procure what they want—and wo be to them if they are found out. The husband would shame and beat his wife for doing what he certainly would have beaten for her refusing to do. As regards the honesty of the men, I give you the opinion of the husband of Checkered Cloud, who was an excellent Indian. "Every Sioux," said he, "will steal if he need, and there be a chance. The best Indian that ever lived, has stolen. I myself once stole some powder."

I have thus, perhaps tediously, endeavored to show, that what is said in this work has been learned by intimate association, and that for years, with the Indian. This association has continued under influences that secured unreservedly their confidence, friendship—and I may say truly, in many instances—their affection. If the perusal of the Legends give pleasure to my friends—how happy am I! To do more than this I hardly dare hope.

M.H.E.

PRELIMINARY REMARKS

ON

THE CUSTOMS OF THE DAHCOTAHS

Indian Spearing Fish Three Miles below Fort Snelling, watercolor on paper, 1846-1848.

I. SIOUX CEREMONIES, SCALP DANCE, &c.

THE SIOUX occupy a country from the Mississippi river to some point west of the Missouri, and from the Chippewa tribe on the north, to the Winnebago on the south; the whole extent being about nine hundred miles long by four hundred in breadth.

Dahcotah is the proper name of this once powerful tribe of Indians. The term Sioux is not recognized, except among those who live near the whites. It is said to have been given by the old French traders, that the Dahcotahs might not know when they were the subjects of conversation. The exact meaning of the word has never been ascertained.

Dahcotah means a confederacy. A number of bands live near each other on terms of friendship, their customs and laws being the same. They mean by the word Dahcotah what we mean by the confederacy of states in our union. The tribe is divided into a number of bands, which are subdivided into villages; every village being governed by its own chief. The honor of being chief is hereditary, though for cause a chief may be deposed and another substituted; and the influence the chief possesses depends much more upon his talents and capacity to govern, than upon mere hereditary descent. To every village there is also a *war-chief*, and as to these are ascribed supernatural powers, their influence is unbounded. Leading every military excursion, the war-chief's command is absolute with his party.

There are many clans among the Sioux, and these are distinguished from each other by the different kinds of medicine they use. Each clan takes a root for its medicine, known only to those initiated into the mysteries of the clan. The name of this root must be kept a secret. Many of these roots are entirely destitute of medicinal power. The clans are governed by a sort of freemasonry system. A Dahcotah would die rather than divulge the secret of his clan. The clans keep up almost a perpetual warfare with each other. Each one supposes the other to be possessed of supernatural powers, by which they can cause the death of any individual, though he may live at a great distance. This belief is the cause of a great deal of bloodshed. When a Dahcotah dies, it is attributed to some one of another clan, and revenge is sought by the relatives of the deceased. All their supposed supernatural powers are invoked to destroy the murderer. They first try the powers of their sacred medicine, imagining they can cast a fatal spell on the offender; if this fails, they have recourse to more destructive weapons, and the axe, knife or gun may by fatally used. After the supposed murderer is killed, his relations retaliate, and thus successive feuds become perpetual.

The Dahcotahs, though a reckless, are a generous people, usually kind and affectionate to their aged, though instances to the contrary frequently occur. Among the E-yanktons, there was a man so feeble and decrepit from age as to be totally unable to take care of himself; not being able to walk, he occasioned great trouble. When the band went out hunting, he entreated the young men to drag him along, that he might not fall a prey to the Chippeways, or to a fate equally dreaded, cold and starvation. For a time they seemed to pity him, and there were always those among the hunting party who were willing to render him assistance. At last he fell to the charge of some young men, who, wearied with carrying him from place to place, told him they would leave him, but he need not die a lingering death. They gave him a gun, and placed him on the ground to be shot at, telling him to try and kill one of the young warriors who were to fire at him; and thus he would have so much more honor to carry with him to the land of the spirits. He knew it was useless to attempt to defend himself. In a few moments he received his death-wound, and was no longer a burden to himself or to others.

The Sioux have a number of superstitious notions, which particularly influence the women. They are slavishly fearful of the spirits of the dead, and a thousand other fancies. Priests and jugglers are venerated from their supposed supernatural powers.

Little is generally known of their religion or their customs. One must live among them to induce them to impart any information concerning their mode of life or religious faith; to a stranger they are always reserved.

Their dances and feasts are not amusements. They all have an object and meaning, and are celebrated year after year, under a belief that neglect will be punished by the Great Spirit by means of disease, want, or the attacks of enemies. All their fear of punishment is confined to what they may suffer in this world. They have no fear of the anger of their deities being continued after death. Revolting as the ceremony of dancing round a scalp seems to us, an Indian believes it to be a sacred duty to celebrate it. The dancing part is performed by the old and young squaws. The medicine men sing, beat the drum, rattle the gourd, and use such other instruments as they contrive. Anything is considered a musical instrument that will assist in creating discordant sounds. One of these is a bone with notches on it, one end of which rests on a tin pan, the other being held in the left hand, while, with a piece of bone in the right, which a medicine man draws over the notches, sounds as discordant and grating as possible are created.

The squaws dance around the scalps in concentric circles, in groups of from four to twelve together, pressing their shoulders against each other, and at every stroke of the drum raising themselves to their utmost height, hopping and sliding a short distance to the left, singing all the time with the medicine men. They keep time perfectly. In the centre, the scalps are attached to a pole stuck in the ground, or else carried on the shoulders of some of the squaws. The scalp is stretched on a hoop, and the pole to which it is attached is several feet long.

It is also covered with vermilion or red earth, and ornamented with feathers, ribbons, beads, and other trinkets, and usually a pair of scissors or a comb.

After dancing for a few minutes, the squaws stop to rest. During this interval one of the squaws, who has had a son, husband, or brother killed by a warrior of the tribe from which the scalp she holds was taken, will relate the particulars of his death, and wind up by saying, "Whose scalp have I now on my shoulders?" At this moment there is a general shout, and the dance again commences. This ceremony continues sometimes, at intervals, for months; usually during the warm weather. After the dance is done, the scalp is buried or put up on the scaffold with some of the deceased of the tribe who took the scalp. So much for the scalp dance—a high religious ceremony, not, as some suppose, a mere amusement.

The *Sacred Feast* is given in honor of the sacred medicine, and is always given by medicine-men or women who are initiated into the mysteries of the medicine dance. The medicine men are invariably the greatest rascals of the band, yet the utmost respect is shown them. Every one fears the power of a medicine man.

When a medicine man intends giving a feast, he goes or sends to the persons whom he wishes to invite. When all are assembled, the giver of the feast opens the medicine bag with some formality. The pipe is lit and smoked by all present; but it is first offered to the Great Spirit. After the smoking, food is placed in wooden bowls, or other vessels that visitors may have brought; for it is not a breach of etiquette to bring dishes with you to the feast. When all are served, the word is given to commence eating, and those that cannot eat all that is given them, must make a present to the host, besides hiring some one present to eat what they fail to consume. To waste a morsel would offend the Great Spirit, and injure or render useless the medicine. Every one having finished eating, the kettle in which the food was cooked is smoked with cedar leaves or grass. Before the cooking is commenced, all the fire within the wigwam is put out, and a fresh one made from flint and steel. In the celebration of the Sacred Feast, the fire and cooking utensils are kept and consecrated exclusively to that purpose. After the feast is over, all the bones are carefully collected and thrown into the water, in order that no dog may get them, nor a woman trample on them.

The Sioux worship the sun. The *sun dance* is performed by young warriors who dance, at intervals of five minutes, for several days. They hop on one foot and then on the other, keeping time to the drum, and making indescribable gestures, each having a small whistle in his mouth, with his face turned towards the sun. The singing and other music is performed by the medicine men. The drum used is a raw hide stretched over a keg, on which a regular beating of time is made with a short stick with a head to it. Women pretend to foretell future events, and, for this reason, are sometimes invited to medicine feasts.

II. INDIAN DOCTORS

WHEN AN INDIAN is sick and wants "the Doctor" as we say, or a medicine man, as they say,—they call them also priests, doctors and jugglers,—a messenger is sent for one, with a pipe filled in one hand, and payment in the other; which fee may be a gun, blanket, kettle or anything in the way of a present. The messenger enters the wigwam (or *teepee*, as the houses of the Sioux are called) of the juggler, presents the pipe, and lays the present or fee beside him. Having smoked, the Doctor goes to the teepee of the patient, takes a seat at some distance from him, divests himself of coat or blanket, and pulls his leggins to his ankles. He then calls for a gourd, which has been suitably prepared, by drying and putting small beads or gravel stones in it, to make a rattling noise. Taking the gourd, he begins to rattle it and to sing, thereby to charm the animal that has entered the body of the sick Sioux. After singing *hi-he-hi-hah* in quick succession, the chorus *ha-ha-ha, hahahah* is more solemnly and gravely chaunted. On due repetition of this the doctor stops to smoke; then sings and rattles again. He sometimes attempts to draw with his mouth the disease from an arm or a limb that he fancies to be affected. Then rising, apparently almost suffocated, groaning terribly and thrusting his face into a bowl of water, he makes all sorts of gestures and noises. This is to get rid of the disease that he pretends to have drawn from the sick person. When he thinks that some animal, fowl or fish, has possession of the sick man, so as to cause disease, it becomes necessary to destroy the animal by shooting it. To accomplish this, the doctor makes a shape of the animal of bark, which is placed in a bowl of water mixed with red earth, which he sets outside of the wigwam where some young men are standing, who are instructed by the doctor how and when to shoot the animal.

When all is ready, the doctor pops his head out of the wigwam, on his hands and knees. At this moment the young men fire at the little bark animal, blowing it to atoms; when the doctor jumps at the bowl, thrusting his face into the water, grunting, groaning and making a vast deal of fuss. Suddenly a woman jumps upon his back, then dismounts, takes the doctor by the hair, and drags him back into the teepee. All fragments of the bark animal are then collected and burned. The ceremony there ceases. If the patient does not recover, the doctor says he did not get the right animal. The reader must be convinced that it is not for want of the most strenuous exertions on the part of the physician.

These are some of the customs of the Dahcotahs, which, however absurd they may appear to us, are held in sacred reverence by them. There are some animals, birds and fishes, that an Indian venerates; and the creature thus sacred, he dare neither kill nor eat. The selection is usually a bear, buffalo, deer, otter, eagle, hawk or snake. One will not eat the right wing of a bird; another dare not eat the left: nor are the women allowed to eat any part that is considered sacred.

The Sioux say it is lawful to take revenge, but otherwise it is not right to murder. When murder is committed, it is an injury to the deceased, not a sin against the Great Spirit. Some of their wise men say that the Great Spirit has nothing to do with their affairs, present or future. They pretend to know but little of a future state. They have dreamy ideas of large cities somewhere in the heavens, where they will go, but still be at war with their enemies and have plenty of game. An Indian woman's idea of future happiness consists in relief from care. "Oh! that I were dead," they will often say, "when I shall have no more trouble." Veneration is much regarded in all Indian families. Thus a son-in-law must never call his father-in-law by his name, but by the title father-in-law, and vice versa. A female is not permitted to handle the sac for war purposes; neither does she dare look into a looking-glass, for fear of losing her eyesight.

The appearance of a brilliant aurora-borealis occasions great alarm. The Indians run immediately for their guns and bows and arrows to shoot at it, and thus disperse it.

III. INDIAN NAMES AND WRITING

THE *NAMES* of the Sioux bands or villages, are as fanciful as those given to individuals. Near Fort Snelling, are the "Men-da-wah-can-tons," or people of the spirit lakes; the "Wahk-patons," or people of the leaves; the "Wahk-pa-coo-tahs," or people that shoot at leaves, and other bands who have names of this kind. Among those chiefs who have been well-known around Fort Snelling, are,

Wah-ba-shaw,	The Leaf.
Wah-ke-on-tun-kah,	Big Thunder.
Wah-coo-ta,	Red Wing.
Muzza Hotah,	Gray Iron.
Ma-pe-ah-we-chas-tah,	The man in the Cloud.
Tah-chun-coo-wash-ta,	Good Road.
Sha-co-pee,	The Sixth.
Wah-soo-we-chasta-ne,	Bad Hail.
Ish-ta-hum-bah,	Sleepy Eyes.

These fanciful names are given to them from some peculiarity in appearance or conduct; or sometimes from an occurrence that took place at the time that they usually receive the name that is ascribed to them for life. There is a Sioux living in the neighborhood of Fort Snelling, called "The man that walks with the women." It is not customary for the Indian to show much consideration for the fair sex, and this young man, exhibiting some symptoms of gallantry unusual among them, received the above name.

The Sioux have ten names for their children, given according to the order of their birth.

The oldest son is called	*Chaskè,*
⟨⟩ second,	*Haparm,*
⟨⟩ third,	*Ha-pe-dah,*
⟨⟩ fourth,	*Chatun,*
⟨⟩ fifth,	*Harka.*
The oldest daughter is called	*Wenonah,*
⟨⟩ second,	*Harpen,*
⟨⟩ third,	*Harpstenah,*
⟨⟩ fourth,	*Waska,*
⟨⟩ fifth,	*We-harka.*

These names they retain until another is given by their relations or friends.

The Dahcotahs say that *meteors* are men or women flying through the air; that they fall to pieces as they go along, finally falling to the earth. They call them "Wah-ken-den-da," or the mysterious passing fire. They have a tradition of a meteor which, they say, was passing over a hill where there was an Indian asleep. The meteor took the Indian on his back, and continued his route till it came to a pond where there many ducks. The ducks seeing the meteor, commenced a general quacking, which so alarmed him that he turned off and went around the pond, and was about to pass over an Indian village. Here he was again frightened by a young warrior, who was playing on the flute. Being afraid of music, he passed around the village, and soon after falling to the earth, released his burden. The Indian then asked the meteor to give him his head strap, which he refused. The Indian offered him a feather of honor for it, and was again refused. The Sioux, determined to gain his point, told the meteor if he would give him the strap, he would kill a big enemy for him. No reply from the meteor. The Indian then offered to kill a wigwam full of enemies—the meteor still mute. The last offer was six wigwams full of dead enemies for the so much coveted strap. The meteor was finally bribed, gave up the head-strap, and the Sioux went home with the great glory of having outwitted a meteor; for, as they met no more, the debt was never paid.

The *language* of the Sioux would, with proper facilities, be easily acquired. It is said, in many respects, to resemble the ancient Greek. Even after having acquired considerable knowledge of the language by study, it is necessary to live among the people in order to understand their fanciful mode of speaking.

One of the chiefs, "Sleepy Eyes," visited a missionary not many weeks since, and on being asked why he did not come at the time appointed, replied, "How could I come when I have no mocassins," meaning that he had no horse. The horse had recently been killed by a man who owed him a grudge; and his way of alluding to the loss was the mocassins. On another occasion, this same chief, having done what he considered a favor for the missionaries, at *Traverse des Sioux*, told them that his coat was worn out, and that he had neither cloth nor thread to mend it; the fact was, that he had no coat at all, no cloth nor thread; his brawny neck and arms were entirely bare, and this was his way of begging for a new coat.

In Indian warfare, the victor takes the scalp of his enemy. If he have time, he takes the entire scalp, including the ears; but if hurried, a smaller scalp-piece is taken. As an inducement to be foremost in battle, the first four that touch the dead body of an enemy, share the honors that are paid to the one who slew the foe and took the scalp. But the victors in Indian fight frequently suffer in this way; a wounded savage feigns death, and, as some warrior approaches to take his scalp, he will suddenly rise, discharge his gun, and fight desperately with the tomahawk until killed. Deeds of valor performed by Indians are as often done from desperation as from any natural bravery. They are educated to warfare, but often show great disinclination to fight; strategy goes farther with them than manly courage does. At Fort Snelling, the Sioux have more than once crouched under the walls of the fort for protection, and on one occasion a chief, who came in to give information of the approach of some Chippeways trembled so as to shake the ornaments about his dress.

IV. INDIAN CHILDREN

THE CHILDREN among the Sioux are early accustomed to look with indifference upon the sufferings or death of a person they hate. A few years ago a battle was fought quite near Fort Snelling. The next day the Sioux children were playing foot-ball merrily with the head of a Chippeway. One boy, and a small boy too, had ornamented his head and ears with curls. He had taken the skin peeled off a Chippeway who was killed in the battle, wound it around a stick until it assumed the appearance of a curl, and tied them over his ears. Another child had a string around his neck with a finger hanging to it as an ornament. The infants, instead of being amused with toys or trinkets, are held up to see the scalp of an enemy, and they learn to hate a Chippeway as soon as to ask for food.

After the battle, the mother of a Sioux who was severely wounded found her way to the fort. She entered the room weeping sadly. Becoming quite exhausted, she seated herself on the floor, and said she wanted some coffee and sugar for her sick son, some linen to bind up his wounds, and a candle to burn at night, and some whiskey *to make her cry!* Her son recovered, and the mother, as she sat by and watched him, had the satisfaction to see the scalps of the murdered Chippeways stretched on poles all through the village, around which she, sixty years old, looked forward with great joy to dance; though *this* was a small gratification compared with her recollection of having formerly cut to pieces the bodies of sundry murdered Chippeway children.

A dreadful creature she was! How vividly her features rise before me. Well do I remember her as she entered my room on a stormy day in January. Her torn moccasins were a mocking protection to her nearly frozen feet; her worn "okendo kenda" hardly covering a wrinkled neck and arms seamed with the scars of many a self-inflicted wound; she tried to make her tattered blanket meet across her chest, but the benumbed fingers were powerless, and her step so feeble, from fatigue and want of food, that she almost fell before the cheerful fire that seemed to welcome her. The smile with which she tried to return my greeting added hideously to the savage expression of her features, and her matted hair was covered with flakes of drifting snow that almost blinded her.

Food, a pipe, and a short nap before the fire, refreshed her wonderfully. At first she would hardly deign an answer to our questions; now she becomes quite talkative. Her small keen eye follows the children as they play about the room; she tells of her children when they were young, and played around her; when their father brought her venison for food.

Where are they? The Chippeways (mark her as she compresses her lips, and see the nervous trembling of her limbs) killed her husband and her oldest son: consumption walked among her household idols. She has one son left, but he loves the white man's *fire-water;* he has forgotten his aged mother—she has no one to bring her food—the young men laugh at her, and tell her to kill game for herself.

At evening she must be going—ten miles she has to walk to reach her teepee, for she cannot sleep in the white man's house. We tell her the storm is howling—it will be dark before she reaches home—the wind blows keenly across the open prairie—she had better lie down on the carpet before the fire and sleep. She points to the walls of the fort—she does not speak; but her action says, "It cannot be; the Sioux woman cannot sleep beneath the roof of her enemies."

She is gone—God help the Sioux woman! the widow and the childless. God help her, I say, for other hope or help has she none.

GODS OF THE DAHCOTAHS

FIRST IN THE order of the gods of the Dahcotahs, comes the Great Spirit. He is the creator of all things, excepting thunder and wild rice. Then there is,

Wakinyan, or Man of the West.

Wehiyayanpa-micaxta, Man of the East.

Wazza, Man of the North.

Itokaga-micaxta, Man of the South.

Onkteri, or Unktahe, God of the Waters.

Hayoka, or Haoka, the antinatural god.

Takuakanxkan, god of motion.

Canotidan, Little Dweller in Woods.
This god is said to live in a forest, in a hollow tree.

Witkokaga, the Befooler, that is, the god who deceives or fools animals so that they can be easily taken.

Mock-pe-en-dag-a-win;

or,

Checkered Cloud, The Medicine Woman*

Indian Battle Scene, Scalping, watercolor on paper, 1846-1848.

WITHIN A few miles of Fort Snelling lives Checkered Cloud. Not that she has any settled habitation; she is far too important a character for

---

* A medicine woman is a female doctor or juggler. No man or woman can assume this office without previous initiation by authority. The medicine dance is a sacred rite, in honor of the souls of the dead; the mysteries of this dance are kept inviolable; its secrets have never been divulged by its members. The medicine men and women attend in cases of sickness. The Sioux have the greatest faith in them. When the patient recovers, it redounds to the honor of the doctor; if he die, they say "The time had come that he should die," or that the "medicine of the person who cast a spell upon the sick person was stronger than the doctor's." They can always

that. Indeed she is not often two days in the same place. Her wanderings are not, however, of any great extent, so that she can always be found when wanted. But her wigwam is about seven miles from the fort, and she is never much farther off. Her occupations change with the day. She has been very busy of late, for Checkered Cloud is one of the medicine women of the Dahcotahs; and as the Indians have had a good deal of sickness among them, you might follow her from teepee to teepee, as she proceeds with the sacred rattle* in her hand, charming away the animal that has entered the body of the Dahcotah to steal his strength.

Then, she is the great legend-teller of the Dahcotahs. If there is a merry-making in the village, Checkered Cloud must be there, to call to the minds of the revellers the traditions that have been handed down from time immemorial.

Yesterday, wrapped in her blanket, she was seated on the St. Peters, near a hole which she had cut in the ice, in order to spear the fish as they passed through the water; and to-day—but while I am writing of her, she approaches the house; even now, her shadow falls upon the room as she passes the window. I need not listen to her step, for her mocassined feet pass noiselessly through the hall. The door is slowly opened, and she is before me!

How tall she is! and with what graceful dignity she offers her hand. Seventy winters have passed over her, but the brightness of her eye is undimmed by time. Her brow speaks of intellect—and the white hair that is parted over it falls unplaited on her shoulders. She folds her blanket round her and seats herself; she has a request to make, I know, but Checkered Cloud is not a beggar, she never asks aught but what she feels she has a right to claim.

———

find a satisfactory solution of the failure of the charm.

* Sacred rattle. This is generally a gourd, but is sometimes made of bark. Small beads are put into it. The Sioux suppose that this rattle, in the hands of one of their medicine men or women, possesses a certain virtue to charm away sickness or evil spirits. They shake it over a sick person, using a circular motion. It is never, however, put in requisition against the worst *spirits* with which the Red Man has to contend.

"Long ago," she says, "the Dahcotah owned lands that the white man now claims; the trees, the rivers, were all our own. But the Great Spirit has been angry with his children; he has taken their forests and their hunting grounds, and given them to others.

" When I was young, I feared not wind nor storm. Days have I wandered with the hunters of my tribe, that they might bring home many buffalo for food, and to make our wigwams. Then, I cared not for cold and fatigue, for I was young and happy. But now I am old; my children have gone before me to the 'House of Spirits'—the tender boughs have yielded to the first rough wind of autumn, while the parent tree has stood and borne the winter's storm.

"My sons have fallen by the tomahawk of their enemies; my daughter sleeps under the foaming waters of the Falls.

"Twenty winters were added to my life on that day. We had encamped at some distance above the Falls, and our hunters had killed many deer. Before we left our village to go on the hunt, we sacrificed to the Spirit of the woods, and we prayed to the Great Spirit. We lifted up our hands and said, 'Father, Great Spirit, help us to kill deer.' The arrows of our hunters never missed, and as we made ready for our return we were happy, for we knew we should not want for food. My daughter's heart was light, for Haparm was with her, and she never was sad but when he was away.

"Just before we arrived at the Falls, she became sick; her hands were burning hot, she refused to eat. As the canoe passed over the Mississippi, she would fill her cup with its waters, to drink and throw over her brow. The medicine men were always at her side, but they said some evil spirit hated her, and prevented their spells from doing her good.

"When we reached to Falls, she was worse; the women left their canoes, and prepared to carry them and the rest of the baggage round the Falls.

"But what should we do with We-no-nah? the flush of fever was on her cheek; she did not know me when I spoke to her; but she kept her eyes fixed upon her lover.

"'We will leave her in the canoe,' said her father; 'and with a line we can carry her gently over the Rapids.' I was afraid, but with her brothers holding the line she must be safe. So I left my child in her canoe, and paddled with the others to the shore.

"As we left her, she turned her eyes toward us, as if anxious to know what we were about to do. The men held the line steadily, and the canoe floated so gently that I began to feel less anxious—but as we approached the rapids, my heart beat quickly at the sound of the waters. Carefully did her brothers hold the line, and I never moved my eyes from the canoe in which she lay. Now the roaring of the waters grew louder, and as they hastened to the rocks over which they would fall they bore with them my child—I saw her raise herself in the canoe, I saw her long hair as it fell on her bosom—I saw no more!

"My sons bore me in their arms to the rest of the party. The hunters had delayed their return that they might seek for the body of my child. Her lover called to her, his voice could be heard above the sound of the waters. 'Return to me, Wenonah, I will never love maiden but you; did you not promise to light the fires in my wigwam?' He would have thrown himself after her, had not the young men prevented him. The body rests not in the cold waters; we found it and buried it, and her spirit calls to me in the silence of the night! Her lover said he would not remain long on the earth; he turned from the Dahcotah maidens as they smiled upon him. He died as a warrior should die!

"The Chippeways had watched for us, they longed to carry the scalp of a Dahcotah home. They did so—but we were avenged.

"Our young men burst in upon them when they were sleeping; they struck them with their tomahawks, they tore their scalps reeking with blood from their heads.

"We heard our warriors at the village as they returned from their war party; we knew by their joyful cries that they had avenged their friends. One by one they entered the village, bearing twenty scalps of the enemy.

"Only three of the Dahcotahs had fallen. But who were the three? My sons, and he who was dear as a son to me, the lover of my child. I fled from their cries of triumph—I longed to plunge the knife into my own heart.

"I have lived on. But sorrow and cold and hunger have bowed my spirit; and my limbs are not as strong and active as they were in my youth. Neither can I work with porcupine as I used to—for age and tears have dimmed my sight. I bring you venison and fish, will you not give me clothes to protect me from the winter's cold?"

Ah! Checkered Cloud—he was a prophet who named you. Though the cloud has varied, now passing away, now returning blacker than before—

though the cheering light of the sun has for a moment dispelled the gloom—'twas but for a moment! for it was sure to break in terrors over your head. Your name is your history, your life has been a checkered cloud! But the storm of the day has yielded to the influence of the setting sun. The thunder has ceased to roll, the wind has died away, and the golden streaks that bound the horizon promise a brighter morning. So with Checkered Cloud, the storm and strife of the earth have ceased; the "battle of life" is fought, and she has conquered. For she hopes to meet the beloved of earth in the heaven of the Dahcotahs.

And who will say that our heaven will not be hers? The God of the Dahcotahs is ours, though they, less happy than we, have not been taught to know him. Christians! are you without blame? Have you thought of the privations, the wants of those who once owned your country, and would own it still but for the strong hand? Have you remembered that their souls are dear in His sight, who suffered for them, as well as for you? Have you given bright gold that their children might be educated and redeemed from their slavery of soul? Checkered Cloud will die as she has lived, a believer in the religion of the Dahcotahs. The traditions of her tribe are written on her heart. She worships a spirit in every forest tree, or every running stream. The features of the favored Israelite are hers; she is perchance a daughter of their lost tribe. When she was young, she would have listened to the missionary as he told her of Gethsemane and Calvary. But age yields not like youth to new impressions; the one looks to the future, the other clings to the past. See! she has put by her pipe and is going, but she is coming oft again to talk to me of her people, that I may tell to my friends the bravery of the Dahcotah warrior, and the beauty of the maiden! the legends of their rivers and sacred isles—the traditions of their rocks and hills!

If I cannot, in recounting the wild stories of this prophetess of the forest, give her own striking words, I shall at least be faithful to the spirit of her recitals. I shall let Indian life speak for itself; these true pictures of its course will tell its whole simple story better than any labored exposition of mine. Here we may see, not the red man of the novel or the drama, but the red man as he appears to himself, and to those who live with him. His better characteristics will be found quite as numerous as ought to be expected under the circumstances; his faults and his sufferings should appeal to the hearts of those who hold the means of his salvation. No intelligent citizen of these United States can without blame forget the aborigines of his country. Their wrongs cry to heaven; their souls will be required of us. To view them as brutes is an insult to Him who made them and us. May this little work do something towards exciting an interest in a single tribe out of the many whose only hope is in the mercy of the white man!

Red Earth;

or,

Mock-a-Doota-Win

Indian Village on the Mississippi near Fort Snelling, watercolor on paper, 1846-1848.

"GOOD ROAD" is one of the Dahcotah chiefs—he is fifty years old and has two wives, but these two have given a deal of trouble; although the chief probably thinks it of no importance whether his two wives fight all the time or not, so that they obey his orders. For what would be a calamity in domestic life to us, is an every day affair among the Dahcotahs.

Good Road's village is situated on the banks of the St. Peter's about seven miles from Fort Snelling. And like other Indian villages it abounds in variety more than anything else. In the teepee the farthest from us, right on the edge of the shore, there are three young men carousing. One is inclined to go to sleep, but the other two will not let him; their spirits are raised and excited by what has made him stupid. Who would suppose they were human beings? See their bloodshot eyes; hear their fiendish laugh and horrid yells; probably before the revel is closed, one of the friends will have buried his knife in the other's heart.

We will pass on to the next teepee. Here we witness a scene almost as appalling. "Iron Arms," one of the most valiant warriors of the band, is stretched in the agonies of death. Old Spirit Killer, the medicine man, is gesticulating by his side, and accompanying his motions with the most horrid noises. But all in vain; the spirit of "Iron Arms," the man of strength, is gone. The doctor says that his medicine was good, but that a prairie dog had entered into the body of the Dahcotah, and he thought it had been a mud-hen. Magnanimous doctor! All honor, that you can allow yourself in error.

While the friends of the dead warrior are rending the air with their cries, we will find out what is going on in the next wigwam. What a contrast!

"The Whirlpool" is seated on the ground smoking; gazing as earnestly at the bright coals as if in them he could read the future or recall the past; and his young wife, whose face, now merry, now sad, bright with smiles at one moment, and lost in thought the next, gained for her the name of "The Changing Countenance," is hushing her child to sleep; but the expression of her features does not change now—as she looks on her child, a mother's deep and devoted love is pictured on her face.

In another, "The Dancing Woman" is wrapped in her blanket pretending to go to sleep. In vain does "The Flying Cloud" play that monotonous courting tune on the flute. The maiden would not be his wife if he gave her all the trinkets in the world. She loves and is going to marry "Iron Lightning," who has gone to bring her—what? a brooch—a new blanket? no, a Chippeway's scalp, that she may be the most graceful of those who dance around it. Her mother is mending the mocassins of the old man who sleeps before the fire.

And we might go round the village and find every family differently employed. They have no regular hours for eating or sleeping. In front of the teepees, young men are lying on the ground, lazily playing checkers, while their wives and sisters are cutting wood and engaged in laborious household duties.

I said Good Road had two wives, and I would now observe that neither of them is younger than himself. But they are as jealous of each other as if they had just turned seventeen, and their lord and master were twenty instead of fifty. Not a day passes that they do not quarrel, and fight too. They throw at each other whatever is most convenient, and sticks of wood are always at hand. And then, the sons of each wife take a part in the battle; they first fight for their mothers, and then for themselves—so that the chief must have been reduced to desperation long ago if it were not for his pipe and his philosophy. Good Road's second wife has Chippeway blood in her veins. Her mother was taken prisoner by the Dahcotahs; they adopted her, and she became the wife of a Dahcotah warrior. She loved her own people, and those who had adopted her too; and in course of time her daughter attained the honorable station of a chief's second wife. Good Road hates the Chippeways, but he fell in love with one of their descendants, and married her. She is a good wife, and the white people have given her the name of "Old Bets."

Last summer "Old Bets" narrowly escaped with her life. The Dahcotahs having nothing else to do, were amusing themselves by recalling all the Chippeways had ever done to injure them; and those who were too lazy to go out on a war party, happily recollected that there was Chippeway blood near them—no farther off than their chief's wigwam; and eight or ten braves vowed they would make an end of "Old Bets." But she heard of their threats, left the village for a time, and after the Dahcotahs had gotten over their mania for shedding blood, she returned, and right glad was Good Road to see her. For she has an open, good humored countenance; the very reverse of that of the first wife, whose vinegar aspect would frighten away an army of small children.

After "Old Bets" returned, Good Road could not conceal his satisfaction. His wife's trip had evidently improved her good looks, for the chief thought she was the handsomest squaw in the village. Her children were always taunting the sons of the first wife, and so it went on, until at last Good Road said he would stand it no longer; he told his oldest wife to go—that he would support her no longer. And for her children, he told them the prairies were large; there were deer and other game—in short, he disinherited them—cut them off with their last meal.

For the discarded wife, life had now but one hope. The only star that shone in the blackness of her heaven, was the undefined prospect of seeing her rival's blood flow. She would greatly have preferred taking her life herself; and as she left the wigwam of the chief, she grasped the handle of her knife—how quick her heart beat! it might be now or never.

But there were too many around to protect Old Bets. The time would come—she would watch for her—she would tear her heart from her yet.

The sons of the old hag did not leave the village; they would keep a watch on their father and his Chippeway wife. They would not easily yield their right to the chieftainship. While they hunted, and smoked, and played at cards, they were ever on the look-out for revenge.

CHAPTER II

"RED EARTH" sits by the door her father's teepee; while the village is alive with cheerfulness, she does not join in any of the amusements going on, but seems to be occupied with what is passing in her own mind.

Occasionally she throws a pebble from the shore far into the river, and the copper-colored children spring after it, as if the water were their own element, striving to get it before it sinks from their view.

Had she been attentive to what is passing around her, she would not have kept her seat, for "Shining Iron," the son of Good Road's second wife, approaches her; and she loves him too little to talk with him when it can be avoided.

"Why are you not helping the women to make the teepee, Red Earth?" said the warrior. "They are laughing while they sew the buffalo-skin together, and you are sitting silent and alone. Why is it so? Are you thinking of 'Fiery Wind?'"

"There are enough women to make the teepee," replied Red Earth, "and I sit alone because I choose to do so. But if I am thinking of 'Fiery Wind' I do right—he is a great warrior!"

"Tell me if you love Fiery Wind?" said the young man, while his eyes flashed fire, and the veins in his temple swelled almost to bursting.

"I do not love you," said the girl, "and that is enough. And you need never think I will become your wife; your spells cannot make me love you.* Where are Fiery Wind and his relations? driven from the wigwam of the Chief by you and your Chippeway mother. But they do not fear you—neither do I!"

And Red Earth looked calmly at the angry face of her lover. For Shining Iron did love her, and he had loved her long. He had loaded her with presents, which she always refused; he had related his honors, his brave acts to her, but she turned a deaf ear to his words. He promised her he would always have venison in her teepee, and that he never would take another wife; she was the only woman he could ever love. But he might as well have talked to the winds. And he thought so himself, for, finding he could not gain the heart of the proud girl, he determined she should never be the wife of any other man, and he told her so.

"You may marry Fiery Wind," said the angry lover, "but if you do, I will kill him."

Red Earth heard, but did not reply to his threats; she feared not for herself, but she trembled at the prospect of danger to the man she loved. And while she turned the bracelets on her small wrists, the warrior left her to her own thoughts. They were far from being pleasant; she must warn her lover of the threats of his rival. For a while she almost determined she would not marry Fiery Wind, for then his life would be safe; but she would not break her promise. Besides, it was hard for her to destroy all the air-built castles which she had built for her happy future.

She knew Shining Iron's bravery, and she doubted not he would fulfill his promise; for a moment prudence suggested that she had better marry him to avoid his revenge. But she grasped the handle of her knife, as if she would plunge it into her own bosom for harboring the dark thought. Never should she be unfaithful; when Fiery Wind returned she would tell him all, and then she would become his wife, and she felt that her own heart was true enough to guard him, her own arm strong enough to slay his enemy.

----

* The Sioux have great faith in spells. A lover will take gum, and after putting some medicine in it, will induce the girl of his choice to chew it, or put it in her way so that she will take it up of her own accord. It is a long time before an Indian lover will take a refusal from the woman he has chosen for a wife.

ALL WOMEN are wilful enough, but Dahcotah women are particularly so. Slaves as they are to their husbands, they lord it over each other, and it is only when they become grandmothers that they seem to feel their dependence, and in many instances yield implicit obedience to the wills of their grandchildren.

They take great delight in watching over and instructing their children's children; giving them lessons in morality,* and worldly wisdom. Thus while Red Earth was making her determination, her old grandmother belonging to the village was acting upon hers.

This old woman was a perfect virago—an "embodied storm." In her time she had cut off the hands and feet of some little Chippeway children, and strung them, and worn them for a necklace. And she feasted yet at the pleasant recollections this honorable exploit induced.

But so tender was she of the feelings of her own flesh and blood, that the thought of their suffering the slightest pain was death to her.

Her son ruled his household very well for a Dahcotah. He had a number of young warriors and hunters growing up around him, and he sometimes got tired of their disturbances, and would use, not the rod but a stick of wood to some purpose. Although it had the good effect of quelling the refractory spirits of the young, it invariably fired the soul of his aged mother. The old woman would cry and howl, and refuse to eat, for days; till, finding this had no effect upon her hard-hearted son, she told him she would do something that would make him sorry, the next time he struck one of his children.

But the dutiful son paid no attention to her. He had always considered women as being inferior to dogs, and he would as soon have thought of giving up smoking, as of minding his mother's threats.

But while Red Earth was thinking of her absent lover, Two Stars was beating his sons again—and when the maiden was left alone by Shining Iron after the warning he had given her, she was attracted by the cries of one of

---

* The idea is ridiculed by some, that an Indian mother troubles herself about the morals of her children; but it is nevertheless true, that she talks to them, and, according to her own ideas of right and wrong, tries to instill good principles into their minds. The grandmothers take a great deal of care of their grandchildren.

the old women of the village, who was struggling 'mid earth and heaven, while old and young were running to the spot, some to render assistance, others to see the fun.

And glorious fun it was! the grandmother had almost hung herself— that is, she seriously intended to do it. But she evidently did not expect the operation to be so painful. When her son, in defiance of her tears and threats, commenced settling his household difficulties in his own way she took her head-strap,* went to a hill just above the village, and deliberately made her preparations for hanging, as cooly too as if she had been used to being hung for a long time. But when, after having doubled the strap four times to prevent its breaking, she found herself choking, her courage gave way—she yelled frightfully; and it was well that her son and others ran so fast, for they had well nigh been too late. As it was, they carried her into the teepee, where the medicine man took charge of her case; and she was quite well again in an hour or two. Report says (but there is a sad amount of scandal in an Indian village) that the son has never offended the mother since; so, like many a wilful woman, she has gained her point.

Red Earth witnessed the cutting down of the old woman, and as she returned to her teepee, her quick ear warned her of coming footsteps. She lingered apart from the others, and soon she saw the eagle feathers of her warrior as he descended the hill towards the village. Gladly would she have gone to meet him to welcome him home, but she knew that Shining Iron was watching her motions, and she bent her steps homeward. She was quite sure that it not be long before he would seek her, and then she would tell him what had passed, and make arrangements for their course of conduct for the future.

Fiery Wind was the nephew of Good Road, but he, like the sons, was in disgrace with the chief, and, like them, he had vowed vengeance against "Old Bets."

---

* The head-strap is made of buffalo skin. It is from eight to ten, or sometimes twenty-four feet long. The women fasten their heavy burdens to this strap, which goes around the forehead; the weight of the burden falls upon the head and back. This occasions the figures of the Indian women to stoop, since they necessarily lean forward in order to preserve their balance.

CHAPTER III

THE GUN is now generally used among the Dahcotahs as a weapon of warfare. But those bands in the neighborhood of Fort Snelling considered it as a necessary part of their war implements, before the distant bands were at all acquainted with its use.

Some time ago, one of the Mun-da-wa-kan-tons gave a gun to a Sisse-ton, who, proud of the gift, went out immediately to use it. On his return to his village he came up with a drove of buffaloes. His first impulse was to use his bow and arrow, but a moment's thought reminded him of the gift of his friend. He loaded the gun, saying at the same time to it, "Now, the Dahcotahs call you 'wah-kun' (supernatural), kill me the fattest cow in the drove." He waited a few moments to see his orders executed, but the gun was not "wah-kun" enough to fire by order alone. Seeing that it did not go off, the Sisse-ton flew into a rage and broke the gun into pieces. "I suppose," said he "that if a Mun-da-wah-can-ton had told you to kill a buffalo, you would have done it, but you do not regard what a Sisse-ton says." So he threw the pieces of the gun away, and found his bow and arrows of far more service.

However naturally the usages of warfare may come to the Indians, they are also made a part of their education.

The children are taught that it is wicked to murder without a cause; but when offence has been given, they are in duty bound to retaliate.

The day after the return of Fiery Wind, the boys of the village were to attack a hornet's nest. This is one of the way of training their sons to warfare. One of the old warriors had seen a hornet's nest in the woods, and he returned to the village, and with the chief assembled all the boys in the village. The chief ordered the boys to take off all their clothes, and gave them each a gun. He then told them how brave their forefathers were—that they never feared pain or danger—and that they must prove themselves worthy sons of such ancestors. "One of these days you will be men, and then you will go on war parties and kill your enemies, and then you will be fit to join in the dog feast. Be brave, and do not fear the sting of the hornet, for if you do, you will be cowards instead of warriors, and the braves will call you women and laugh at you."

This was enough to animate the courage of the boys—some of them not more than five years old pushed ahead of their elder brothers, eager to show their fathers, who accompanied them, how little they fear their enemies, as they termed the hornets. And formidable enemies they were too—for many of the little fellows returned sadly stung, with swollen limbs, and closed eyes; but they bore their wounds as well as brave men would have endured their pain on a battle-field.

After leaving their village, they entered the woods farther from the banks of the river. The guide who had seen the nest led the way, and the miniature warriors trod as lightly as if there was danger of rousing a sleeping foe. At last the old man pointed to the nest, and without a moment's hesitation, the young Dahcotahs attacked it. Out flew the hornets in every direction. Some of the little boys cried out with pain from the stings of the hornets on their unprotected limbs—but the cries of Shame! shame! from one of the old men soon recalled them to their duty, and they marched up again not a whit discomfited. Good Road cheered them on. "Fight well, my warriors," said he; "you will carry many scalps home, you are brave men."

It was not long before the nest was quite destroyed, and then the old men said they must take a list of the killed and wounded. The boys forced a loud laugh when they replied that there were no scalps taken by the enemy, but they could not deny that the list of the wounded was quite a long one. Some of them limped, in spite of their efforts to walk upright, and one little fellow had to be assisted along by his father, for both eyes were closed; and, although stung in every direction and evidently suffering agony, the brave boy would not utter a complaint.

When they approached the village, the young warriors formed into Indian file, and entered as triumphantly as their fathers would have done, had they borne twenty Chippeway scalps with them.

The mothers first applauded the bravery of their sons; and then applied herbs to their swollen limbs, and the mimic war furnished a subject of amusement for the villages for the remainder of the day.

CHAPTER IV

IT WOULD be well for the Dahcotahs if they only sought the lives of their enemies. But they are wasting in numbers far more by their internal dissensions than from other causes. Murder is so common among them, that it is even less than a nine days' wonder; all that is thought necessary is to bury the dead, and then some relative must avenge his quarrel.

Red Earth told her lover of the threat of Shining Iron, and the young man was thus put on his guard. The sons of Good Road's first wife were also told of the state of things, and they told Fiery Wind that they would take up his quarrel, glad of an opportunity to avenge their own and their mother's wrongs. It was the month of April, or as the Dahcotahs say in "the moon that geese lay," that Red Earth took her place by the side of her husband, thus asserting her right to be mistress of his wigwam. While she occupied herself with her many duties, she never for a moment forgot the threat of Shining Iron. But her cares and anxieties for her husband's safety were soon over. She had not long been a wife before her enemy lay a corpse; his life was a forfeit to his love for her, and Red Earth had a woman's heart. Although she could but rejoice that the fears which had tormented her were now unnecessary, yet when she remembered how devotedly the dead warrior had loved her, how anxiously he had tried to please her, she could not but shed a few tears of sorrow for his death. But they were soon wiped away—not for the world would she have had her husband see them.

The oldest sons of Good Road were true to their word—and the son of Old Bets was not the only subject for their vengeance. His sister was with him at the moment that they chose to accomplish their purpose; and when an Indian commences to shed blood, there is no knowing how soon he will be satisfied. Shining Iron died instantly, but the sister's wounds were not fatal—she is slowly recovering.

It was but yesterday that we visited the grave of the dead warrior. On a hill near the St. Peters his body is buried. The Indians have enclosed the grave, and there is a "Wah-kun stone," to which they sacrifice, at his head. No one reposes near him. Alone he lies, undisturbed by aught except the winds that sigh over him. The first flowers of Spring are blooming on the spot where he played in childhood, and here, where he reposes, he often sat to mourn the unkindness of Red Earth, and vow vengeance on his successful rival.

But he is not unwatched. His spirit is ever near, and perhaps he will again live on earth.* His friends believe that he may hold communion with

---

* The Sioux believe in the transmigration of souls. Many of the Indians near Fort Snelling say they have lived before on earth. The jugglers remember many incidents that occurred during some former residence on earth, and they will tell them to you with all the gravity imaginable.

Unk-ta-he,—that from that God he will learn the mysteries of the Earth and Water; and when he lives again in another form, he will instruct the Dahcotahs in their religion, and be a great medicine man.

Good Road is quite reconciled to his sons, for he says it was a brave deed to get rid of an enemy. In vain does Old Bets ask for vengeance on the murderers. Good Road reminds her that Shining Iron had made a threat, and it was not proper he should live; and the chief insisted more upon this, when he added that these children of her's were by a former husband, and it was natural his sons should resent their father's preference for them.

So after all Old Bets doubts whether she, or the Chief's first wife, has got the best of it; and as she dresses the wounds of her daughter, she wishes that the Dahcotahs had killed her mother instead of adopting her— lamenting, too, that she should ever have attained to the honor of being Good Road's wife.

Wenona;

or,

THE VIRGIN'S FEAST

On the Mississippi 140 miles above Prairie du Chien, watercolor on paper, 1846-1848.

NEVER DID the sun shine brighter than on a cold day in December, when the Indians at "Little Crow's" village were preparing to go on a deer hunt. The Mississippi was frozen, and the girls of the village had the day before enjoyed one of their favorite amusements—a ball-play on the ice. Those who owned the bright cloths and calicoes which were hung up before their eyes, as an incentive to win the game, were still rejoicing over their treasures; while the disappointed ones were looking sullen, and muttering of partiality being shown to this one because she was beautiful, and to that, because she was the sister of the chief.

"Look at my head!" said Harpstenah; "Wenona knew that I was the swiftest runner in the band, and as I stooped to catch the ball she struck me a blow that stunned me, so that I could not run again."

But the head was so ugly, and the face too, that there was no pity felt for her; those dirty, wrinkled features bore witness to her contempt for the cleansing qualities of water. Her uncombed hair was hanging in masses about her ears and face, and her countenance expressed cruelty and passion. But Harpstenah had nothing to avenge; when she was young she was passed by, as there was nothing in her face or disposition that could attract; and now in the winter of life she was so ugly and so desolate, so cross and so forlorn, that no one deemed her worthy even of a slight. But for all that, Harpstenah could hate, and with all the intensity of her evil heart did she hate Wenonah, the beautiful sister of the chief.

Yesterday had been as bright as to-day, and Grey Eagle, the medicine man, had hung on a pole the prizes that were to be given to the party that succeeded in throwing the ball into a space marked off.

The maidens of the village were all dressed in their gayest clothing, with ornaments of beads, bracelets, rings, and ribbons in profusion. They cared not half so much for the prizes, as they rejoiced at the opportunity of displaying their graceful persons. The old women were eager to commence the game, for they longed to possess the cloth for their leggins, and the calico for the "okendokendas."*

The women, young and old, were divided into two parties; but as one party threw the ball towards the space marked off, the others threw it back again far over their heads, and then all ran back, each party endeavoring to reach it first, that they might succeed in placing the ball in the position which was to decide the game.

But the ball is not thrown by the hand, each woman has a long stick with a circular frame at the end of it; this they call a bat stick, and, simple as it looks, it requires great skill to manage it.

Wenona was the swiftest runner of one party, and Harpstenah, old and ugly as she was, the best of the other. How excited they are! the snow-covered hills, majestic and silent, look coldly enough upon their sport; but

---

* "Okendokendas." This is the Sioux word for calico. It is used as the name for a kind of short gown, which is worn by the Sioux women, made generally of calico, sometimes of cloth.

what care they? the prize will soon be won.

The old medicine man cheered them on. "Run fast, Wenona! take care that Harpstenah does not win the game. Ho, Harpstenah! if you and your leggins are old, you may have the cloth yet."

Now Wenona's party is getting on bravely, but the ball has been caught and thrown back by the other party. But at last it is decided. In the struggle for the ball, Harpstenah received a blow from an old squaw as dismal looking as herself, and Wenona catches the ball and throws it into the appointed place. The game is ended, and the medicine man comes forward to distribute the prizes.

The warriors have looked on, admiring those who were beautiful and graceful, and laughing at the ugly and awkward.

But Wenona cared little for the prizes. She was a chief's sister, and she was young and beautiful. The handsomest presents were given her, and she hardly looked at the portion of the prizes which fell to her lot.

Smarting with pain from the blow she had received (and she spoke falsely when she said Wenona had struck her), stung with jealousy at the other party having won the game, Harpstenah determined on revenge. "If I am old," she said, "I will live long enough to bring misery on her; ugly as I may be, I will humble the proud beauty. What do I eat? the worthless heads of birds are given to the old woman for whom nobody cares, but my food will be to see the eye of Wenona fall beneath the laugh of scorn. I will revenge the wrongs of my life on her."

Commend me to a Dahcotah woman's revenge! Has she been slighted in love? blood must be shed; and if she is not able to accomplish the death of her rival, her own life will probably pay the forfeit. Has disgrace or insult been heaped upon her? a life of eighty years is not long enough to bring down vengeance on the offender. So with Harpstenah. Her life had not been a blessing to herself—she would make it a curse to others.

CHAPTER II

IN THE PREPARATIONS for the deer hunt, the ball-play has been forgotten. The women are putting together what will be necessary for their comfort during their absence, and the men are examining their guns and bows and arrows. The young girls anticipate amusement and happiness, for they will assist their lovers to bring in the deer to the camp; and the jest and merry laugh, and the words of love are spoken too. The ball-play has been forgotten by all but Harpstenah.

But it is late in the afternoon; and as they do not start till the morning, something must be done to pass the long evening. "If this were full," said a young hunter, kicking at the same time an empty keg that had once contained whiskey, "if this were full, we would have a merry night of it."

"Yes," said Grey Iron, whose age seemed to have brought him wisdom, "the night would be merry, but where would you be the day after. Did you not, after drinking that very whiskey, strike a white woman, for which you were taken to the fort by the soldiers, and kept as a prisoner?"

The young man's look of mortification at this reproof did not save him from the contemptuous sneer of his companions, for all despise the Dahcotah who has thus been punished. No act of bravery can wipe away his disgrace.

But Wenona sat pale and sad in her brother's wigwam. The bright and happy looks of yesterday were all gone. Her sister-in-law has hushed her child to sleep, and she is resting from the fatigues of the day. Several old men, friends of Little Crow's father, are sitting round the fire; one has fallen asleep, while the others talk of the wonderful powers of their sacred medicine.

"Why are you sad, Wenona," said the chief, turning to her; "why should the eyes of a chief's sister be filled with tears, and her looks bent on the ground?"

"You need not ask why I am not happy," said Wenona: "Red Cloud brought presents to you yesterday; he laid them at the door of your wigwam. He wants to buy me, and you have received his gifts; why do you not return them? you know I do not love him."

"Red Cloud is a great warrior," replied the chief; "he wears many feathers of honor; you must marry him."

The girl wrapped herself in her blanket and lay down. For a time her sighs were heard—but at length sleep came to her relief, and her grief was forgotten in dreams. But morn has come and they are to make an early start. Was ever such confusion? Look at that old hag knocking the very senses out of her daughter's head because she is not ready! and the girl, in order to avoid the blows, stumbles over an unfortunate dog, who commences a horrible barking and whining, tempting all the dogs of the village to outbark and outwhine him.

There goes "White Buffalo" with his two wives, the first wife with the teepee on her back and her child on top of it. No wonder she looks so cross, for the second wife walks leisurely on. Now is her time, but let her beware! for White Buffalo is thinking seriously of taking a third.

But they are all off at last. Mothers with children, and corn, and teepees, and children with dogs on their backs. They are all gone, and the village looks desolate and forsaken.

CHAPTER III

THE PARTY encamped about twenty miles from the village. The women plant the poles of their teepees firmly in the ground and cover them with a buffalo skin. A fire is soon made in the centre and corn put on to boil. Their bread is kneaded and put in the ashes to bake, but flour is not very plenty among them.

The next day parties were out in every direction; tracks of deer were seen in the snow, and the hunters followed them up. The beautiful animal flies in terror from the death which comes surer and swifter than her own light footsteps. The hunter's knife is soon upon her, and while warmth and even life are left, the skin is drawn off.

After the fatigues of the day comes the long and pleasant evening. A bright fire burned in the wigwam of the chief, and many of the Indians were smoking around it, but Wenona was sad, and she took but little part in the laughter and merriment of the others.

Red Cloud boasted of his bravery and his deeds of valor; even the old men listened to him with respect, for they knew that his name was a terror to his enemies. But Wenona turned from him! she hated to hear the sound of his voice.

The old men talked of the mighty giant of the Dahcotahs, he who needed not to take his gun to kill the game he wanted; the glance of his eye would strike with death the deer, the buffalo, or even the bear.

The song, the jest, the legend, by turns occupied them until they separated to sleep. But as the warriors stepped into the open air, why does the light of the moon fall upon faces pale with terror? "See!" said the chief, "how flash the mysterious lights! there is danger near, some dreadful calamity is threatening us."

"We will shoot at them," said Red Cloud; "we will destroy their power," And the Indians discharged their guns in quick succession towards the northern horizon, which was brilliantly illuminated with the Aurora Borealis; thus hoping to ward off coming danger.

The brother and sister were left alone at the door of the teepee. The stern warrior's looks expressed superstitious terror, while the maiden's face was calm and fearless. "Do you not fear the power of the woman who sits in the north, Wenona? she shows those flashes of light to tell us of coming evil."

"What should I fear," said Wenona; "I, who will soon join my mother, my father, my sisters, in the land of spirits? Listen to my words, my brother: there are but two of us; strife and disease have laid low the brave, the good, the beautiful; we are the last of our family; you will soon be alone.

"Before the leaves fell from the trees, as I sat on the banks of the Mississippi, I saw the fairy of the water. The moon was rising, but it was not yet bright enough for me to see her figure distinctly. But I knew her voice; I had often heard it in my dreams. 'Wenona,' she said (and the waves were still that they might hear her words), 'Wenona, the lands of the Dahcotah are green and beautiful—but there are fairer prairies than those on earth. In that bright country the forest trees are ever green, and the waves of the river flow on unchilled by the breath of winter. You will not long be with the children of the earth. Even now your sisters are calling you, and your mother is telling them that a few more months will bring you to their side!'

"The words were true, my brother, but I knew not that your harshness would hasten my going. You say that I shall marry Red Cloud; sooner will I plunge my knife into my heart; sooner shall the waves of the Mississippi roll over me. Brother, you will soon be alone!"

"Speak not such words, my sister," said the chief; "it shall be as you will. I have not promised Red Cloud. I thought you would be happy if you were his wife, and you shall not be forced to marry him. But why should you think of death? you saw our braves as they shot at the lights in the north. They have frightened them away. Look! they flash no more. Go in, and sleep, and tomorrow I will tell Red Cloud that you love him not."

And the cloudless moon shone on a happy face, and the bright stars seemed more bright as Wenona gazed upon them; but as she turned to enter the wigwam, one star was seen falling in the heavens, and the light that followed it was lost in the brightness of the others. And her dreams were not happy, for the fairy of the water haunted them. "Even as that star, Wenona, thou shalt pass from all that thou lovest on earth; but weep not, thy course is upward!"

THE HUNTERS were so successful that they returned to their village soon. The friends of Wenona rejoiced in her happy looks, but to Harpenstah they were bitterness and gall. The angry countenance of Red Cloud found an answering chord in her own heart.

"Ha!" said she to him, as he watched Wenona and her lover talking together, "what has happened? Did you not say you would marry the chief's sister—why then are you not with her? Red Cloud is a great warrior, why should he be sad because Wenona loves him not? Are there not maidens among the Dahcotahs more beautiful than she? She never loved you; her brother, too, has treated you with contempt. Listen to my words, Red Cloud; the Virgin's Feast is soon to be celebrated, and she will enter the ring for the last time. When she comes forward, tell her she is unworthy. Is she not a disgrace to the band? Has she not shamed a brave warrior? Will you not be despised when another is preferred to you?"

The words of the tempter are in his ear—madness and hatred are in his heart.

"I said I would take her life, but my revenge will be deeper. Wenona would die rather than be disgraced." And as he spoke Harpstenah turned to leave him, for she saw that the poison had entered his soul.

CHAPTER IV

AMONG THE Dahcotahs, women are not excluded from joining in their feasts or dances; they dance the scalp dance while the men sit round and sing, and they join in celebrating many of the customs of their tribe. But the

Virgin's Feast has reference to the women alone; its object is not to celebrate the deeds of the warrior, but rather to put to the test the virtue of the maiden.

Notice was given among the Indians that the Virgin's Feast was to be celebrated at Little Crow's village; the time was mentioned, and all who chose to attend were welcome to do so.

The feast was prepared in the neighborhood of the village. The boiled corn and venison were put in wooden bowls, and the Indians sat round, forming a ring. Those who were to partake of the feast were dressed in their gayest apparel; their long hair plaited and falling over their shoulders. Those who are conscious of error dare not approach the feast, for it is a part of the ceremony that they shall be exposed by any one present. Neither rank nor beauty must interpose to prevent the punishment. Nay, sometimes the power of innocence and virtue itself is not sufficient to guard the Dahcotah maiden from disgrace.

And was Wenona unworthy? The white snow that covered the hills was not more pure than she. But Red Cloud cared not for that. She had refused to be the light of his wigwam, and thus was he avenged.

Wenona advanced with the maidens of the village. Who can describe her terror and dismay when Red Cloud advances and leads her from the sacred ring? To whom shall the maiden turn for help? To her brother? his angry countenance speaks not of comfort. Her friends? the smile of scorn is on their lips. Her lover? he has left the feast.

Her determination is soon made; her form is seen as she flies to the woods. Death is the refuge of the friendless and the wronged.

But as night came on the relatives of Wenona wondered that she did not return. They sought her, and they found her lifeless body; the knife was deep in her heart.

She knew she was innocent, but what did that avail her? She was accused by a warrior, and who would believe her if she denied the charge?

And why condemn her that she deprived herself of life, which she deemed worthless, when embittered by unmerited contempt. She knew not that God has said, "Thou shalt do no murder." The command had never sounded in her ears.

She trusted to find a home in the House of Spirits—she may have found heaven in the mercy of God.

The fever of the following summer spared neither age nor youth, and Red Cloud was its first victim. As the dying Harpenstah saw his body carried out to be placed upon the scaffold—"He is dead," she cried, "and Wenona was innocent! He hated her because she slighted him; I hated her because she was happy. He had his revenge, and I mine; but Wenona was falsely accused, and I told him to do it!" and the eyes were closed—the voice was hushed in death.

Wenona was innocent; and when the Virgin's Feast shall be celebrated in her native village again, how will the maidens tremble as they approach the sacred ring! Can they forget the fate of their beautiful companion?

And when the breath of summer warms to life the prairie flowers—when the long grass shall wave under the scaffold where repose the mortal remains of the chief's sister—how often will the Dahcotah maidens draw near to contrast the meanness, the treachery, the falsehood of Red Cloud, with the constancy, devotion, and firmness of Wenona!

THE DAHCOTAH CONVERT

⁎
∧∧∧∧∧∧

Permanent Residence, Sioux, watercolor on paper, 1846-1848.

"TELL ME," said Hiatu-we-noken-chah, or 'woman of the night,' "the Great Spirit whom you have taught me to fear, why has he made the white woman rich and happy, and the Dahcotah poor and miserable?" She spoke with bitterness when she remembered the years of sorrow that had made up the sum of her existence.

But how with the missionary's wife? had her life been one bright dream—had her days been always full of gladness—her nights quiet and free from care? Had she never longed for the time of repose, that darkness might cover her as with a mantle—and when 'sleep forsook the wretched,' did she not pray for the breaking of the day, that she might again forget all in the performance of the duties of her station? Could it be that the Creator had balanced the happiness of one portion of his children against the wretchedness of the rest? Let her story answer.

Her home is now among the forests of the west. As a child she would tremble when she heard of the savage whose only happiness was in shedding the blood of his fellow creatures. The name of an "Indian" when uttered by her nurse would check the boisterous gayety of the day or the tedious restlessness of the night.

As she gathered flowers on the pleasant banks of the Sciota, would it not have brought paleness to her cheek to have whispered her that not many years would pass over her, before she would be far away from the scenes of her youth?

And as she uttered the marriage vow, how little did she think that soon would her broken spirit devote time, energies, life, to the good of others; as an act of duty and, but for the faith of the Christian, of despair. For several years she only wept with others when they sorrowed; fair children followed her footsteps, and it was happiness to guide their voices, as they, like the morning stars, sang together; or to listen to their evening prayer as they folded their hands in childlike devotion ere they slept.

And when the father returned from beside the bed of death, where his skill could no longer alleviate the parting agonies of the sufferer: how would he hasten to look upon the happy faces of his children, in order to forget the scene he had just witnessed. But, man of God as he was, there was not always peace in his soul; yet none could see that he had cause for care. He was followed by the blessings of those who were ready to perish. He essayed to make the sinner repent, and to turn the thoughts of the dying to Him who suffered death on the cross.

But for months the voice of the Spirit spake to his heart; he could not forget the words—"Go to the wretched Dahcotahs, their bodies are suffering, and their souls, immortal like thine, are perishing. Soothe their temporal cares, and more, tell them the triumphs of the Redeemer's love."

But it was hard to give up friends, and all the comforts with which he was surrounded: to subject his wife to the hardships of a life in the wilderness, to deprive his children of the advantages of education and good influences, and instead—to show them life as it is with those who know not God. But the voice said, "Remember the Dahcotahs." Vainly did he struggle with the conflict of duty against inclination.

The time has come when the parents must weep for themselves. No longer do the feet of their children tread among the flowers; fever has paralyzed their strength, and vainly does the mother call upon the child, whose eyes wander in delirium, who knows not her voice from a stranger's. Nor does the Destroyer depart when *one* has sunk into a sleep from which there is no awakening until the morn of the resurrection. He claims another, and who shall resist that claim!

As the father looks upon the still forms of his children, as he sees the compressed lips, the closed eyes of the beings who were but a few days ago full of life and happiness, the iron enters his soul; but as the Christian remembers who has afflicted him, his spirit rises above his sorrow. Nor is there now any obstacle between him and the path of duty. The one child that remains must be put in charge of those who will care for her, and he will go where God directs.

But will the mother give up the last of her children? it matters not now where she lives, but she must part with husband or child! Self has no part in her schemes; secure in her trust in God she yields up her child to her friend, and listens not to the suggestions of those who would induce her to remain where she would still enjoy the comforts of life. Nothing should separate her from her husband. "Entreat me not to leave thee; where thou goest I will go, where thou diest I will die, and there will I be buried."

And as the Dahcotah woman inquires of the justice of God, the faces of her children rise up before her—first in health, with bright eyes and lips parted with smiles, and then as she last saw them—their hands white to transparency, the hue of death upon their features; the shrouds, the little coffins, the cold lips, as she pressed them for the last time.

The Dahcotah looked in astonishment at the grief which for a few moments overcame the usual calmness of her kind friend; and as she wondered why, like her, she should shed bitter tears, she heard herself thus addressed—

"Do not think that you alone have been unhappy. God afflicts all his children. There is not a spot on the earth which is secure from sorrow. Have I not told you why? This world is not your home or mine. Soon will our bodies lie down in the earth—and we would forget this, if we were always happy.

"And you should not complain though your sorrows have been great. Do not forget the crown of thorns which pressed the brow of the Saviour, the cruel nails that pierced his hands and feet, the desertion of his friends, his fear that God his Father had forsaken him. And remember that after death the power of those who hated him ceased; the grave received but could not keep his body. He rose from the dead, and went to Heaven, where he has prepared a place for all who love him; for me and mine, I trust, and for you too, if you are careful to please him by serving him yourself, and by endeavoring to induce your friends to give up their foolish and wicked superstitions, and to worship the true God who made all things."

CHAPTER II

THE DAHCOTAHS believe in the existence of a Great Spirit, but they have very confused ideas of his attributes. Those who have lived near the missionaries, say that the Great Spirit lived forever, but their own minds would never have conceived such an idea. Some say that the Great Spirit has a wife.

They say that this being created all things but thunder and wild rice; and that he gave the earth and all animals to them, and that their feasts and customs were the laws by which they are to be governed. But they do not fear the anger of this deity after death.

Thunder is said to be a large bird; the name that they give to thunder is the generic term for all animals that fly. Near the source of the St. Peters is a place called Thunder-tracks—where the footprints of the thunder-bird are seen in the rocks, twenty-five miles apart.

The Dahcotahs believe in an evil spirit as well as a good, but they do not consider these spirits as opposed to each other; they do not think that they are tempted to do wrong by this evil spirit; their own hearts are bad. It would be impossible to put any limit to the number of spirits in whom the Dahcotahs believe; every object in nature is full of them. They attribute death as much to the power of these subordinate spirits as to the Great Spirit, but most frequently they suppose death to have been occasioned by a spell having been cast upon them by some enemy.

The sun and moon are worshipped as emblems of their deity.

Sacrifice is a religious ceremony among them; but no missionary has yet been able to find any reference to the one great Atonement made for sin; none of their customs or traditions authorize any such connection. They sacrifice to all the spirits; but they have a stone, painted red, which they call the Grandfather, and on or near this, they place their most valuable articles, their buffalo robes, dogs, and even horses; and on one occasion a father killed a child as a kind of sacrifice. They frequently inflict severe bruises or cuts upon their bodies, thinking thus to propitiate their gods.

The belief in an evil spirit is said by some not to be a part of the religion of the Dahcotahs. They perhaps obtained this idea from the whites. They have a far greater fear of the spirits of the dead, especially those whom they have offended, than of Wahkon-tun-kah, the Great Spirit.

ONE OF the punishments they most dread is that of the body of an animal entering theirs to make them sick. Some of the medicine men, the priests, and the doctors of the Dahcotahs, seem to have an idea of the immortality of the soul but intercourse with the whites may have originated this. They know nothing of the resurrection.

They have no custom among them that indicates the belief that man's heart should be holy. The faith in spirits, dreams, and charms, the fear that some enemy, earthly or spiritual, may be secretly working their destruction by a spell, is as much a part of their creed, as the existence of the Great Spirit.

A good dream will raise their hopes of success in whatever they may be undertaking to the highest pitch; a bad one will make them despair of accomplishing it. Their religion is a superstition, including as few elements of truth and reason as perhaps any other of which the particulars are known. They worship they "know not what," and this from the lowest motives.

When they go out to hunt, or on a war party, they pray to the Great Spirit—"Father, help us to kill the buffalo." "Let us soon see deer"— or, "Great Spirit help us to kill our enemies."

They have no hymns of praise to their Deity; they fast occasionally at the time of their dances. When they dance in honor of the sun, they refrain from eating for two days.

The Dahcotahs do not worship the work of their hands; but they consider every object that the Great Spirit has made, from the highest mountain to the smallest stone, as worthy of their idolatry.

They have a vague idea of a future state; many have dreamed of it. Some of their medicine men pretend to have had revelations from bears and other animals; and they thus learned that their future existence would be but a continuation of this. They will go on long hunts and kill many buffalo; bright fires will burn in their wigwams as they talk through the long winter's night of the traditions of their ancients; their women are to tan deerskin for their mocassins, while their young children learn to be brave warriors by attacking and destroying wasps' or hornets' nests; they will celebrate the dog feast to show how brave they are, and sing in triumph as they dance round the scalps of their enemies. Such is the Heaven of the Dahcotahs! Almost every Indian has the image of an animal or a bird tattoed on his breast or arm, which can charm away an evil spirit, or prevent his enemy from bringing trouble or death upon him by a secret shot. The power of life rests with mortals, especially with their medicine men; they believe that if an enemy be shooting secretly at them, a spell or charm must be put in requisition to counteract their power.

The medicine men or women, who are initiated into the secrets of their wonderful medicines (which secret is as sacred with them as free-masonry is to its members) give the feast which they call the medicine feast.

Their medicine men, who profess to administer to the affairs of soul and body are nothing more than jugglers, and are the worst men of the tribe: yet from fear alone they claim the entire respect of the community.

There are numerous clans among the Dahcotahs each using a different medicine, and no one knows what this medicine is but those who are initiated into the mysteries of the medicine dance, whose celebration is attended with the utmost ceremony.

A Dahcotah would die before he would divulge the secret of his clan. All the different clans unite at the great medicine feast.

And from such errors as these must be the Dahcotah turn if he would be a Christian! And the heart of the missionary would faint within him at the work which is before him, did he not remember who has said, "Lo, I am with you always!"

And it was long before the Indian woman could give up the creed of her nation. The marks of the wounds in her face and arms will to the grave bear witness of her belief in the faith of her fathers, which influenced her in youth. Yet the subduing of her passions, the quiet performance of her duties, the neatness of her person, and the order of her house, tell of the influence of a better faith, which sanctifies the sorrows of this life, and rejoices her with the hope of another and a better state of existence.

But such instances are rare. These people have resisted as encroachments upon their rights the efforts that have been made for their instruction. Kindness and patience, however, have accomplished much, and during the last year they have, in several instances, expressed a desire for the aid and instructions of missionaries. They seem to wish them to live among them; though formerly the lives of those who felt it their duty to remain were in constant peril.

They depend more, too, upon what the ground yields them for food, and have sought for assistance in ploughing it.

There are four schools sustained by the Dahcotah mission; in all there are about one hundred and seventy children; the average attendance about sixty.

The missionaries feel that they have accomplished something, and they are encouraged to hope for still more. They have induced many of the Dahcotahs to be more temperate; and although few, comparatively, attend worship at the several stations, yet of those few some exhibit hopeful signs of conversion.

There are five mission stations among the Dahcotahs; at "Lac qui parle," on the St. Peter's river, in sight of the beautiful lake from which the station takes its name; at "Travers des Sioux" about eighty miles from Fort Snelling; at Xapedun, Oak-grove, and Kapoja, the last three being within a few miles of Fort Snelling.

There are many who think that the efforts of those engaged in instructing the Dahcotahs are thrown away. They cannot conceive why men of education, talent, and piety, should waste their time and attainments upon a people who cannot appreciate their efforts. If the missionaries reasoned on worldly principles, they would doubtless think so too; but they devote the energies of soul and body to Him who made them for His own service.

They are pioneers in religion; they show the path that others will walk in far more easily at some future day; they undertake what others will carry on—what God himself will accomplish. They have willingly given up the advantages of this life, to preach the gospel to the degraded Dahcotahs. They are translating the Bible into Sioux; many of the books are translated, and to their exertions it is owing that the praise of God has been sung by the children of the forest in their own language.

CHAPTER III

HOWEVER ABSURD may be the religion of the Dahcotahs, they are zealous in their devotion to it. Nothing is allowed to interfere with it. Are their women planting corn, which is to be in a great measure depended upon for food during the next winter? whatever be the consequences, they stop to celebrate a dance or a feast, either of which is a part of their religion. How many Christians satisfy their consciences by devoting one day of the week to God, feeling themselves thus justified in devoting the other six entirely to the world! But it is altogether different with the Dahcotahs, every act of their life is influenced by their religion, such as it is.

They believe they are a great people, that their country in unrivaled in beauty, their religion without fault. Many of the Dahcotahs, now living near Fort Snelling, say that they have lived on the earth before in some region far distant, that they died, and for a time their spirits wandered through the world seeking the most beautiful and delightful country to live in, and that after examining all parts of the earth they fixed upon the country of the Dahcotahs.

In fact, dreams, spells and superstitious fears, constitute a large part of the belief of the Dahcotahs. But of all their superstitious notions the most curious is the one which occasions the dance called Ho-saw-kah-u-tap-pe, or Fish dance, where the fish is eaten raw.

Some days since, an Indian who lives at Shah-co-pee's village dreamed of seeing a cormorant, a bird which feeds on fish. He was very much alarmed, and directed his friend to go out and catch a fish, and to bring the first one he caught to him.

The Indian did so, and the fish, which was a large pike, was painted with blue clay. Preparations were immediately made to celebrate the Fish dance, in order to ward off any danger of which the dream might have been the omen.

A circle was formed of brush, on one side of which the Indians pitched a wigwam. The war implements were then brought inside the ring, and a pole stuck up in the centre, with the raw fish, painted blue, hung upon it.

The men then enter the ring, almost naked; their bodies painted black, excepting the breast and arms, which are varied in color according to the fancy of each individual.

Inside the ring is a bush for each dancer; in each bush a nest, made to resemble a cormorant's nest; and outside the ring is an Indian metamorphosed for the occasion into a wolf—that is, he has the skin of a wolf drawn over him, and hoops fixed to his hands to enable him to run easier on all fours; and in order to sustain the character which he has assumed, he remains outside, lurking about for food.

All being ready, the medicine men inside the wigwam commence beating a drum and singing. This is the signal for all the cormorants (Indians), inside the ring, to commence quacking and dancing and using their arms in imitation of wings, keeping up a continual flapping. Thus for some time they dance up to and around the fish—when the bravest among them will snap at the fish, and if he have good teeth will probably bite off a piece, if not, he will slip his hold and flap off again.

Another will try his luck at this delicious food, and so they continue, until they have made a beginning in the way of eating the fish. Then each cormorant flaps up and takes a bite, and then flaps off to his nest, in which the piece of fish is concealed, for fear the wolves may get it.

After a while, the wolf is seen emerging from his retreat, painted so hideously as to frighten away the Indian children. The cormorants perceive the approach of the wolf, and a general quacking and flapping takes place, each one rushing to his nest to secure his food.

This food each cormorant seizes and tries to swallow, flapping his wings and stretching out his neck as a young bird will when fed by its mother.

After the most strenuous exertions they succeed in swallowing the raw fish. While this is going on, the wolf seizes the opportunity to make a snap at the remainder of the fish, seizes it with his teeth, and makes his way out of the ring, as fast as he can, on all fours. The whole of the fish, bones and all, must be swallowed; not the smallest portion of it can be left, and the fish must only be touched by the mouth—never with the hands. This dance is performed by the men alone—their war implements must be sacred from the touch of the women.

Such scenes are witnessed every day at the Dahcotah villages. The missionary sighs as he sees how determined is their belief in such a religion. Is it not a source of rejoicing to be the means of turning one fellow-creature from a faith like this?

A few years ago and every Dahcotah woman reverenced the fish-dance as holy and sacred—even too sacred for her to take a part in it. She believed the medicine women could foretell future events; and, with an injustice hardly to be accounted for, she would tell you it was lawful to beat a girl as much as you chose, but a sin to strike a boy!

She gloried in dancing the scalp dance—aye, even exulted at the idea of taking the life of an enemy herself.

But there are instances in which these things are all laid aside beneath the light of Christianity; instances in which the poor Dahcotah woman sees the folly, the wickedness of her former faith; blesses God who inclined the missionary to leave his home and take up his abode in the country of the savage; and sings to the praise of God in her own tongue as she sits by the door of her wigwam. She smiles as she tells you that her "face is dark, but that she hopes her heart has been changed; and that she will one day sing in heaven, where the voices of the white people and of the converted Dahcotahs, will mingle in a song of love to Him 'who died for the whole world.'"

WABASHAW

∧∧∗∧∧∧

Wah-ba-sha Village on the Mississippi, watercolor on paper, 1846-1848.

CHAPTER I

WABASHAW (or, The Leaf) is the name of one of the Dahcotah chiefs. His village is on the Mississippi river, 1,800 miles from its mouth.

The teepees are pitched quite near the shore, and the many bluffs that rise behind them seem to be their perpetual guards.

The present chief is about thirty-five years old—as yet he has done not much to give him a reputation above the Dahcotahs about him. But his father was a man whose life and character were such as to influence his people to a great degree.

Wabashaw the elder (for the son inherits his father's name) is said by the Dahcotahs to have been the first chief in their tribe.

Many years ago the English claimed authority over the Dahcotahs, and an English traveller having been murdered by some Dahcotahs of the band of which Wabashaw was a warrior, the English claimed hostages to be given up until the murderer could be found.

The affairs of the nation were settled then by men who, having more mind than the others, naturally influenced their inferiors. Their bravest men, their war chief too, no doubt exercised a control over the rest.

Wabashaw was one of the hostages given up in consequence of the murder, and the Governor of Canada required that these Dahcotahs should leave the forests of the west, and remain for a time as prisoners in Canada. Little as is the regard for the feelings of the savage now, there was still less then.

Wabashaw often spoke of the ill treatment he received on his journey. It was bad enough to be a prisoner, and to be leaving home; it was far worse to be struck, for the amusement of idle men and children—to have the war eagle's feather rudely torn from his head to be trampled upon—to have the ornaments, even the pipes of the nation, taken away, and destroyed before his eyes.

But such insults often occurred during their journey, and the prisoners were even fettered when at last they reached Quebec.

Here for a long time they sighed to breathe the invigorating air of the prairies; to chase the buffalo; to celebrate the war dance. But when should they join again in the ceremonies of their tribe? When? Alas! they could not even ask their jailer when; or if they had, he would only have laughed at the strange dialect that he could not comprehend. But the Dahcotahs bore with patience their unmerited confinement, and Wabashaw excelled them all. His eye was not as bright as when he left home, and there was an unusual weakness in his limbs—but never should his enemies know that he suffered. And when those high in authority visited the prisoners, the haughty dignity of Wabashaw made them feel that the Dahcotah warrior was a man to be respected.

But freedom came at last. The murderers were given up; and a interpreter in the prison told Wabashaw that he was no longer a prisoner; that he would soon again see the Father of many waters; and that more, he had been made by the English a chief, the first chief of the Dahcotahs.

It was well nigh too late for Wabashaw. His limbs were thin, and his strength had failed for want of the fresh air of his native hills.

Little did the prisoners care to look around as they retraced their steps. They knew they were going home. But when the waters of the Mississippi again shone before them, when the well-known bluffs met their eager gaze; when the bending river gave to view their native village, then, indeed, did the new-made chief cast around him the "quiet of a loving eye." Then, too, did he realize what he had suffered.

He strained his sight—for perhaps his wife might have wearied of waiting for him—perhaps she had gone to the Land of spirits, hoping to meet him there.

His children, too—the young warriors, who were wont to follow him and listen to his voice, would they welcome him home?

As he approached the village a cloud had come between him and the sun. He could see many upon the shore, but who were they? The canoe swept over the waters, keeping time to the thoughts of those who were wanderers no longer.

As they neared the shore, the cloud passed away and the brightness of the setting sun revealed the faces of their friends; their cries of joy rent the air—to the husband, the son, the brother, they spoke a welcome home!

Wabashaw, by the command of the English Governor, was acknowledged by the Dahcotahs their first chief; and his influence was unbounded. Every band has a chief, and the honor descends from father to son; but there has never been one more honored and respected than Wabashaw.

CHAPTER II

WABASHAW'S VILLAGE is sometimes called Keusca. This word signifies to break through, or set aside; it was given in consequence of an incident which occurred some time ago, in the village.

"Sacred Wind" was a daughter of one of the most powerful families among the Dahcotahs; for although a chief lives as the meanest of his band, still there is a great difference among the families. The number of a family constitutes its importance; where a family is small, a member of it can be injured with little fear of retaliation; but in a large family there are sure to be found some who will not let an insult pass without revenge. Sacred Wind's father was living; a stalwart old warrior, slightly bent with the weight of years. Though his face was literally seamed with wrinkles, he could endure fatigue, or face danger, with the youngest and hardiest of the band.

Her mother, a fearfully ugly old creature, still mended mocassins and scolded; bidding fair to keep up both trades for years to come. Then there were tall brothers, braving hardships and danger, as if a Dahcotah was only born to be scalped, or to scalp; uncles, cousins, too, there were, in abundance, so that Sacred Wind did belong to a powerful family.

Now, among the Dahcotahs, a cousin is looked upon as a brother; a girl would as soon think of marrying her grandfather, as a cousin. I mean an ordinary girl, but Sacred Wind was not of that stamp; she was destined to be a heroine. She had many lovers, who wore themselves out playing the flute, to as little purpose as they braided their hair, and painted their faces. Sacred Wind did not love one of them.

Her mother, was always trying to induce her to accept some one of her lovers, urging the advantages of each match; but it would not do. The girl was eighteen years old, and not yet a wife; though most of the Dahcotah women are mothers long before that.

Her friends could not imagine why she did not marry. They were wearied with arguing with her; but not one of them ever suspected the cause of her seeming coldness of heart.

Her grandmother was particularly officious. She could not do as Sacred Wind wished her—attend to her own affairs, for she had none to attend to; and grandmothers, among the Sioux, are as loving and devoted as they are among white people; consequently, the old lady beset the unfortunate girl, day and night, about her obstinacy.

"Why are you not now the mother of warriors," she said, "and besides, who will kill game for you when you are old? The "Bear," has been to the traders; he has bought many things, which he offers your parents for you; marry him and then you will make your old grandmother happy."

"I will kill myself," she replied, "if you ask me to marry the Bear. Have you forgotten the Maiden's rock? There are more high rocks than one on the banks of the Mississippi, and my heart is as strong as Wenona's. If you torment me so, to marry the Bear, I will do as she did—in the house of spirits I shall have no more trouble."

This threat silenced the grandmother for the time. But a young girl who had been sitting with them, and listening to the conversation, rose to go out; and as she passed Sacred Wind, she whispered in her ear, "Tell her why you will not marry the Bear; tell her that Sacred Wind loves her cousin; and that last night she promised him she never would marry any one but him."

Had she been struck to the earth she could not have been paler. She thought her secret was hid in her own heart. She had tried to cease thinking of "The Shield;" keeping away from him, dreading to find true what she only suspected. She did not dare acknowledge even to herself that she loved a cousin.

But when The Shield gave her his handsomest trinkets, when he followed her when she left her laughing and noisy companions to sit beside the still waters—when he told her that she was the most beautiful girl among the Dahcotahs—when he whispered her that he loved her dearly, and would marry her in spite of mothers, grandmothers, customs and religion too— then she found that her cousin was dearer to her than all the world—that she would gladly die with him—she could never live without him.

But still, she would not promise to marry him. What would her friends say? and the spirits of the dead would torment her, for infringing upon the sacred customs of her tribe. The Shield used many arguments, but all in vain. She told him she was afraid to marry him, but that she would never marry any one else. Sooner should the waves cease to beat against the shores of the spirit lakes, than she forget to think of him.

But this did not satisfy her cousin. He was determined she should be his wife; he trusted to time and his irresistible person to overcome her fears.

The Shield's name was give to him by his father's friends. Shields were formerly used by the Sioux; and the Eyanktons and Sissetons still use them. They are made of buffalo skin, of a circular form; and are used as a protection against the arrows of their enemies.

"You need not fear your family, Sacred Wind," said her cousin, "nor the medicine men, nor the spirits of the dead. We will go to one of the villages, and when we are married, we will come back. Let them be angry, I will stand between you and them, even as my father's shield did between him and the foe that sought his life."

But she was firm, and promised nothing more than that she would not marry the Bear, or any one else; and they returned to her father's teepee, little thinking that any one had overheard their conversation. But the "Swan" had heard every word of it.

She loved The Shield, and she had seen him follow his cousin. After hearing enough to know that her case was a hopeless one, she made up her mind to make Sacred Wind pay dearly for the love which she herself could not obtain.

She did not at once tell the news. She wanted to amuse herself with her victim before she destroyed her; and she had hardly yet made up her mind as to the way which she would take to inform the family of Sacred Wind of the secret she had found out.

But she could not resist the temptation of whispering to Sacred Wind her knowledge of the true reason why she would not marry the Bear. This was the first blow, and it struck to the heart; it made a wound which was long kept open by the watchful eye of jealousy.

The grandmother, however, did not hear the remark; if she had she would not have sat still smoking—not she! she would have trembled with rage that a Dahcotah maiden, and her grandchild, should be guilty of the enormous crime of loving a cousin. An eruption of Vesuvius would have given but a faint idea of her fury.

Most fortunately for herself, the venerable old medicine woman died a few days after. Had she lived to know of the fatal passion of her granddaughter, she would have longed to seize the thunderbolts of Jupiter (if she had been aware of their existence) to hurl at the offenders; or like Niobe, have wept herself to stone.

Indeed the cause of her death showed that she could not bear contradiction.

There was a war party formed to attack the Chippeways, and the "Eagle that Screams as she Flies" (for that was the name of Sacred Wind's grandmother) wanted to go along.

She wished to mutilate the bodies after they were scalped. Yes, though near ninety years old, she would go through all the fatigues of a march of three hundred miles, and think it nothing, if she could be repaid by tearing the heart from one Chippeway child.

There were, however, two old squaws who had applied first, and the Screaming Eagle was rejected.

There were no bounds to her passion. She attempted to hang herself and was cut down; she made the village resound with her lamentations; she called upon all the spirits of the lakes, rivers, and prairies, to torment the war party; nothing would pacify her. Two days after the war party left, the Eagle that Screams as she Flies expired, in a fit of rage!

When the war-party returned, The Shield was the observed of all observers; he had taken two scalps.

Sacred Wind sighed to think he was her cousin. How could she help loving the warrior who had returned the bravest in the battle?

The Swan saw that she loved in vain. She knew that she loved The Shield more in absence; why then hope that he would forget Sacred Wind when he saw her no more?

When she saw him enter the village, her heart beat fast with emotion; she pressed her hand upon it, but could not still its tumult. "He has come," she said to herself, "but will his eye seek mine? will he tell *me* that the time has been long since he saw the woman he loved?"

She follows his footsteps—she watches his every glace, as he meets his relations. Alas! for the Swan, the wounded bird feels not so acutely the arrow that pierces, as she that look of recognition between the cousins!

But the unhappy girl was roused from a sense of her griefs, to a recollection of her wrongs. With all the impetuosity of a loving heart, she thought she had a right to the affections of The Shield. As the water reflected her features, so should his heart give back the devoted love of hers.

But while she lived, she was determined to bring sorrow upon her rival; she would not "sing in dying." That very evening did she repeat to the family of Sacred Wind the conversation she had overheard, adding that the love of the cousins was the true cause of Sacred Wind's refusing to marry.

Time would fail me to tell of the consequent sufferings of Sacred Wind. She was scolded and watched, shamed, and even beaten. The medicine men threatened her with all their powers; no punishment was severe enough for the Dahcotah who would thus transgress the laws of their nation.

The Shield was proof against the machinations of his enemies, for he was a medicine man, and could counteract all the spells that were exerted against him. Sacred Wind bore everything in patience but the sight of the Bear. She had been bought and sold, over and over again; and the fear of her killing herself was the only reason why her friends did not force her to marry.

One evening she was missing, and the cries of her mother broke upon the silence of the night; canoes were flying across the water; friends were wandering in the woods, all seeking the body of the girl.

But she was not to be found in the river, or in the woods. Sacred Wind was not dead, she was only married.

She was safe in the next village, telling The Shield how much she loved him, and how cordially she hated the Bear; and although she trembled when she spoke of the medicine men, her husband only laughed at her fears, telling her, that now that she was his wife, she need fear nothing.

But where was the Swan? Her friends were assisting in the search for Sacred Wind. The father had forgotten his child, the brother his sister. And the mother, who would have first missed her, had gone long ago, to the land of the spirits.

The Swan had known of the flight of the lovers—she watched them as their canoe passed away, until it became a speck in the distance, and in another moment the waters closed over her.

Thus were strangely blended marriage and death. The Swan feared not to take her own life. Sacred Wind, with a nobler courage, a more devoted love, broke through the customs of her nation, laid aside the superstitions of the tribe, and has thus identified her courage with the name of her native village.

THE DAHCOTAH BRIDE

ᴬᴬᴬᴬᴬᴬ

From Ft. Snelling looking up [the Mississippi River], watercolor on paper, 1846-1848.

THE VALLEY of the Upper Mississippi presents many attractions to the reflecting mind, apart from the admiration excited by its natural beauty. It is at once an old country and a new—the home of a people who are rapidly passing away—and of a nation whose strength is ever advancing. The white man treads upon the footsteps of the Dahcotah—the war dance of the warrior gives place to the march of civilization—and the saw-mill is heard where but a few years ago were sung the deeds of the Dahcotah braves.

Years ago, the Dahcotah hunted where the Mississippi takes its rise—the tribe claiming the country as far south as St. Louis. But difficulties with the neighboring tribes have diminished their numbers and driven them farther north and west; the white people have needed their lands, and their course is onward. How will it end? Will this powerful tribe cease to be a nation on the earth? Will their mysterious origin never be ascertained? And must their religion and superstitions, their customs and feasts pass away from memory as if they had never been?

Who can look upon them without interest? hardly the philosopher—surely not the Christian. The image of God is defaced in the hearts of the savage. Cain-like does the child of the forest put forth his hand and stain it with a brother's blood. But are there no deeds of darkness done in our own favored land?

But the country of the Dahcotah—let it be new to those who fly at the beckon of gain—who would speculate in the blood of their fellow-creatures, who for gold would, aye do, sell their own souls—it is an old country to me. What say the boundless prairies? how many generations have roamed over them? when did the buffalo first yield to the arrow of the hunter? And look at the worn bases of the rocks that are washed by the Father of waters. Hear the Dahcotah maiden as she tells of the lover's leap—and the warrior as he boasts of the victories of his forefathers over his enemies, long, long before the hated white man had intruded upon their lands, or taught them the fatal secret of intoxicating drink.

The Dahcotahs feel their own weakness—they know they cannot contend with the power of the white man. Yet there are times when the passion and vehemence of the warriors in the neighborhood of Fort Snelling can hardly be brought to yield the necessity of control; and were there a possibility of success, how soon would the pipe of peace be thrown aside, and the yell and whoop of war be heard instead! And who would blame them? Has not the blood of our bravest and best been poured out like water for a small portion of a country— when the whole could never make up for the loss sustained by one desolate widow or fatherless child?

The sky was without a cloud when the sun rose on the Mississippi. The morning mists passed slowly away as if they loved to linger round the hills. Pilot Knob rose above them, proud to be the burial place of her warrior children, while on the opposite side of the Mine Soto* the frowning walls of

---

* Mine Soto, or Whitish Water, the name that the Sioux give to the St. Peter's River. The mud or clay in the water has a whitish look.

Fort Snelling, told of the power of their enemies. Not a breath disturbed the repose of nature, till the voice of the song birds rose in harmony singing the praise of the Creator.

But a few hours have passed away, and how changed the scene. Numbers of canoes are seen rapidly passing over the waters, and the angry savages that spring from them as hastily ascending the hill. From the gates of the fort, hundreds of Indians are seen collecting from every direction, and all approaching the house of the interpreter. We will follow them.

Few have witnessed so wild a scene. The house of the interpreter employed by government is near the fort, and all around it were assembled the excited Indians. In front of the house is a piazza, and on it lay the body of a young Dahcotah; his black hair plaited, and falling over his swarthy face. The closed eye and compressed lips proclaimed the presence of death. Life had but recently yielded to the sway of the stern conqueror. A few hours ago Beloved Hail had eaten and drank on the very spot where his body now reposed.

Bending over his head is his wife; tears fall like rain from her eyes; and as grief has again overcome her efforts at composure, see how she plunges her knife into her arm: and as the warm blood flows from the wound calls upon the husband of her youth!

"My son! my son! bursts from the lips of his aged mother, who weeps at his feet; while her bleeding limbs bear witness to the wounds which she had inflicted upon herself in the agony of her soul. Nor are these the only mourners. A crowd of friends are weeping round his body. But the mother has turned to the warriors as they press through the crowd; tears enough have been shed, it is time to think of revenge. "Look at your friend," she says, "look how heavily lies the strong arm, and see, he is still, though his wife and aged mother call upon him. Who has done this? who has killed the brave warrior? bring me the murderer, that I may cut him in pieces."

It needed not to call upon the warriors who stood around. They were excited enough. Bad Hail stood near, his eyes bloodshot with rage, his lip quivering, and every trembling limb telling of the tempest within. Shah-co-pee, the orator of the Dahcotahs, and "The Nest," their most famous hunter; the tall form of the aged chief "Man in the cloud" leaned against the railing, his sober countenance strangely contrasting with the fiend-like look of his wife; Grey Iron and Little Hill, with brave after brave, all crying vengeance to the foe, death to the Chippeway!

CHAPTER II

BUT YESTERDAY the Dahcotahs and Chippeways, foes from time immemorial, feasted and danced together, for there was peace between them. They had promised to bury the hatchet; the Chippeways danced near the fort, and the Dahcotahs presented them with blankets and pipes, guns and powder, and all that the savage deems valuable. Afterwards, the Dahcotahs danced, and the generous Chippeways exceeded them in the number and value of their gifts. As evening approached, the bands mingled their amusements—together they contended in the foot-race, or, stretching themselves upon the grass, played at checkers.

The Chippeways had paid their annual visit of friendship at Fort Snelling, and, having spent their time happily, they were about to return to their homes. Their wise men said they rejoiced that nothing had occurred to disturb the harmony of the two tribes. But their vicinity to the Fort prevented any outbreak; had there been no such restraint upon their actions, each would have sought the life of his deadly foe.

"Hole in the Day" was the chief of the Chippeways. He owed his station to his own merit; his bravery and firmness had won the respect and admiration of the tribe when he was but a warrior, and they exalted him to the honor being their chief. Deeds of blood marked his course, yet were his manners gentle and his voice low. There was a dignity and a courtesy about his every action that would have well befitted a courtier.

He watched with interest the trials of strength between the young men of his own tribe and the Dahcotahs. When the latter celebrated one of their national feasts, when they ate the heart of the dog while it was warm with life, just torn from the animal, with what contempt did he gaze upon them!

The amusements of the dog feast, or dance, have closed, and the Chippeway chief has signified to his warriors that they were to return home on the following day. He expressed a wish to see several of the chiefs of the Dahcotahs, and a meeting having been obtained, he thus addressed them—

"Warriors! it has been the wish of our great father that we should be friends; blood enough has been shed on both sides. But even if we preferred to continue at war, we must do as our great father says. The Indian's glory is passing away; they are as the setting sun; while the white man is as the sun rising in all his power. We are the falling leaves; the whites are the powerful horses that trample them under foot. We are about to return home, and it is well that nothing has happened to occasion strife between us. But I wish you to know that there are two young men among us who do not belong to my band. They are pillagers, belonging to another band, and they may be troublesome. I wish you to tell your young men of this, that they may be on their guard."

After smoking together, the chiefs separated. "Hole in the Day" having thus done all that he deemed proper, returned with his warriors to his teepee.

Early in the morning the Chippeways encamped near St. Anthony's falls; the women took upon themselves all the fatigue and labor of the journey, the men carrying only the implements of war and hunting. The Chippeway chief was the husband of three wives, who were sisters; and, strange to say, when an Indian fancies more than one wife, he is fortunate if he can obtain sisters, for they generally live in harmony, while wives who are not related are constantly quarreling; and the husband does not often interfere, even if words are changed to blows.

In the mean time, the two pillagers were lurking about; now remaining a short time with the camp of the Chippeways, now absenting themselves for a day or two. But while the Chippeways were preparing to leave the Falls, the pillagers were in the neighborhood of Fort Snelling. They had accompanied Hole in the Day's band, with the determination of killing an enemy. The ancient feud still rankled in their hearts; as yet they had had no opportunity of satisfying their thirst for blood; but on this morning they were concealed in the bushes, when Red Boy and Beloved Hail, two Dahcotahs, were passing on horseback. It was but a moment—and the deed was done. Both the Chippeways fired, and Beloved Hail fell.

Red Boy was wounded, but not badly; he hurried in to tell the sad news, and the two Chippeways were soon out of the power of their enemies. They fled, it is supposed, to Missouri.

The friends of the dead warrior immediately sought his body, and brought it to the house of the interpreter. There his friends came together;

and as they entered one by one, on every side pressing forward to see the still, calm, features of the young man; they threw on the body their blankets, and other presents, according to their custom of honoring the dead.

Troops are kept at Fort Snelling, not only as a protection to the whites in the neighborhood, but to prevent, if possible, difficulties between the different bands of Indians; and as every year brings the Chippeways to Fort Snelling, either to transact business with the government or on a visit of pleasure, the Chippeways and Dahcotahs must be frequently thrown together. The commanding officer of the garrison notifies the two bands, on such occasions, that no hostilities will be permitted; so there is rarely an occurrence to disturb their peace.

But now it is impossible to restrain the excited passions of the Dahcotahs. Capt. B———, who was then in command at Fort Snelling, sent word to the Chippeway chief of the murder that had been committed, and requested him to bring all his men in, as the murderer must be given up.

But this did not satisfy the Dahcotahs; they longed to raise the tomahawk which they held in their hands. They refused to wait, but insisted upon following the Chippeways and revenging themselves; the arguments of the agent and other friends of the Dahcotahs were unavailing; nothing would satisfy them but blood. The eyes, even of the women, sparkled with delight, at the prospect of the scalps they would dance round; while the mother of Beloved Hail was heard to call for the scalp of the murderer of her son!

Seeing the chiefs determined on war, Capt. B——— told them he would cease to endeavor to change their intentions; "but as soon," said he, "as you attack the Chippeways, will I send soldiers to your villages; and who will protect your women and children?"

This had the desired effect, and the warriors, seeing the necessity of waiting for the arrival of the Chippeways, became more calm.

Hole in the Day with his men came immediately to the Fort, where a conference was held at the gate. There were assembled about three hundred Dahcotahs and seventy Chippeways, with the officers of the garrison and the Indian agent.

It was ascertained that the murder had been committed by the two pillagers, for none of the other Chippeway warriors had been absent from the camp. Hole in the Day, however, gave up two of his men, as hostages to be kept at Fort Snelling until the murderers should be given up.

The Dahcotahs, being obliged for the time to defer the hope of revenge, returned to their village to bury their dead.

CHAPTER III

WE RARELY consider the Indian as a member of a family—we associate him with the tomahawk and scalping-knife. But the very strangeness of the customs of the Dahcotahs adds to their interest; and in their mourning they have all the horror of death without an attendant solemnity.

All the agony and grief that a Christian mother feels when she looks for the last time at the form which will so soon moulder in the dust, an Indian mother feels also. The Christian knows that the body will live again; that the life-giving breath of the Eternal will once more re-animate the helpless clay; that the eyes which were brilliant and beautiful in life will again look brightly from the now closed lids—when the dead shall live—when the beloved child shall "rise again."

The Dahcotah woman has no such hope. Though she believes that the soul will live forever in the "city of spirits," yet the infant she has nursed at her bosom, the child she loved and tended, the young man whose strength and beauty were her boast, will soon be ashes and dust.

And if she have not the hope of the Christian, neither has she the spirit. For as she cuts off her hair and tears her clothes, throwing them under the scaffold, what joy would it bring to her heart could she hope herself to take the life of the murderer of her son.

Beloved Hail was borne by the Indians to his native village, and the usual ceremonies attending the dead performed, but with more than usual excitement, occasioned by the circumstances of the death of their friend.

The body of a dead Dahcotah is wrapped in cloth or calico, or sometimes put in a box, if one can be obtained, and placed upon a scaffold raised a few feet from the ground. All the relations of the deceased then sit round it for about twenty-four hours; they tear their clothes; run knives through the fleshy parts of their arms, but there is no sacrifice which they can make so great as cutting off their hair.

The men go in mourning by painting themselves black and they do not wash the paint off until they take the scalp of an enemy, or give a medicine-dance.

While they sit round the scaffold, one of the nearest relations commences a doleful crying, when all the others join in, and continue their wailing for some time. Then for a while tears are wiped away. After smoking for a short time another of the family commences again, and the others join in. This is continued for a day and night, and the each one goes to his own wigwam.

The Dahcotahs mourned thus for Beloved Hail. In the evening the cries of his wife were heard as she called for her husband, while the rocks and the hills echoed the wail. He will return no more—and who will hunt the deer for his wife and her young children!

The murderers were never found, and the hostages, after being detained for eighteen months at Fort Snelling, were released. They bore their confinement with admirable patience, the more so as they were punished for the fault of others. When they were released, they were furnished with guns and clothing. For fear they would be killed by the Dahcotahs, their release was kept a secret, and the Dahcotahs knew not that the two Chippeways were released, until they were far on their journey home. But one of them never saw his native village again. The long confinement had destroyed his health, and being feeble when he set out, he soon found himself unequal to the journey. He died a few days before the home was reached; and the welcome that his companion received was a sad one, for he brought the intelligence of the death of this comrade.

CHAPTER IV

BUT WE WILL do as the Dahcotahs did—turn from the sadness and horror of an Indian's death, to the gayety and happiness of an Indian marriage. The Indians are philosophers, after all—they knew that they could not go after the Chippeways, so they made the best of it and smoked. Beloved Hail was dead, but they could not bring him to life, and they smoked again: besides, "Walking Wind" was to be married to "The War Club," whereupon they smoked harder than ever.

There are two kinds of marriages among the Dahcotahs, buying a wife and stealing one. The latter answers to our runaway matches, and in some respects the former is the ditto of one conducted as it ought to be among ourselves. So after all, I suppose, Indian marriages are much like white people's.

But among the Dahcotahs it is an understood thing that, when the young people run away, they are to be forgiven at any time they choose to return, if it should be the next day, or six months afterwards. This saves a world of trouble. It prevents the necessity of the father looking daggers at the son-in-law, and then loving him violently; the mother is spared the trial of telling her daughter that she forgives her though she has broken her heart; and, what is still better, there is not the slightest occasion whatever for the bride to say she is wretched, for having done what she certainly would do over again to-morrow, were it undone.

So that it is easy to understand why the Dahcotahs have the advantage of us in runaway matches, or as *they* say in "stealing a wife;" for it is the same thing, only more honestly stated.

When a young man is unable to purchase the girl he loves best, or if her parents are unwilling she should marry him, if he have gained the heart of the maiden he is safe. They appoint a time and place to meet; take whatever will be necessary for their journey; that is, the man takes his gun and powder and shot, and the girl her knife and wooden bowl to eat and drink out of; and these she intends to hide in her blanket. Sometimes they merely go to the next village to return the next day. But if they fancy a bridal tour, away they go several hundred miles with the grass for their pillow, the canopy of heaven for their curtains, and the bright stars to light and watch over them. When they return home, the bride goes at once to chopping wood, and the groom to smoking, without the least form or parade.

Sometimes a young girl dare not run away; for she has a miserly father or mother who may not like her lover because he had not enough to give them for her; and she knows they will persecute her and perhaps shoot her husband. But this does not happen often. Just as, once in a hundred years in a Christian land, if a girl will run away with a young man, her parents run after her, and in spite of religion and common sense bring her back, have her divorced, and then in either case the parties must, as a matter of course, be very miserable.

But the marriage that we are about to witness, is a "marriage in high life" among the Dahcotahs, and the bride is regularly bought, as often occurs with us.

"Walking Wind" is not pretty; even the Dahcotahs, who are far from being connoisseurs in beauty, do no consider her pretty. She is, however, tall and well made, and her feet and hands (as is always the case with the Dahcotah women) are small. She has a quantity of jet-black hair, that she braids with a great deal of care. Her eyes are very black, but small, and her dark complexion is relieved by more red than is usually seen in the cheeks of the daughters of her race. Her teeth are very fine, as everybody knows—for she is always laughing, and her laugh is perfect music.

Then Walking Wind is, generally speaking, so good tempered. She was never known to be very angry but once, when Harpstenah told her she was in love with "The War Club;" she threw the girl down and tore half the hair out of her head. What made it seem very strange was, that she was over head and ears in love with "The War Club" at that very time; but she did not choose anybody should know it.

War Club was a flirt—yes, a male coquette—and he had broken the hearts of half the girls in the band. Besides being a flirt, he was a fop. He would plait his hair and put vermilion on his cheeks; and, after seeing that his leggins were properly arranged, he would put the war eagle feathers in his head, and folding his blanket round him, would walk about the village, or attitudinize with all the airs of Broadway dandy. War Club was a great warrior too, for on his blanket was marked the Red Hand, which showed he had killed his worst enemy—for it was his father's enemy, and he had hung the scalp up at his father's grave. Besides, he was a great hunter, which most of the Dahcotahs are.

No one, then, could for a moment doubt the pretensions of War Club, or that all the girls of the village should fall in love with him; and he, like a downright flirt, was naturally very cold and cruel to the poor creatures who loved him so much.

Walking Wind, besides possessing many other accomplishments, such as tanning deer-skin, making mocassins, &c., was a capital shot. On one occasion, when the young warriors were shooting at a mark, Walking Wind was pronounced the best shot among them, and the War Club was quite subdued. He could bear everything else; but when Walking Wind beat him shooting—why—the point was settled; he must fall in love with her, and, as a natural consequence, marry her.

Walking Wind was not so easily won. She had been tormented so long herself, that she was in duty bound to pay back in the same coin. It was a Duncan Gray affair—only reversed. At last she yielded; her lover gave her so many trinkets. True, they were brass and tin; but Dahcotah maidens cannot sigh for pearls and diamonds, for they never even heard of them; and the philosophy of the thing is just the same, since everybody is outdone by somebody. Besides, her lover played the flute all night long near her father's wigwam, and, not to speak of the pity that she felt for him, Walking Wind was confident she never could sleep until that flute stopped playing, which she knew would be as soon as they were married. For all the world knows that no husband, either white or copper-colored, ever troubles himself to pay any attention of that sort to his wife, however devotedly romantic he may have been before marriage.

Sometimes the Dahcotah lover buys his wife without her consent; but the War Club was more honorable that that: he loved Walking Wind, and he wanted her to love him.

When all was settled between the young people, War Club told his parents that he wanted to marry. The old people were glad to hear it, for they like their ancient and honorable names and houses to be kept up, just as well as lords and dukes do; so they collected everything they owned for the purpose of buying Walking Wind. Guns and blankets, powder and shot, knives and trinkets, were in requisition instead of title-deeds and settlements. So, when all was ready, War Club put the presents on a horse, and carried them to the door of Walking Wind's wigwam.

He does not ask for the girl, however, as this would not be Dahcotah etiquette. He lays the presents on the ground and has a consultation, or, as the Indians say, a "talk" with the parents, concluding by asking them to give him Walking Wind for his wife.

And, what is worthy to be noticed here is, that, after having gone to so much trouble to ask a question, he never for a moment waits for an answer, but turns round, horse and all, and goes back to his wigwam.

The parents then consult for a day or two, although they from the first moment have made up their minds as to what they are going to do. In due time the presents are taken into the wigwam, which signifies to the lover that he is a happy man. And on the next day Walking Wind is to be a bride.

CHAPTER V

EARLY IN the morning, Walking Wind commenced her toilet—and it was no light task to deck the Indian bride in all her finery.

Her mocassins were worked with porcupine, and fitted closely her small feet; the leggins were ornamented with ribbons of all colors; her cloth shawl, shaped like a mantilla, was worked with rows of bright ribbons, and the sewing did honor to her own skill in needle-work. Her breast was covered with brooches, and a quantity of beads hung round her neck. Heavy ear-rings are in her ears—and on her head is a diadem of war eagle's feathers. She has a bright spot of vermilion on each cheek, and—behold an Indian bride!

When she is ready, as many presents as were given for her are collected and put on a horse; and the bride, accompanied by three or four of her relations, takes the road to the wigwam of the bridegroom.

When they arrive within a hundred yards of the wigwam, Walking Wind's father calls for the War Club to come out. He does not come, but sends one of his relations to receive the bride. Do not suppose that Walking Wind's father takes offense at the bridegroom's not coming when he is called; for it is as much a part of the ceremony, among the Dahcotahs, for one of the bride's relations to call for the bridegroom, and for the groom to refuse to come, as it is for us to have the ring put upon the third finger of the left hand.

As soon as the warrior deputed by the husband elect to receive the bride makes his appearance, the Indians raise a shout of applause, and all run towards him as he approaches them, and while they are running and shouting they are firing off their guns too.

But the ceremony is not over yet. Walking Wind, in order to complete the ceremonies, to be a wife, must jump upon the back of her husband's relative, and be thus carried into the wigwam of which she is to be the mistress.

What a situation for a bride! Walking Wind seriously thinks of rebelling; she hesitates—while the man stands ready to start for the wigwam as soon as the luggage is on. The bride draws back and pouts a little, when some of her friends undertake to reason with her; and she, as if to avoid them, springs upon the back of the Dahcotah, who carries her into the wigwam.

But where on earth is the bridegroom? Seated on the ground in the teepee, looking as placid and unconcerned as if nothing was going on. Of course he rises to receive his bride? Not he; but Walking Wind is on her feet again, and she takes her seat, without any invitation, by the side of him, who is literally to be her lord and master—and they are man and wife. As much so, as if there were a priest and a ring, pearls and bride-cake. For the Dahcotah reveres the ceremony of marriage, and he thinks with solemn awe of the burial rites of his nation, as we do. These rites have been preserved from generation to generation, told from father to son, and they will be handed down until the Dahcotahs are no more, or until religion and education take the place of superstition and ignorance—until God, our God, is known and worshiped among a people who as yet have hardly heard His name.

SHAH-CO-PEE;

THE ORATOR OF THE SIOUX

Distant View of Fort Snelling, watercolor on paper, 1847.

SHAH-CO-PEE (or Six) is one of the chiefs of the Dahcotahs; his village is about twenty-five miles from Fort Snelling. He belongs to the bands that are called Men-da-wa-can-ton, or People of the Spirit Lakes.

No one who has lived at Fort Snelling can ever forget him, for at what house has he not called to shake hands and smoke; to say that he is a great chief, and that he is hungry and must eat before he starts for home? If the hint is not immediately acted upon, he adds that the sun is dying fast, and it is time for him to set out.

Shah-co-pee is not so tall or fine looking as Bad Hail, nor has he the fine Roman features of old Man in the Cloud. His face is decidedly ugly; but there is an expression of intelligence about his quick black eye and fine forehead, that makes him friends, notwithstanding his many troublesome qualities.

At present he is in mourning; his face is painted black. He never combs his hair, but wears a black silk handkerchief tied across his forehead.

When he speaks he uses a great deal of gesture, suiting the action to the word. His hands, which are small and well formed, are black with dirt; he does not descend to the duties of the toilet.

He is the orator of the Dahcotahs. No matter how trifling the occasion, he talks well; and assumes an air of importance that would become him if he were discoursing on matters of life and death.

Some years ago, our government wished the Chippeways and Dahcotahs to conclude a treaty of peace among themselves. Frequently have these two bands made peace, but rarely kept it any length of time. On this occasion many promises were made on both sides; promises which would be broken by some inconsiderate young warrior before long, and then retaliation must follow.

Shah-co-pee has great influence among the Dahcotahs, and he was to come to Fort Snelling to be present at the council of peace. Early in the morning he and about twenty warriors left their village on the banks of the St. Peters, for the Fort.

When they were very near, so that their actions could be distinguished, they assembled in their canoes, drawing them close together, that they might hear the speech which their chief was about to make them.

They raised the stars and stripes, and their own flag, which is a staff adorned with feathers from the war eagle; and the noon-day sun gave brilliancy to their gay dresses, and the feathers and ornaments that they wore.

Shah-co-pee stood straight and firm in his canoe—and not the less proudly that the walls of the Fort towered above him.

"My boys," he said (for thus he always addressed his men), "the Dahcotahs are all braves; never has a coward been known among the People of the Spirit Lakes. Let the women and children fear their enemies, but we will face our foes, and always conquer.

"We are going to talk with the white men; our great Father wishes us to be at peace with our enemies. We have long enough shed the blood of the Chippeways; we have danced round their scalps, and our children have kicked their heads about in the dust. What more do we want? When we are in council, listen to the words of the Interpreter as he tells us what our great Father says, and I will answer him for you; and when we have eaten and smoked the pipe of peace, we will return to our village."

The chief took his seat with all the importance of a public benefactor. He intended to have all the talking to himself, to arrange matters according to his own ideas; but he did it with utmost condescension, and his warriors were satisfied.

Besides being an orator, Shah-co-pee is a beggar, and one of a high order too, for he will neither take offense nor a refusal. Tell him one day that you will not give him pork and flour, and on the next he returns, nothing daunted, shaking hands, and asking for pork and flour. He always gains his point, for you are obliged to give in order to get rid of him. He will take up his quarters at the Interpreter's, and come down upon you every day for a week just at meal time—as he is always blessed with a ferocious appetite, it is much better to capitulate, come to terms by giving him what he wants, and let him go. And after he has once started, ten to one if he does not come back to say he wants to shoot and bring you some ducks; you must give him powder and shot to enable him to do so. That will probably be the last of it.

CHAPTER II

IT WAS A beautiful morning in June when we left Fort Snelling to go on a pleasure party up the St. Peters, in a steamboat, the first that had ever ascended that river. There were many drawbacks in the commencement, as there always are on such occasions. The morning was rather cool, thought some, and as they hesitated about going, of course their toilets were delayed to the last moment. And when all were fairly in the boat, wood was yet to be found. Then something was the matter with one of the wheels—and the mothers were almost sorry they had consented to come; while the children, frantic with joy, were in danger of being drowned every moment, by the energetic movements they made near the sides of the boat, by way of indicating their satisfaction at the state of things.

In the cabin, extensive preparations were making in case the excursion brought on a good appetite. Everybody contributed loaf upon loaf of bread and cake; pies, coffee and sugar; cold meats of every description; with milk and cream in bottles. Now and then, one of these was broken or upset, by way of adding to the confusion, which was already intolerable.

Champaigne and cold Cogniac were brought by the young gentlemen, only for fear the ladies should be sea-sick; or, perhaps, in case the gentlemen should think it positively necessary to drink the ladies' health.

When we thought all was ready, there was still another delay. Shah-co-pee and two of his warriors were seen coming down the hill, the chief making an animated appeal to some one on board the boat; and as he reached the shore he gave us to understand that his business was concluded, and that he would like to go with us. But it was very evident that he considered his company a favor.

The bright sun brought warmth, and we sat on the upper deck admiring the beautiful shores of the St. Peter's. Not a creature was to be seen for some distance on the banks, and the birds as they flew over our heads seemed to be the fit and only inhabitants of such a region.

When tired of admiring the scenery, there was enough to employ us. The table was to be set for dinner; the children had already found out which basket contained the cake, and they were casting admiring looks towards it.

When we were all assembled to partake of some refreshments, it was delightful to find that there were not enough chairs for half the party. We borrowed each other's knives and forks too, and etiquette, that petty tyrant of society, retired from the scene.

Shah-co-pee found his way to the cabin, where he manifested strong symptoms of shaking hands over again; in order to keep him quiet, we gave him plenty to eat. How he seemed to enjoy a piece of cake that had accidentally dropped into the oyster-soup! and with equal gravity would he eat apple-pie and ham together. And then his cry of "wakun"* when the cork flew from the champaigne bottle across the table!

———

*Mysterious

How happily the day passed—how few such days occur in the longest life!

As Shah-co-pee's village appeared in sight, the chief addressed Col. D_____, who was at that time in command of Fort Snelling, asking him why we had come on such an excursion.

"To escort you home," was the ready reply; "you are a great chief, and worthy of being honored, and we have chosen this as the best way of showing our respect and admiration of you."

The Dahcotah chief believed all; he never for a moment thought there was anything like jesting on the subject of his own high merits; his face beamed with delight on receiving such a compliment.

The men and women of the village crowded on the shore as the boat landed, as well they might, for a steamboat was a new sight to them.

The chief sprang from the boat, and swelling with pride and self admiration he took the most conspicuous station on a rock near the shore, among his people, and made them a speech.

We could not but admire his native eloquence. Here, with all that is wild in nature surrounding him, did the untaught orator address his people. His lips gave rapid utterance to thoughts which did honor to his feelings, when we consider who and what he was.

He told them that the white people were their friends; that they wished them to give up murder and intemperance, and to live quietly and happily. They taught them to plant corn, and they were anxious to instruct their children. "When we are suffering," said he, "during the cold weather, from sickness or want of food, they give us medicine and bread."

And finally he told them of the honor that had been paid him. "I went, as you know, to talk with the big Captain of the Fort, and he, knowing the bravery of the Dahcotahs, and that I was a great chief, has brought me home, as you see. Never has a Dahcotah warrior been thus honored!"

Never indeed! But we took care not to undeceive him. It was a harmless error, and as no efforts on our part could have diminished his self importance, we listened with apparent, indeed with real admiration of his eloquent speech. The women brought ducks on board, and in exchange we gave them bread; and it was evening as we watched the last teepee of Shah-co-pee's village fade away in the distance.

But sorrow mingles with the remembrance of that bright day. One of those who contributed most to its pleasures is gone from us—one whom all esteemed and many loved, and justly, for never beat a kinder or a nobler heart.

CHAPTER III

SHAH-CO-PEE HAS looked rather grave lately. There is trouble in the wigwam.

The old chief is the husband of three wives, and they and their children are always fighting. The first wife is old as the hills, wrinkled and haggard; the chief cares no more for her than he does for the stick of wood she is chopping. She quarrels with everybody but him, and this prevents her from being quite forgotten.

The day of the second wife is past too, it is of no use for her to plait her hair and put on her ornaments; for the old chief's heart is wrapped up in his third wife.

The girl did not love him, how could she? and he did not succeed in talking her into the match; but he induced the parents to sell her to him, and the young wife went weeping to the teepee of the chief.

Hers was a sad fate. She hated her husband as much as he loved her. No presents could reconcile her to her situation. The two forsaken wives never ceased annoying her, and their children assisted them. The young wife had not the courage to resent their ill treatment, for the loss of her lover had broken her heart. But that lover did not seem to be in such despair as she was—he did not quit the village, or drown himself, or commit any act of desperation. He lounged and smoked as much as ever. On one occasion when Shah-co-pee was absent from the village the lovers met.

They had to look well around them, for the two old wives were always on the look out for something to tell of the young one; but there was no one near. The wind whistled keenly round the bend of the river as the Dahcotah told the weeping girl to listen to him.

When had she refused? How had she longed to hear the sound of his voice when wearied to death with the long boastings of the old chief.

But how did her heart beat when Red Stone told her that he loved her still—that he had only been waiting an opportunity to induce her to leave her old husband, and go with him far away.

She hesitated a little, but not long; and when Shah-co-pee returned to his teepee his young wife was gone—no one had seen her depart—no one knew where to seek for her. When the old man heard that Red Stone was gone too, his rage knew no bounds. He beat his two wives almost to death, and would have given his handsomest pipe-stem to have seen the faithless one again.

His passion did not last long; it would have killed him if it had. His wives moaned all through the night, bruised and bleeding, for the fault of their rival; while the chief had recourse to the pipe, the never-failing refuge of the Dahcotah.

"I thought," said the chief, "that some calamity was going to happen to me (for being more composed, he began to talk to the other Indians who sat with him in his teepee, somewhat after the manner and in the spirit of Job's friends). I saw Unk-a-tahe, the great fish of the water, and it showed its horns; and we know that that is always a sign of trouble."

"Ho!" replied an old medicine man, "I remember when Unk-a-tahe got in under the falls (of St. Anthony) and broke up the ice. The large pieces of ice went swiftly down, and the water forced its way until it was frightful to see it. The trees near the shore were thrown down, and the small islands were left bare. Near Fort Snelling there was a house where a white man and his wife lived. The woman heard the noise, and, waking her husband, ran out; but as he did not follow her quick enough, the house was soon afloat and he was drowned."

There was an Indian camp near this house, for the body of Wenona, the sick girl who was carried over the Falls, was found here. It was placed on a scaffold on the shore, near where the Indians found her, and Checkered Cloud moved her teepee, to be near her daughter. Several other Dahcotah families were also near her.

But what was their fright when they heard the ice breaking, and the waters roaring as they carried everything before them? The father of Wenona clung to his daughter's scaffold, and no entreaties of his wife or others could induce him to leave.

"Unk-a-tahe has done this," cried the old man, "and I care not. He carried my sick daughter under the waters, and he may bury me there too."

And while the others fled from the power of Unk-a-tahe, the father and mother clung to the scaffold of their daughter.

They were saved, and they lived by the body of Wenona until they buried her. The power of Unk-a-tahe is great!" so spoke the medicine man, and Shah-co-pee almost forgot his loss in the fear and admiration of this monster of the deep, this terror of the Dahcotahs.

He will do well to forget the young wife altogether; for she is far away, making mocassins for the man she loves. She rejoices at her escape from the old man, and his two wives; while he is always making speeches to his men, commencing by saying he is a great chief, and ending with the assertion that Red Stone should have respected his old age, and not have stolen from him the only wife he ever loved.

CHAPTER IV

SHAH-CO-PEE CAME, a few days ago, with twenty other warriors, some of them chiefs, on a visit to the commanding officer of Fort Snelling.

The Dahcotahs had heard that the Winnebagoes were about to be removed, and that they were to pass through their hunting grounds on their way to their future homes. They did not approve of this arrangement. Last summer the Dahcotahs took some scalps of the Winnebagoes, and it was decided at Washington that the Dahcotahs should pay four thousand dollars of their annuities as an atonement for the act. This caused much suffering among the Dahcotahs; fever was making great havoc among them, and to deprive them of their flour and other articles of food was only enfeebling their constitutions, and rendering them an easy prey for disease. The Dahcotahs thought this very hard at the time; they have not forgotten the circumstance, and they think that they ought to be consulted before their lands are made a thoroughfare by their enemies.

They accordingly assembled, and, accompanied by the Indian agent and the interpreter, came to Fort Snelling to make their complaint. When they were all seated, (all on the floor but one, who looked most uncomfortable, mounted on a high chair), the agent introduced the subject, and it was discussed for a while; the Dahcotahs paying the most profound attention, although they could not understand a word of what was passing; and when there was a few moments' silence, the chiefs rose each in his turn to protest against the Winnebagoes passing through their country. They all spoke sensibly and well; and when one finished, the others all intimated their approval by crying, "Ho!" as a kind of chorus. After a while Shah-co-pee rose; his manner said "I am Sir Oracle." He shook hands with the commanding officer, with the agent and interpreter, and then with some strangers who were visiting the fort.

His attitude was perfectly erect as he addressed the officer.

"We are the children of our great Father, the President of the United States; look upon us, for we are your children too. You are placed here to see that the Dahcotahs are protected, that their rights are not infringed upon."

While the Indians cried Ho! ho! with great emphasis, Shah-co-pee shook hands all round again, and then resumed his place and speech.

"Once this country all belonged to the Dahcotahs. Where had the white man a place to call his own on our prairies? He could not even pass through our country without our permission!

"Our great Father has signified to us that he wants our lands. We have sold some of them to him, and we are content to do so, but he has promised to protect us, to be a friend to us, to take care of us as a father does of his children.

"When the white man wishes to visit us, we open the door of our country to him; we treat him with hospitality. He looks at our rocks, our river, our trees, and we do not disturb him. The Dahcotah and the white man are friends.

"But the Winnebagoes are not our friends, we suffered for them not long ago; our children wanted food; our wives were sick; they could not plant corn or gather the Indian potato. Many of our nation died; their bodies are now resting on their scaffolds. The night birds clap their wings as the winds howl over them!

"And we are told that our great Father will let the Winnebagoes make a path through our hunting grounds: they will subsist upon our game; every bird or animal they kill will be a loss to us.

"The Dahcotah's lands are not free to others. If our great Father wishes to make any use of our lands, he should pay us. We object to the Winnebagoes passing through our country; but if it is too late to prevent this, then we demand a thousand dollars for every village they shall pass."

Ho! cried the Indians again; and Shah-co-pee, after shaking hands once more, took his seat.

I doubt if you will ever get the thousand dollars a village, Shah-co-pee; but I like the spirit that induces you to demand it. May you live long to make speeches and beg bread—the unrivaled orator and most notorious beggar of the Dahcotahs!

Oye-kar-mani-vim;

The Track-Maker

Valley of the St. Peters, watercolor on paper, 1848.

CHAPTER I

IT WAS THE summer of 183–, that a large party of Chippeways
visited Fort Snelling. There was peace between them and the Sioux. Their
time was passed in feasting and carousing; their canoes together flew over the
waters of the Mississippi. The young Sioux warriors found strange beauty in
the oval faces of the Chippeway girls; and the Chippeways discovered (what
was actually the case) that the women of the Dahcotahs were far more
graceful than those of their own nation.

But as the time of the departure of the Chippeways approached, many a

Chippeway maiden wept when she remembered how soon she would bid adieu to all her hopes of happiness. And Flying Shadow was saddest of them all. She would gladly have given up everything for her lover. What were home and friends to her who loved with all the devotion of a heart untrammeled by forms, fresh from the hand of nature? She listened to his flute in the still evening, as if her spirit would forsake her when she heard it no more. She would sit with him on the bluff which hung over the Mississippi, and envy the very waters which would remain near him, when she was far away. But her lover loved his nation ever more than he did her; and though he would have died to have saved her from sorrow, yet he knew she could never be his wife. Even were he to marry her, her life would ever be in danger. A Chippeway could not long find a home among the Dahcotahs.

The Track-maker bitterly regretted that they had ever met, when he saw her grief at the prospect of parting. "Let us go," he said, "to the Falls, where I will tell you the story you asked me."

The Track-maker entered the canoe first, and the girl followed; and so pleasant was the task of paddling her lover over the quiet waters, that it seemed but a moment before they were in sight of the torrent.

"It was there," said the Sioux, "that Wenona and her child found their graves. Her husband, accompanied by some other Dahcotahs, had gone some distance above the falls to hunt. While there, he fell in love with a young girl whom he thought more beautiful than his wife. Wenona knew that she must no longer hope to be loved as she had been.

"The Dahcotahs killed much game, and then broke up their camp and started for their homes. When they reached the falls, the women got ready to carry their canoes and baggage round.

"But Wenona was going on a longer journey. She would not live when her husband loved her no more, and, putting her son in her canoe, she soon reached the island that divides the falls.

"Then she put on all her ornaments, as if she were a bride; she dressed her boy too, as a Dahcotah warrior; she turned to look once more at her husband, who was helping his second wife to put the things she was to carry, on her back.

"Soon her husband call to her; she did not answer him, but placed her child high up in the canoe, so that his father could see him, and getting in herself she paddled towards the rapids.

"Her husband saw that Unk-tahe would destroy her, and he called to her to come ashore. But he might have called to the roaring waters as well, and they would have heeded him as soon as she.

"Still he ran along the shore with his arms uplifted, entreating her to come ashore.

"Wenona continued her course towards the rapids—her voice was heard above the waters as she sang her death song. Soon the mother and child were seen no more—the waters covered them.

"But her spirit wanders near this place. An elk and fawn are often seen, and we know they are Wenona and her child."

"Do you love me as Wenona loved?" continued the Sioux, as he met the looks of the young girl bent upon him.

"I will not live when I see you no more," she replied. "As the flowers die when the winter's cold falls upon them, so will my spirit depart when I no longer listen to your voice. But when I go to the land of the spirits I shall be happy. My spirit will return to earth; but it will be always near you."

Little didst thou dream that the fate of Wenona would be less sad than thine. She found the death she sought, in the waters whose bosom opened to receive her. But thou wilt bid adieu to earth in the midst of the battle—in the very presence of him, for whose love thou wouldst venture all. Thy spirit will flee trembling from the shrieks of the dying mother, the suffering child. Death will come to thee as a terror, not as a refuge.

CHAPTER II

WHEN THE Chippeways broke up their camp near Fort Snelling, they divided into two parties, one party returning home by the Mississippi, the other by way of the St. Croix.

They parted on the most friendly terms with the Sioux, giving presents, and receiving them in return.

Some pillagers, who acknowledge no control, had accompanied the Chippeways. These pillagers are in fact highwaymen or privateers—having no laws, and acting from the impulses of their own fierce hearts.

After the Chippeways had left, the pillagers concealed themselves in a path near Lake Calhoun. This lake is about seven miles from Fort Snelling.

Before they had been concealed one hour, two Dahcotahs passed, father and son. The pillagers fired, and the father was killed instantly; but the son escaped, and made his way home in safety. The boy entered the village calling for his mother, to tell her the sad news; her cries of grief gave the alarm, and soon the death of the Sioux was known throughout the village. The news flew from village to village on the wings of the wind; Indian runners were seen in every direction, and in twenty-four hours there were three hundred warriors on foot in pursuit of the Chippeways.

Every preparation was made for the death-strife. Not a Sioux warrior but vowed he would with his own arm avenge the death of his friend. The very tears of the wife were dried when the hope of vengeance cheered her heart.

The Track-maker was famous as a warrior. Already did the aged Dahcotahs listen to his words; for he was both wise and brave. He was among the foremost to lead the Dahcotahs against the Chippeways; and though he longed to raise his tomahawk against his foes, his spirit sunk within him when he remembered the girl he loved. What will be her fate! Oh! that he had never seen her. But it was no time to think of her. Duty called upon him to avenge the death of his friend.

CHAPTER III

WOE TO THE unsuspecting Chippeways! ignorant of the murder that had been committed, they were leisurely turning their steps homeward, while the pillagers made their escape with the scalp of the Dahcotah.

The Sioux travelled one day and night before they came up with the Chippeways. Nothing could quench their thirst but blood. And the women and children must suffer first. The savage suffers a twofold death; before his own turn comes, his young children lie breathless around him, their mother all unconscious by their side.

The Chippeways continued their journey, fearing nothing. They had camped between the falls of St. Anthony and Rum river; they were refreshed, and the men proceeded first, leaving their women and children to follow. They were all looking forward with pleasure to seeing their homes again. The women went leisurely along; the infant slept quietly—what should it fear close to its mother's heart! The young children laughed as they hid themselves behind the forest trees, and then emerged suddenly to frighten the others. The Chippeway maidens rejoiced when they remembered that their rivals, the Dahcotah girls, would no longer seduce their lovers from their allegiance.

Flying Shadow wept, there was nothing to make her happy, she would see the Track-maker no more, and she looked forward to death as the end of her cares. She concealed in her bosom the trinkets he had given her; every feature of his face was written on her heart—that heart that beat only for him, that so soon would cease to beat at all!

But there was a fearful cry, that banished even him from her thoughts. The war-whoop burst suddenly upon the defenseless women.

Hundreds of Dahcotah warriors rose up to blind the eyes of the terror-stricken mothers. Their children are scalped before their eyes; their infants are dashed against the rocks, which are not more insensible to their cries than their murderers.

It is a battle of strength against weakness. Stern warrior, it needs not to strike the mother that blow! she dies in the death of her children.*

The maidens clasp their small hands—a vain appeal to the merciless wretches, who see neither beauty nor grace, when rage and revenge are in their hearts. It is blood they thirst for, and the young and innocent fall like grass before the mower.

Flying Shadow sees her lover! he is advancing towards her! What does his countenance say? There is sadness in his face, and she hopes—aye, more than hopes—she knows he will save her. With all a woman's trust she throws herself in his arms. "Save me! save me!" she cries; "do not let them slay me before your eyes; make me your prisoner!+ you said that you loved me, spare my life!"

-----

* The Dahcotahs believe, or many of them believe, that each body has four souls. One wanders about the earth and requires food; a second watches over the body; the third hovers round its native village, while the fourth goes to the land of the spirits.

+ When the Sioux are tired of killing, they sometimes take their victims prisoners, and, generally speaking, treat them with great kindness.

Who shall tell his agony? For a moment he thought he would make her his prisoner. Another moment's reflection convinced him that that would be of no avail. He knew that she must die, but he could not take her life.

Her eyes were trustingly turned upon him; her soft hand grasped his arm. But the Sioux warriors were pressing upon them, he gave her one more look, he touched her with his spear,*and he was gone.

And Flying Shadow was dead. She felt not the blow that sent her reeling to the earth. Her lover had forsaken her in the hour of danger, and what could she feel after that?

The scalp was torn from her head by one of those who had most admired her beauty; and her body was trampled upon by the very warriors who had so envied her lover.

The shrieks of the dying women reached the ears of their husbands and brothers. Quickly did they retrace their steps, and when they reached the spot, they bravely stood their ground; but the Dahcotahs were too powerful for them,—terrible was the struggle!

The Dahcotahs continued the slaughter, and the Chippeways were obliged at last to give way. One of the Chippeways seized his frightened child and placed him upon his back. His wife lay dead at his feet; with his child clinging to him, he fought his way through.

Two of the Dahcotahs followed him, for he was flying fast; and they feared he would soon be out of their power. They thought, as they nearly came up to him, that he would loose his hold on his child; but the father's heart was strong within him. He flies, and the Sioux are close upon his heels! He fires and kills one of them. The other Sioux follows: he has nothing to encumber him—he must be victor in such an unequal contest. But the love that was stronger than death nerved the father's arm. He kept firing, and the Sioux retreated. The Chippeway and his young son reached their home in safety, there to mourn the loss of others whom they loved.

The sun set upon a bloody field; the young and old lay piled together; the hearts that had welcomed the breaking of the day were all unconscious of its close.

———

* When a Dahcotah touches an enemy with his spear, he is privileged to wear a feather of honor, as if he had taken a scalp.

The Sioux were avenged; and the scalps that they brought home (nearly one hundred when the party joined them from the massacre at Saint Croix) bore witness to their triumph.

The other party of Sioux followed the Chippeways who had gone by way of the St. Croix. While the Chippeways slept, the war-cry of the Sioux aroused them. And though they fought bravely, they suffered as did their friends, and the darkness of night added terror to the scene.

The Dahcotahs returned with the scalps to their villages, and as they entered triumphantly, they were greeted with shouts of applause. The scalps were divided among the villages, and joyful preparations were made to celebrate the scalp-dance.

The scalps were stretched upon hoops, and covered with vermilion, ornamented with feathers, ribbons and trinkets.

On the women's scalps were hung a comb, or a pair of scissors, and for months did the Dahcotah women dance around them. The men wore mourning for their enemies, as is the custom among the Dahcotahs.

When the dancing was done, the scalps were buried with the deceased relatives of the Sioux who took them.

And this is Indian, but what is Christian warfare? The wife of the hero lives to realize her wretchedness; the honors paid by his countrymen are a poor recompense for the loss of his love and protection. The life of the child too, is safe, but who will lead him in the paths of virtue, when his mother has gone down to the grave.

Let us not hear of civilized warfare! It is all the work of the spirits of evil. God did not make man to slay his brother, and the savage alone can present an excuse. The Dahcotah dreams not that it is wrong to resent an injury to the death; but the Christian knows that God has said, Vengeance is mine!

CHAPTER IV

THE TRACK-MAKER had added to his fame. He had taken many scalps, and the Dahcotah maidens welcomed him as a hero—as one who would no longer refuse to acknowledge the power of their charms. They asked him eagerly of the fight—whom he had killed first—but they derived but little satisfaction from his replies. They found he resisted their advances, and they left him to his gloomy thoughts.

Every scene he looked upon added to his grief. Memory clung to him, recalling every word and look of Flying Shadow. But that last look, could he ever forget it?

He tried to console himself with the thoughts of his triumph. Alas! her smile was sweeter than the recollection of revenge. He had waded in the blood of his enemies; he had trampled upon the hearts of the men he hated; but he had broken the heart of the only woman he had ever loved.

In the silence of the night her death-cry sounded in his ear; and he would start as if to flee from the sound. In his dreams he saw again that trustful face, that look of appeal—and then the face of stone, when she saw that she had appealed in vain.

He followed the chase, but there he could not forget the battle scene. "Save me! save me!" forever whispered every forest leaf, or every flowing wave. Often did he hear her calling him, and he would stay his steps as if he hoped to meet her smile.

The medicine men offered to cure his disease; but he knew that it was beyond their art, and he cared not how soon death came, nor in what form.

He met the fate he sought. A war party was formed among the Dahcotahs to seek more scalps, more revenge. But the Track-maker was weary of glory.

He went with the party, and never returned. Like *her*, he died in battle; but the death that she sought to avert, was a welcome messenger to him. He felt that in the grave all would be forgotten.

Eta Keazah;

OR,

Sullen Face

Prairie near the mouth of the St. Peters. Buffalo Hunt, watercolor on paper, 1846-1848.

WENONA WAS the light of her father's wigwam—the pride of the band of Sissetons, whose village is on the shores of beautiful Lake Travers. However cheerfully the fire might burn in the dwelling of the aged chief, there was darkness for him when she was away—and the mother's heart was always filled with anxiety, for she knew that Wenona had drawn upon her the envy of her young companions, and she feared that some one of them would cast a spell* upon her child,

---

* The Indians fear that from envy or jealousy some person may cast a fatal spell upon them to produce sickness, or even death. This superstition seems almost identical with the Obi or Obeat of the West India negroes.

that her loveliness might be dimmed by sorrow or sickness.

The warriors of the band strove to outdo each other in noble deeds, that they might feel more worthy to claim her hand;—while the hunters tried to win her good will by presents of buffalo and deer. But Wenona thought not yet of love. The clear stream that reflected her form told her she was beautiful; yet her brother was the bravest warrior of the Sissetons; and her aged parents too—was not their love enough to satisfy her heart! Never did brother and sister love each other more; their features were the same, yet man's sternness in him was changed to woman's softness in her. The "glance of the falcon" in his eye was the "gaze of the dove" in hers. But at times the expression of his face would make you wonder that you ever could have thought him like his twin sister.

When he heard the Sisseton braves talk of the hunts they had in their youth, before the white man drove them from the hunting-grounds of their forefathers;—when instead of the blanket they wore the buffalo robe;—when happiness and plenty were in their wigwams—and when the voices of weak women and famished children were never heard calling for food in vain—then the longing for vengeance that was written on his countenance, the imprecations that were breathed from his lips, the angry scowl, the lightning from his eye, all made him unlike indeed to his sister, the pride of the Sissetons!

When the gentle breeze would play among the prairie flowers, then would she win him from such bitter thoughts. "Come, my brother, we will go and sit by the banks of the lake, why should you be unhappy! the buffalo is still to be found upon our hunting-grounds—the spirit of the lake watches over us—we shall not want for food."

He would go, because she asked him. The quiet and beauty of nature were not for him; rather would he have stood alone when the storm held its sway; when the darkness was only relieved by the flash that laid the tall trees of the forest low; when the thunder bird clapped her wings as she swept through the clouds above him. But could he refuse to be happy when Wenona smiled? Alas! that her gentle spirit should not always have been near to soften his!

But as the beauty and warmth of summer passed away, so did Wenona's strength begin to fail; the autumn wind, that swept rudely over the prairie flowers, so that they could not lift their heads above the tall grass, seemed to pass in anger over the wigwam of the old man—for the eye of the Dahcotah maiden was losing its brightness, and her step was less firm, as she wandered with her brother in her native woods. Vainly did the medicine men practice their cherished rites—the Great Spirit had called—and who could refuse to hear his voice? she faded with the leaves—and the cries of the mourners were answered by the wailing winds, as they sang her requiem.

A few months passed away, and her brother was alone. The winter that followed his sister's death, was a severe one. The mother had never been strong, and she soon followed her daughter—while the father's age unfitted him to contend with sorrow, infirmity, and want.

Spring returned, but winter had settled on the heart of the young Sisseton; she was gone who alone could drive away the shadow from his brow, what wonder then that his countenance should always be stern. The Indians called him Eta Keazah, or Sullen Face.

But after the lapse of years, the boy, who brooded over the wrongs of his father, eagerly seeks an opportunity to avenge his own. His sister has never been forgotten; but he remembers her as we do a beautiful dream; and she is the spirit that hovers round him while his eyes are closed in sleep.

But there are others who hold a place in his heart. His wife is always ready to receive him with a welcome, and his young son calls upon him to teach him to send the arrow to the heart of the buffalo. But the sufferings of his tribe, from want of food and other privations, are ever before his eyes. Vengeance upon the white man, who has caused them!

CHAPTER II

WINTER IS the season of trial for the Sioux, especially for the women and children. The incursions of the English half-breeds and Cree Indians, into the Sisseton country, have caused their buffalo to recede, and so little other game is to be found, that indescribable sufferings are endured every winter by the Sissetons.

Starvation forces the hunters to seek for the buffalo in the depth of winter. Their families must accompany them, for they have not the smallest portion of food to leave with them; and who will protect them from the Chippeways!

However inclement the season, their home must be for a time on the open prairie. As far as the eye can reach, it is a desert of snow. Not a stick of timber can be seen. A storm is coming on too; nothing is heard but the howling blast, which mocks the cries of famished children. The drifting of the snow makes it impossible to see what course they are to take; they have only to sit down and let the snow fall upon them. It is a relief when they are quite covered with it, for it shelters them from the keenness of the blast!

Alas! for the children; the cry of those who can speak is, Give me food! while the dying infant clings to its mother's breast, seeking to draw, with its parting breath, the means of life.

But the storm is over; the piercing cold seizes upon the exhausted frames of the sufferers.

The children have hardly strength to stand; the father places one upon his back and goes forward; the mother wraps her dead child in her blanket, and lays it in the snow; another is clinging to her, she has no time to weep for the dead; nature calls upon her to make an effort for the living. She takes her child and follows the rest. It would be a comfort to her, could she hope to find her infant's body when summer returns to bury it. She shudders, and remembers that the wolves of the prairie are starving too!

Food is found at last; the strength of the buffalo yields to the arrow of the Sioux. We will have food and not die, is the joyful cry of all, and when their fierce appetites are appeased, they carry with them on their return to their village, the skins of the animals with the remainder of the meat.

The sufferings of famine and fatigue, however, are followed by those of disease; the strength of many is laid low. They must watch, too, for their enemies are at hand.

CHAPTER III

IN THE SUMMER of 1844 a large party of half-breeds and Indians from Red river,—English subjects,—trespassed upon the hunting grounds of the Sioux. There were several hundred hunters, and many carts drawn by oxen for the purpose of carrying away the buffalo they had killed. One of this party had left his companions, and was riding alone at some distance from them. A Dahcotah knew that his nation would suffer from the destruction of their game—fresh in his memory, too, were the sufferings of the past winter. What wonder then that the arrow which was intended for the buffalo, should find its way to the heart of the trespasser!

This act enraged the half-breeds; they could not find the Sioux who committed it—but a few days after they fell in with a party of others, who were also hunting, and killed seven of them. The rest escaped, and carried the news of the death of their braves to their village. One of the killed was a relative of Sullen Face. The sad news spread rapidly through the village, and nothing was heard but lamentation. The women cut long gashes on their arms, and as the blood flowed from the wound they would cry, Where is my husband? my son? my brother?

Soon the cry of revenge is heard above that of lamentation. "It is not possible," said Sullen Face, "that we can allow these English to starve us, and take the lives of our warriors. They have taken from us the food that would nourish our wives and children; and more, they have killed seven of our bravest men! we will have revenge—we will watch for them, and bring home their scalps, that our women may dance round them!"

A war party was soon formed, and Sullen Face, at the head of more than fifty warriors, stationed himself in the vicinity of the road by which the half-breeds from Red river drive their cattle to Fort Snelling.

Some days after, there was an unusual excitement in the Sioux village on Swan lake, about twenty miles northwest of Traverse des Sioux. A number of Indians were gazing at an object not very distant, and in order to discover what it was, the chief of the village, Sleepy Eyes, had sent one of his young men out, while the rest continued to regard it with looks of curiosity and awe.

They observed that as the Sioux approached it, he slackened his pace, when suddenly he gave a loud cry and ran towards the village.

He soon reached them, and pale with terror, exclaimed, "It is a spirit, it is white as the snow that covers our prairies in the winter. It looked at me and spoke not." For a short time, his fears infected the others, but after a while several determined to go and bring a more satisfactory report to their chief. They returned with the body, as it seemed only, of a white man; worn to a skeleton, with his feet cut and bleeding, unable to speak from exhaustion; nothing but the beating of his heart told that he lived.

The Indian women dressed his feet, and gave him food, wiped the blood from his limbs, and, after a consultation, they agreed to send word to the missionaries at Traverse des Sioux, that there was a white man sick and suffering with them.

The missionaries came immediately; took the man to their home, and with kind nursing he was soon able to account for the miserable situation in which he had been found.

"We left the state of Missouri," said the man, whose name was Bennett, "for the purpose of carrying cattle to Fort Snelling. My companions' names were Watson and Turner. We did not know the road, but supposed a map would guide us, with what information we could get on the way. We lost our way, however, and were eagerly looking for some person who could set us right. Early one morning some Sioux came up with us, and seemed inclined to join our party. One of them left hastily as if sent on a message; after a while a number of warriors, accompanied by the Indian who had left the first party, came towards us. Their leader had a dark countenance, and seemed to have great influence over them. We tried to make them understand that we had lost our way; we showed them the map, but they did not comprehend us.

"After angrily addressing his men for a few moments, the leader shot Watson through the shoulder, and another sent an arrow through his body and killed him. They then struck Watson's brother and wounded him.

"In the mean time the other Indians had been killing our cattle; and some of the animals having run away, they made Watson, who was sadly bruised with the blows he had received from them, mount a horse and go with them to hunt the rest of the cattle. We never heard of him again. The Indians say he disappeared from among the bushes, and they could not find him; but the probability is that they killed him. Some seemed to wish to kill Turner and myself—but after a while they told us to go, giving us our horses and a little food. We determined to retrace our steps. It was the best thing we could do; but our horses gave out, and we were obliged to leave them and proceed on foot.

"We were soon out of provisions, and having no means of killing game, our hearts began to fail us. Turner was unwell, and on arriving at a branch of

Crow river, about one hundred miles northwest of Fort Snelling, he found himself unable to swim. I tried to carry him across on my back, but could not do it; he was drowned, and I barely succeeded in reaching the shore. After resting, I proceeded on my journey. When I came in sight of the Indian village, much as I needed food and rest, I dreaded to show myself, for fear of meeting Watson's fate. I was spared the necessity of deciding. I fainted and fell to the ground. They found me, and proved kinder than I anticipated.

"Why they should have molested us I know not. There is something in it that I do not understand."

But it is easily explained. Sullen Face supposed them to belong to the party that had killed his friends, and through this error he had shed innocent blood.

CHAPTER IV

WHO THAT has seen Fort Snelling will not bear testimony to its beautiful situation! Whichever way we turn, nature calls for our admiration. But beautiful as it is by day, it is at night that its majesty and loveliness speak to the soul. Look to the north (while the Aurora Borealis is flashing above us, and the sound of the waters of St. Anthony's Falls meets the ear), the high bluffs of the Mississippi seem to guard its waters as they glide along. To the south, the St. Peter's has wandered off, preferring gentle prairies to rugged cliffs. To the east we see the "meeting of the waters;" gladly as the returning child meets the welcoming smile of the parent, do the waves of the St. Peter's flow into the Mississippi. On the west, there is prairie far as the eye can reach.

But it is to the free only that nature is beautiful. Can the prisoner gaze with pleasure on the brightness of the sky, or listen to the rippling of the waves? they make him feel his fetters the more.

> I am here, with my heavy chain!
> And I look on a torrent sweeping by,
> And an eagle rushing to the sky,
> And a host to its battle plain.

        Must I pine in my fetters here!
                With the wild wave's foam and the free bird's flight,
                And the tall spears glancing on my sight,
        And the trumpet in mine ear?

The summer of 1845 found Sullen Face a prisoner at Fort Snelling. Government having been informed of the murder of Watson by two Dahcotah Indians, orders were received at Fort Snelling that two companies should proceed to the Sisseton country, and take the murderers, that they might be tried by the laws of the United States.

Now for excitement, the charm of garrison life. Officers are of course always ready to "go where glory waits" them, but who ever heard of one being ready to go when the order came?

Alas! for the young officer who has a wife to leave; it will be weeks before he meets again her gentle smile!

Still more—alas for him who has no wife at all! for he has not a shirt with buttons on it, and most of what he has are in the wash. He will have to borrow of Selden; but here's the difficulty, Selden is going too, and is worse off than himself. But no matter! what with pins and twine and trusting to chance, they will get along.

Then the married men are inquiring for tin reflectors, for hard bread, though healthy, is never tempting. India rubber cloaks are in requisition too.

Those who are going, claim the doctor in case of accidents. Those who stay, their wives at least, want him for fear of measles; while the disciple of Esculapius, though he knows there will be better cooking if he remain at home, is certain there will be food for fun if he go. It is soon decided—the doctor goes.

Then the privates share in the pleasure of the day. How should a soldier be employed but in active service? besides, what a capital chance to desert! One, who is tired of calling "All's well" through the long night, with only the rocks and trees to hear him, hope that it will be his happy fate to find out there is danger near, and to give the alarm. Another vows, that if trouble won't come, why he will bring it by quarrelling with the first rascally Indian he meets. All is ready. Rations are put up for the men;—hams, buffalo tongues, pies and cake for the officers. The battalion marches out to the sound of the drum and fife;—they are soon down the hill—they enter their boats; handkerchiefs are waved from the fort, caps are raised and flourished over the water—they are almost out of sight—they are gone.

When the troops reached their destination, Sullen Face and Forked Horn were not there, but the chief gave them three of his warriors (who were with the party of Sullen Face at the time of the murder), promising that when the two murderers returned they would come to Fort Snelling, and give themselves up.

There was nothing then to prevent the immediate return of our troops. Their tramp had been a delightful one, and so far success had crowned their expedition. They were in the highest spirits. But a little incident occurred on their return, that was rather calculated to show the transitoriness of earthly joys. One dark night, when those who were awake were thinking, and those who slept were dreaming of their welcome home, there was evidently a disturbance. The sleepers roused themselves; guns were discharged. What could it be?

The cause was soon ascertained. To speak poetically, the birds had flown—in plain language, the prisoners had run away. They were not bound, their honor had been trusted to;—but you cannot place much reliance on the honor of an Indian with a prison in prospect. I doubt if a white man could be trusted under such circumstances. True, there was a guard, but, as I said, 'twas a dark night.

The troops returned in fine health, covered with dust and fleas, if not with glory.

CHAPTER V

IT IS TIME to return to Sullen Face. He and Forked Horn, on their return to the village, were informed of what had occurred during their absence. They offered to fulfil the engagement of the chief, and accompanied by others of the band, they started for Fort Snelling. The wife of Sullen Face had insisted upon accompanying him, and influenced by a presentiment that he should never return to his native village, he allowed her to do so. Their little boy quite forgot his fatigue as he listened to his father's voice, and held his hand. When they were near the fort, notice of their approach was sent to the commanding officer.

The entire force of the garrison marched out to receive the prisoners. A large number of Indians assembled to witness the scene—their gay dresses and wild appearance adding to its interest.

Sullen Face and Forked Horn, with the Sioux who had accompanied them, advanced to meet the battalion. The little boy dressed as a warrior, his war-eagle plumes waving proudly over his head, held his father's hand. In a moment the iron grasp of the soldier was on the prisoner's shoulder; they entered the gate of the fort; and he, who had felt that the winds of Heaven were not more free than a Dahcotah warrior, was now a prisoner in the power of the white man. But he entered not his cell until he had sung a warrior's song. Should his enemies think that he feared them? Had he not yielded himself up?

It was hard to be composed in parting with his wife and child. "Go my son," he said, "you will soon be old enough to kill the buffalo for your mother." But to his wife he only said, "I have done no wrong, and fear not the power of my enemies." The Sissetons returned to the village, leaving the prisoners at Fort Snelling, until they should be sent to Dubuque for trial.

They frequently walked about the fort, accompanied by a guard. Sullen Face seemed to be indifferent to his fate, and was impressed with the idea that he never would return to his home.

"Beautiful country!" said he, as he gazed towards the point where the waters of the Mississippi and St. Peter's meet. "I shall never look upon you again, the waters of the rivers unite, but I have parted forever from country and friends. My spirit tells me so. Then welcome death! they guard me now with sword and bayonet, but the soul of the Dahcotah is free."

After their removal to Dubuque, the two prisoners from Fort Snelling, with others who had been concerned in the murder, suffered much from sickness. Sullen Face would not complain, but the others tried to induce him to make his escape. He, at first, refused to do so, but finding his companions determined upon going, he at last consented.

Their plans succeeded, and after leaving the immediate neighborhood, they broke their shackles with stones. They were obliged, however, to hide themselves for a time among the rocks, to elude the sheriff and his party. They were not taken, and as soon as they deemed it prudent, they resumed their route.

Two of the prisoners died near Prairie du Chien. Sullen Face, Forked Horn, and another Sioux, pursued their journey with difficulty, for they were near perishing from want of food. They found a place where the Winnebagoes had encamped, and they parched the corn that lay scattered on the ground.

Disease had taken a strong hold upon the frame of Sullen Face; he constantly required the assistance of his companions. When they were near Prairie le Gros, he became so ill that he was unable to proceed. He insisted upon his friends leaving him; this they at first refused to do, but fearing they would be found and carried back to prison, they consented—and the dying warrior found himself alone.

Some Indians who were passing by saw him and gently carried him to their wigwam. But he heeded not their kindness. Death had dimmed the brightness of his eye, and his fast-failing strength told of the long journey to the spirits' land.

"It was not thus," he said, "that I thought to die! Where are the warriors of the Sissetons? Do they listen to my death song? I hoped to have triumphed over the white man, but his power had prevailed. My spirit drooped within his hated walls? But hark! there is music in my ears—'tis the voice of the sister of my youth—"Come with me my brother, we wait for you in the house of the spirits! we will sit by the banks of a lake more beautiful than that by which we wandered in our childhood; you will roam over the hunting grounds of your forefathers, and there the white man may never come."

His eyes are closing fast in death, but his lips murmur—"Wenona! I come! I come!"

Tᴏɴᴡᴀ-ʏᴀʜ-ᴘᴇ-ᴋɪɴ;

Tʜᴇ Sᴘɪᴇs

Indian Graves at the mouth of St. Peters, watercolor on paper, 1847.

CHAPTER I.

IT WAS IN the spring of 1848, that several Dahcotahs were carefully making their way along the forests near the borders of the Chippeway country. There had recently been a fight near the spot where they were, and the Dahcotahs were seeking the bodies of their friends who had been slain, that they might take them home to bury them.

They moved noiselessly along, for their enemies were near. Occasionally, one of them would imitate the cry of a bird or of some animal, so that if the attention of their enemies should be drawn to the spot, the slight noise they made in moving might be attributed to any but the right cause.

They had almost given up the hope of finding their friends, and this was the close of their last day's efforts to that intent. In the morning they intended to return to their village.

It was a bright clear evening, and the rays of the setting sun fell upon some objects further on. For a time the Dahcotahs gazed in silence; but no movement gave sign of what it was that excited their curiosity. All at once there was a fearful foreboding; they remembered why they were there, and they determined to venture near enough to find out what was the nature of the object on which the rays of the sun seemed to rest as if to attract their notice.

A few more steps and they were relieved from their terrible suspense, but their worst fears were realized.

The Dahcotahs recently killed had been skinned by the Chippeways, while their bodies were yet warm with life, and the skins were stretched upon poles; while on separate poles the hands were placed, with one finger of each hand pointing to the Dahcotah country. The savages were in a fearful rage. They had to endure a twofold insult.

There were the bodies of their friends, treated as if they were but beasts, and evidently put there to be seen by the Dahcotahs. And besides, the hands pointing to the country of the Dahcotahs—did it not plainly say to the spies, go back to your country and say to your warriors, that the Chippeways despise them, that they are not worthy to be treated as men?

The spies returned as cautiously as they had ventured near the fatal spot, and it was not until they were out of reach of danger from their foes, that they gave vent to their indignation. Then their smothered rage burst forth. They hastened to return and tell the event of their journey. They forgot how grieved the wives and sisters of the dead would be at being deprived of the solace of burying the remains of their friends—they only thought of revenge for the insult they had received.

When they arrived at their village, they called together their chiefs and braves, and related to them what they had seen. A council of war was held, which resulted in immediate preparations being made to resent the indignity offered to their friends, and the insult to the whole tribe.

The war-dance is always celebrated before a war party goes out to find an enemy, and there is in every village a war chief, who conducts the party. The war dance is performed inside of a wigwam, and not out of door, as is usually represented.

The "Owl" felt himself qualified in every respect to conduct the present party. He was a great warrior, and a juggler besides; and he had a reputation acquired from an act performed when he was a very young man, which showed as much cunning as bravery; for one of these qualities is as necessary to a Dahcotah war chief as the other.

He was one of a party of Dahcotahs who went to war against the Chippeways, but without success. On their way back "the Owl" got separated from the rest of the party, and he climbed a tree to see if he could discover his comrades. While in the tree a war party of the Chippeways came in sight and stopped quite near the tree to make their camp.

The Owl was in a sad predicament; he knew not what to do to effect his escape. As he knew he had not the power to contend with his enemies, he determined to have recourse to stratagem. When it was quite dark he commenced hooting like an owl, having previously transformed himself into one. The Chippeways looked up towards the tree and asked the owl what he was doing there. The owl replied that he had come to see a large war party of Dahcotahs who would soon pass by. The Chippeways took the hint, and took to their heels too, and ran home. The Owl then resumed his form, got down from the tree and returned home.

This wonderful incident, which he related of himself, gave him a great reputation and a name besides; for until now he had been called Chaskè, a name always given to the oldest son; but the Indians after this gave him the name of the Owl.

It being decided that the war party should leave as soon as their preparations could be made, the war chief sent for those who were to dance. The dance was performed every third or fourth night until the party left. For each dance the war chief had a new set of performers; only so many were asked at a time as could conveniently dance inside the wigwam. While some were dancing, others were preparing for the expedition, getting extra mocassins made, drying meat, or parching corn.

When all was ready, the party set out, with every confidence in their war chief. He was to direct them where to find the enemy, and at the same time to protect them from being killed themselves.

For a few days they hunted as they went along, and they would build large fires at night, and tell long stories, to make the time pass pleasantly.

The party was composed of about twenty warriors, and they all obeyed implicitly the orders of their war chief, who appointed some warriors to see that his directions were carried out by the whole party. Woe to him who violates a single regulation! his gun is broken, his blanket cut to pieces, and he is told to return home. Such was the fate of Iron Eyes, who wandered from the party to shoot a bird on the wing, contrary to the orders of their chief. But although disgraced and forbidden to join in the attempt to punish the Chippeways for the outrage they had commited, he did not return to his village; he followed the tracks of the war party, determining to see the fun if he could not partake of it.

On the fourth night after they left home, the warriors were all assembled to hear the war song of their chief. They were yet in their own country, seated on the edge of a prairie, and back of them as far as the eye could reach, there was nothing to be seen but the half melted snow; no rocks, no trees, relieved the sameness of the view. On the opposite side of the Mississippi, high bluffs, with their worn sides and broken rocks, hung over the river; and in the centre of its waters lay the sacred isles, whose many trees and bushes wanted only the warm breath of summer to display their luxuriance. The war chief commenced. He prophesied that they would see deer on the next day, but that they must begin to be careful, for they would then have entered their enemies' country. He told them how brave they were, and that he was braver still. He told them the Chippeways were worse than prairie dogs. To all of which the warriors responded, Ho!

When they found themselves near their enemies, the chief forbade a gun being fired off; no straggling was allowed; none but the spies were to go beyond a certain distance from the party.

But after they entered the Chippeway country the duties of the war chief were still more important. He had to prophesy where the enemy was to be found, and about their number; and besides, he had to charm the spirits of their enemies, that they might be unable to contend with the Dahcotahs. The spirits on this occasion took the form of a bear.

About nine o'clock at night this ceremony commences. The warriors all lie down as if asleep, when the war chief signifies the approach of the spirits to his men, by the earnestness of his exertions in singing.

The song continues, and increases in energy as the spirit gets nearer to the hole in the ground, which the chief dug and filled with water, previous to commencing his song. Near this hole he placed a hoop, against which are laid all the war implements of the chief. Before the song commences the warriors sit and look steadfastly at their leader. But when the spirit approaches this hole, the warriors hardly dare breathe, for fear of frightening it away.

At last the spirit gets close to the hole. The war chief strikes it with his rattle and kills it; this ensures to the Dahcotahs success in battle. And most solemnly did the Owl assert to his soldiers, the fact that he had thus dealt with the bear spirit, while they as earnestly believed it.

The next morning, four of the warriors went in advance as spies; one of them carried a pipe, presented as an offering to deceive the spirits of their enemies. About noon they sat down to rest, and waited until the remainder of the party came up. When they were all together again, they rested and smoked; and other spies were appointed, who took the pipe and went forward again.

They had not proceeded far when they perceived signs of their enemies. In the sand near the borders of a prairie were the footprints of Chippeways, and fresh too. They congratulated each other by looks, too cautious even to whisper. In a few moments a hundred Chippeways could be called up, but still the Dahcotahs plunge into the thick forest that skirts the edge of the prairie, in order to find out what prospect they have for delighting themselves with the long wished for revenge.

It was not long before a group of Chippways was discovered, all unapprehensive of evil. At their camp the Chippeways had made pickets, for they knew they might expect retaliation; but those who fell a sacrifice were not expecting their foes.

The spies were not far ahead—they returned to the party, and then retraced their steps. The low cries of animals were imitated to prevent any alarm being given by the breaking of a twig or the rustling of the leaves. They were very near the Chippeways, when the war chief gave the signal on a bone whistle, and the Dahcotahs fired. Every one of the Chippeways fell—two men, three women, and two children.

Then came the tomahawk and scalping knife—the former to finish the work of death, the latter to bear a trophy to their country, to say, Our comrades are avenged. Nor was that all. The bodies were cut to pieces, and then the warriors commenced their homeward journey.

They allowed themselves but little rest until they were out of their enemies' country. But when they were out of the reach of attack, when their feet trod again upon Dahcotah soil, then they stopped to stretch each scalp on a hoop, which was attached to a slender pole. This is always the work of the war chief.

They look eagerly for the welcome sight of home. The cone-shaped teepees rise before their view. They know that their young wives will rejoice to see the scalps, as much as to know that the wanderers have returned.

When they are near their village the war chief raises the song of victory; the other warriors join their voices to his. The welcome sound rouses the inhabitants of the village from their duties or amusements. The warriors enter the village in triumph, one by one, each bearing the scalp he took; and the stout warrior, the aged woman, and the feeble child, all press forward to feast their eyes with the sight of the scalps.

There was a jubilee in the village for weeks. Day and night did the savages dance round the scalps. But how soon may their rejoicings be lost in cries of terror! Even now they tremble at the sound of their own voices when evening draws near—for it is their turn to suffer. They expect their foes, but they do not dread them the less.

CHAPTER II

MANY OF THE customs of the Dahcotahs are to be attributed to their superstitions. Their teepees are always made of buffalo-skins; nothing would induce them to use deer-skin for that purpose. Many years ago a woman made a teepee of deer-skin, and was taken suddenly ill, and died immediately after. Some reason must be found for the cause of her death, and as no other was known, the Indians concluded that she brought her death upon herself by using deer-skin for her teepee. They have always, since, used buffalo-skin for that purpose.

Nothing would induce a Dahcotah woman to look into a looking-glass; for the medicine men say that death will be the consequence.

But there is no superstition which influences them more than their belief in Haokah, or the Giant. They say this being is possessed of superhuman powers: indeed he is deemed so powerful, as to be able to take the thunder in his hand and cast it to the ground. He dresses in many colors, and wears a forked hat. One side of his face is red, the other blue, his eyes are also of different colors. He always carries a bow and arrow in his hand, but never has occasion to use it, as one look will kill the animal he wants.

They sing songs to this giant, and once in a long time dance in honor of him; but so severe is the latter custom, that it is rarely performed. The following incident will show how great is their reverence for this singular being. An Indian made a vapor bath, and placed inside of it a rude image of the giant, made of birch bark. This he intended to pray to while bathing.

After the hot stone was placed inside of the wigwam, several Indians went in to assist in giving the bath to their sick friend. One of them commenced pouring the water of the hot stone, and the water flew on the others, and scalded them badly; the image of the giant was also displaced; the Indians never dreamed of attributing their burns to the natural cause, but concluded that the giant was displeased at their placing his image there, and they considered it as an instance of his mercy that they were not scalded to death.

However defective may be the religion of the Dahcotahs, they are faithful in acting up to all its requirements. Every feast and custom among them is celebrated as a part of their religion.

After the scalp-dance had been performed long enough, the Dahcotahs of the villages turned their attention to making sugar. Many groves of sugar trees were in sight of their village, and on this occasion the generous sap rewarded their labors.

Nor were they ungrateful; for when the medicine men announced that they must keep the sugar-feast, all left their occupation, anxious to celebrate it. Neither need it be concluded that this occasioned them no loss of time; for they were all occupied with the construction of their summer wigwams, which are made of the bark of trees, which must be peeled off in the spring.

But every villager assembled to keep the feast. A certain quantity of sugar was dealt out to each individual, and any one of them who could not eat all that was given him was obliged to pay leggins, or a blanket, or something valuable, to the medicine man. On this occasion, indeed on most occasions, the Dahcotahs have no difficulty in disposing of any quantity of food.

When the feast was over, however, the skill of their doctors was in requisition; for almost all of them were made quite ill by excess, and were seen at evening lying at full length on the ground, groaning and writhing with pain.

CHAPTER III

THE DAY AFTER the sugar feast, the Owl told his wife to get ready her canoe, as he wanted to spear some fish. She would rather have staid at home, as she was not fully recovered from her last night's indisposition. But there was no hesitating when the war chief spoke; so she placed her child upon her back, and seated herself in the stern of the canoe, paddling gently along the shore where the fish usually lie. Her husband stood in the bow of the canoe with a spear about six feet in length. As he saw the fish lying in the water, he threw the spear into them, still keeping hold of it.

When the war chief was tired, his wife would stop paddling, and nurse her child while he smoked. If the Owl were loquaciously inclined, he would point out to his wife the place where he shot a deer, or where he killed the man who had threatened his life. Indeed, if you took his word for it, there was not a foot of ground in the country which had not been a scene of some exploit.

The woman believed them all; for, like a good wife, she shone by the reflected light of her husband's fame.

When they returned home, she made her fire and put the fish to cook, and towards evening many of the Indians were assembled in the wigwam of the war-chief, and partook of the fish he had caught in the morning.

"Unk-ta-he,"* said one of the oldest men in the tribe (and reverenced as a medicine man of extraordinary powers), "Unk-ta-he is as powerful as the thunder-bird. Each wants to be the greatest god of the Dahcotahs, and they have had many battles. My father was a great medicine man; he was killed

———

*The God of the Waters

many years ago, and his spirit wandered about the earth. The Thunder-bird wanted him, and Unk-ta-he wanted him, for they said he would make a wonderful medicine man. Some of the sons of Unk-ta-he fought against the sons of Thunder, and the young thunder-birds were killed, and then Unk-ta-he took the spirit of my father, to teach him many mysterious things.

"When my father had lived a long time with Unk-ta-he in the waters under the earth, he took the form of a Dahcotah again, and lived in this village. He taught me all that I know, and when I go to the land of the spirits, my son must dance alone all night, and he will learn from me the secret of the medicine of our clan."

All listened attentively to the old man, for not an Indian there but believed that he could by a spell cause their instant death; and many wonderful miracles had the "Elk" wrought in his day.

In the corner of the wigwam sat the Bound Spirit, whose vacant look told the sad tale of her want of reason. Generally she sat quiet, but if the cry of an infant fell upon her ear, she would start, and her shriek could be heard throughout the village.

The Bound Spirit was a Sisseton. In the depth of winter, she had left her village to seek her friends in some of the neighboring bands. She was a widow, and there was no one to provide her food.

Accompanied by several other Indians, she left her home, which was made wretched by her desolate condition—that home where she had been very happy while her husband lived. It had since been the scene of her want and misery.

The small portion of food they had taken for their journey was exhausted. Rejoiced would they have been to have had the bark of trees for food; but they were on the open prairie. There was nothing to satisfy the wretched cravings of hunger, and her child—the very child that clung to her bosom—was killed by the unhappy mother, and its tender limbs supplied to her the means of life.

She reached the place of destination, but it was through instinct, for forgetting and forgotten by all was the wretched maniac who entered her native village.

The Indians feared her; they longed to kill her, but were afraid to do so. They said she had no heart.

Sometimes she would go in the morning to the shore, and there, with only her head out of water, would she lie all day.

Now, she has been weeping over the infant who sleeps by her. She is perfectly harmless, and the wife of the war chief kindly gives her food and shelter whenever she wishes it.

But it is not often she eats—only when desperate from long fasting—and when her appetite is satisfied, she seems to live over the scene, the memory of which has made her what she is.

After all but she had eaten of the fish, the Elk related to them the story of the large fish that obstructed the passage of the St. Croix river. The scene of this tradition was far from them, but the Dahcotahs tell each other over and over again the stories which have been handed down from their fathers, and these incidents are known throughout the tribe. "Two Dahcotahs went to war against their enemies. On returning home, they stopped at the Lake St. Croix, hungry and much fatigued.

"One of them caught a fish, cooked it, and asked his comrade to eat, but he refused. The other argued with him, and begged of him to eat, but still he declined.

"The owner of the fish continued to invite his friend to partake of it, until he, wearied by his importunities, consented to eat, but added with a mysterious look, 'My friend, I hope you will not get out of patience with me.' After saying this, he ate heartily of the fish.

"He then seemed to be very thirsty, and asked his companion to bring him some water out of the lake; he did so, but very soon the thirst, which was quenched for a time only, returned; more was given him, but the terrible thirst continued, and at last the Indian, who had begged his companion to eat, began to be tired of bringing him water to drink. He therefore told him he would bring him no more, and requested him to go down to the water and drink. He did so, and after drinking a great quantity, while his friend was asleep, he turned himself into a large fish and stretched himself full length across the St. Croix.

"This fish for a long time obstructed the passage of the St. Croix; so much so that the Indians were obliged to go round it by land.

"Some time ago the Indians were on a hunting excursion up the river, and when they got near the fish a woman of the party darted ahead in her canoe.

"She made a dish of bark, worked the edges of it very handsomely, filled it with water, and placed some red down in it. She then placed the dish near the fish in the river, and entreated the fish to go to its own elements, and not to obstruct the passage of the river and give them so much trouble.

"The fish obeyed, and settled down in the water, and has never since been seen.

"The woman who made this request of the fish, was loved by him when he was a Dahcotah, and for that reason he obeyed her wishes."

Nor was this the only legend with which he amused his listeners. The night was half spent when they separated to rest, with as firm a faith in the stories of the old medicine man, as we have in the annals of the Revolution.

THE MAIDEN'S ROCK;

OR,

WENONA'S LEAP

Maidens Leap, watercolor on paper, 1846-1848.

LAKE PEPIN is a widening of the Mississippi river. It is about twenty miles in length, and from one to two miles wide.

The country along its banks is barren. The lake has little current, but is dangerous for steamboats in a high wind. It is not deep, and abounds in fish, particularly the sturgeon. On its shores the traveller gathers white and red agates, and sometimes specimens streaked with veins of gold color. The lover reads the motto from his mistress' seal, not thinking that the beautiful stone which made the impression, was found on the banks of Lake Pepin.

At the south end of the lake, the Chippeway river empties into the Mississippi.

The Maiden's rock is a high bluff, whose top seems to lean over towards the water. With this rock is associated one of the most interesting traditions of the Sioux.

But the incident is well-known. Almost every one has read it a dozen times, and always differently told. Some represent the maiden as delivering an oration from the top of the rock, long enough for an address at a college celebration. It has been stated that she fell into the water, a circumstance which the relative situation of the rock and river would render impossible.

Writers have pretended, too, that the heroine of the rock was a Winnebago. It is a mistake, the maiden was a Dahcotah.

It was from the Dahcotahs that I obtained the incident, and they believe that it really occurred. They are offended if you suggest the possibility of its being a fiction. Indeed they fix a date to it, reckoning by the occurrences of great battles, or other events worthy of notice.

But to the story—and I wish I could throw into it the feeling and energy of the old medicine woman who related it.

About one hundred and fifty years ago, the band of Dahcotahs to which Wenona belonged, lived near Fort Snelling. Their village was on the site now occupied by Good Road's band.

The whole band made preparations to go below Lake Pepin, after porcupines. These animals are of great value among the Dahcotahs; their flesh is considered excellent as an article of food, and the women stain their quills to ornament the dresses of the men, their mocassins, and many other articles in use among them. A young girl of this band had received repeated offers of marriage from a Dahcotah, whom she hated with the same degree of intensity that she loved his rival.

She dared not marry the object of her choice, for she knew it would subject herself and him to the persecutions of her family. She declared she never would consent to be the wife of the man whom her parents had chosen for her, though he was young and brave, and, what is most valued by the friends of an Indian girl, he was said to be the best hunter of the tribe.

"Marry him, my daughter," said the mother, "your father is old; he cannot now hunt deer for you and me, and what shall we do for food?

Chaskè will hunt the deer and buffalo, and we shall be comfortable and happy."

"Yes," said her father, "your mother speaks well. Chaskè is a great warrior too. When your brother died, did he not kill his worst enemy and hang up his scalp at his grave?"

But Wenona persevered in her refusal. "I do not love him, I will not marry him," was her constant reply.

But Chaskè, trusting to time and her parent's influence, was not discouraged. He killed game and supplied the wants of the family. Besides, he had twice bought her, according to Indian custom.

He had given her parents cloth and blankets, calico and guns. The girl entreated them not the receive them, but the lover refused to take them back, and, finally, they were taken into the wigwam.

Just as the band was about leaving the village for the hunt, he came again with many presents; whatever would make the family comfortable on their journey, and a decided promise was then given that the maiden should become his wife.

She knew it would be useless to contend, so she seemed to be willing to submit to her fate. After encamping for a time opposite the Maiden's Rock to rest from their journey, the hunters determined to go further down the river. They had crossed over to the other side, and were seated nearly under the rock.

Their women were in their canoes coming over, when suddenly a loud cry was heard from an old woman, the mother of Wenona.

The canoe had nearly reached the shore, and the mother continued to shriek, gazing at the projecting rock.

The Indians eagerly inquired of her what was the matter? "Do you not see my daughter?" she said; "she is standing close to the edge of the rock!"

She was there indeed, loudly and wildly singing her dirge, and invocation to the Spirit of the Rock, calm and unconcerned in her dangerous position, while all was terror and excitement among her friends below her.

The hunters, so soon as they perceived her, hastily ascended the bluff, while her parents called to her and entreated her to go back from the edge of the rock. "Come down to us, my child," they cried; "do not destroy your life; you will kill us, we have no child but you."

Having finished her song, the maiden answered her parents. "You have forced me to leave you. I was always a good daughter, and never disobeyed you; and could I have married the man I love, I should have been happy, and would never have left you. But you have been cruel to me; you have turned my beloved from the wigwam; you would have forced me to marry a man I hated; I go the the house of the spirits."

By this time the hunters had nearly reached her. She turned towards them for a moment with a smile of scorn, as if to intimate to them that their efforts were in vain. But when they were quite near, so that they held out their arms towards her in their eagerness to draw her from her dangerous station, she threw herself from the rock.

The first blow she received from the side of the rock must have killed her, for she fell like a dead bird, amidst the shouts of the hunters above, and the shrieks of the women below.

He body was arrayed in her handsomest clothing, placed upon a scaffold, and afterwards buried.

But the Dahcotahs say that her spirit does not watch over her earthly remains; for her spirit was offended when she brought trouble upon her aged mother and father.

Such is the story by the Dahcotahs; and why not apply to them for their own traditions?

Neither is there any reason to doubt the actual occurrence of the incident.

Not a season passes away but we hear of some Dahcotah girl who puts an end to her life in consequence of jealousy, or from the fear of being forced to marry some one she dislikes. A short time ago a very young girl hung herself, rather than become the wife of a man who was already the husband of one of her sisters.

The parents told her they had promised her, and insisted upon her fulfilling the engagement. Even her sister did not object, nay, rather seemed anxious to forward the scheme, which would give her a rival from among her nearest relations.

The young girl finally ran away, and the lover, leaving his wife, pursued the fugitive, and soon overtook her. He renewed his entreaties, and finding her still obstinate, he told her that she should become his wife, and that he would kill her if she made any more trouble.

This last argument seemed to have the desired effect, for the girl expressed her willingness to return home.

After they arrived, the man went to his wigwam to tell his wife of the return of her sister, and that everything was now in readiness for their marriage.

But one hour after, the girl was missing; and when found, was hanging to a tree, forever free from the power of her tormentors. Her friends celebrated the ceremonies of death instead of marriage.

It must be conceded that an Indian girl, when desperate with her love affairs, chooses a most unromantic way of ending her troubles. She almost invariably hangs herself; when there are so many beautiful lakes near her where she could die an easier death, and at the same time one that would tell better, than where she fastens an old leather strap about her neck, and dies literally by choking. But there is this to be taken into consideration. When she hangs herself near the village, she can manage affairs so that she can be cut down if she concludes to live a little longer; for this frequently occurs, and the suicide lives forty and sometimes sixty years after. But when Wenona took the resolution of ending her earthly sorrows, no doubt there were other passions beside love influencing her mind.

Love was the most powerful. With him she loved, life would have been all happiness—without him, all misery. Such was the reasoning of her young heart.

But she resented the importunity of the hunter whose pretensions her parents favored. How often she had told him she would die before she would become his wife; and he would smile, as if he had but little faith in the words of a woman. Now he should see that her hatred to him was not assumed; and she would die such a death that he might know that she feared neither him nor a death of agony.

And while her parents mourned their unkindness, her lover would admire that firmness which made death more welcome than the triumph of his rival.

And sacred is the spot where the devoted girl closed her earthly sorrows. Spirits are ever hovering near the scene. The laugh of the Dahcotah is checked when his canoe glides near the spot. He points to the bluff, and as the shades of evening are throwing dimness and a mystery around the beauty of the lake, and of the mountains, he fancies he can see the arms of the girl as she tosses them wildly in the air. Some have averred they heard her voice as she called to the spirits of the rock, and ever will the traveller, as he passes the bluff, admire the wondrous beauty of the picture, and remember the story of the lover's leap.

There is a tradition among the Dahcotahs which fixes a date to the incident, as well as to the death of the rival lovers of Wenona.

They say that it occurred about the time stated, and that the band of Indians went and obtained the porcupines, and then they returned and settled on the St. Croix river.

Shortly after the tragical death of Wenona, the band went again down the Mississippi, and they camped at what they call the medicine wood. Here a child died, and the body was laid on a scaffold. The father in the middle of the night went out to mourn for his child. While he leant against the scaffold weeping, he saw a man watching him. The stranger did not appear to be a Dahcotah, and the mourner was alarmed, and returned to the camp. In the morning he told the Indians of the circumstance, and they raised the camp and went into the pine country.

The body of the child was carried along, and in the night the father went out again to lament its death. The same figure appeared to him, and again he returned, alarmed at the circumstance.

In the morning the Indians moved their camp again, and at night the same occurrence took place.

The Dahcotahs are slaves to superstition, and they now dreaded a serious evil. Their fears were not confirmed in the way they anticipated, for their foes came bodily, and when daylight appeared, one thousand Chippeway warriors appeared before them, and the shrill whistle and terrible whoop of war was heard in earnest.

Dreadful were the shouts of the Chippeways, for the Dahcotahs were totally unprepared for them, and many were laid low at the first discharge of the rifles.

The merciless Chippeways continued the work of death. The women and children fled to their canoes, but the Chippeways were too quick for them; and they only entered their canoes to meet as certain a fate as those who remained.

The women had not their paddles with them, and there was an eddy in the current; as soon as the canoe was pushed from the shore, it would whirl round, and the delighted Chippeways caught the canoes, and pulled them ashore again, while others let fall upon their victims the uplifted tomahawk.

When the Chippeways had killed until they were tired, they took what they wanted from the Sioux camp, and started for home, taking one Dahcotah boy prisoner. The party had not travelled far, when a number of Dahcotahs attacked the Chippeways, but the latter succeeded in killing many of the Dahcotahs. One of the latter fled, and was in his canoe on the lake St. Croix, when the Chippeways suddenly came upon him.

The little Dahcotah saw his only chance for liberty—he plunged in the water and made for the canoe of the Dahcotah. In a moment he had reached and entered it, and the two Dahcotahs were out of sight before the arrows of their enemies could reach them.

A very few of that band escaped; one of them says that when they were first attacked by the Chippeways, he saw he had but one chance, so he dived down to the bottom of the river, and the Chippeways could not see him.

He found the water at the bottom of the river very cold, and when he had gone some distance, he ventured where the water was warmer, which he knew was near the shore. He then came out of the water and made his escape.

Even this latter trifling incident has been handed down from father to son, and is believed universally by the Dahcotahs. And according to their tradition, the lovers and family of Wenona perished in this battle. At all events, there is no one who can prove that their tradition or my translation may not be true.

THE INDIAN IN A TRANCE

∧∧⋆∧∧∧

Red Wing's Village 70 miles [downstream on the Mississippi from] the Falls of St. Anthony, watercolor, 1846-1848.

ABOUT FORTY YEARS ago, Ahak-tah, "The Male Elk," was taken sick with a sore throat. It was in the winter too, and sickness and cold together are hard to bear. Want was an evil from which they were suffering; though the Dahcotahs were not so poor then as they are now. They had not given so much of their lands to the white people; and they depended more upon their own exertions for support than they do at present.

The medicine men did all they could to cure Ahaktah; they tried to charm away the animal that had entered into his body; they used the sacred rattle. But Ahaktah's throat got worse; he died, and while his wives and children wept for him, he had started on his long journey to the land of spirits.

He was wrapped in scarlet cloth, and laid upon a scaffold. His wives sat weeping in their teepee, when a cry from their young children drew their attention to the door. There stood he for whom they mourned. The dead man again took his place among those who sat beside the household fire. Tears of grief were shed no more—food was given to Ahaktah, and when he was refreshed he thus addressed his wondering family:—

"While you were weeping for me, my spirit was on its way to the great city where our fathers, who have taught us all the wonders of our sacred medicine, of Haokah the giant, and of the Thunder bird, are now living. Twice has the sun ceased to shine since I left you, and in that short time I have seen many strange things. First, I passed through a beautiful country; the forest-trees were larger than any you have ever seen. Birds of all colors filled them, and their music was as loud as when our medicine men play for us to celebrate the scalp dance. The broad river was full of fish, and the loon screamed as she swam across the lakes. I had no difficulty in finding my way, for there was a road through this country. It seemed as if there must have been many travellers there, though I saw no one.

"This great road was made by the spirits of those who were killed in battle. No warrior, however brave he may have been, has ever assisted in making this road, except those who sang their death songs under the tomahawk of their enemies. Neither did any woman ever assist. She is not considered worthy to touch the war implements of a Dahcotah warrior, and she was not permitted to do anything towards completing the path in which the braves of the Dahcotahs would walk, when they joined their forefathers in the land of spirits.

"As I pursued my journey, I saw near the banks of the river a teepee; I entered it, and saw paint and all that a warrior needed to dress himself in order to be fit to enter the city of spirits. I sat down and plaited my hair, I put vermilion on my cheeks, and arranged the war-eagle feathers in my head. Here, I said to myself, did my father rest when he was on the same journey. I was tired, but I could not wait—I longed to see my friends who had travelled this path before me—I longed to tell them that the Dahcotahs were true to the customs of their forefathers—I longed to tell them that we had drank deep of the blood of the Chippeways, that we had eaten the hearts of our enemies, that we had torn their infants from their mothers' breasts, and dashed them to the earth.

"I continued my journey, looking eagerly around me to see some one, but all was desolate; and beautiful as everything was, I would have been glad to have seen the face of a friend.

"It was evening when a large city burst upon my sight. The houses were built regularly on the shores of the river. As far as I could see, the homes of the spirits of my forefathers were in view.

"But still I saw no one. I descended the hill towards the river, which I must cross to reach the city of spirits. I saw no canoe, but I feared nothing, I was so near my journey's end. The river was wide and deep, and the waves were swiftly following one another, when I plunged among them; soon I reached the opposite shore, and as I again stood on the land, I heard some one cry, 'Here he comes! here he comes!' I approached the nearest house and entered; everything looked awful and mysterious.

"In the corner of the room sat a figure whom I recognized. It was my mother's brother, Flying Wind, the medicine man. I remembered him, for it was he who taught me to use my bow and arrow.

"In a bark dish, in the corner of the room, was some wild rice. I was very hungry, for I had not eaten since I left the earth. I asked my uncle for some rice to eat, but he did not give it to me. Had I eaten of the food for spirits, I never should have returned to earth.

"At last my uncle spoke to me. 'My nephew,' said he, 'why are you travelling without a bow and arrow? how can you provide yourself with food when you have no means of killing game? When my home was on the Mississippi, the warriors of the Dahcotahs were never without their bows and arrows—either to secure their food or to strike to the hearts of their enemies.'

"I then remembered that I had been travelling without my bow and arrows. 'But where,' said I to my uncle, 'where are the spirits of my forefathers? where is my brother who fell under the tomahawk of his enemy? where is my sister who threw herself into the power of Unktahe, rather than to live and see her rival the wife of the Sun? where are the spirits of the Dahcotah braves whose deeds are still told from father to son among us?'

"'The Dahcotah braves are still watching for their enemies—the hunters are bringing in the deer and the buffalo—our women are planting corn and tanning deer-skin. But you will not now see them; your step is firm and your eye is bright; you must return to earth, and when your limbs are feeble, when your eye is dim, then will you return and find your home in the city of spirits.'

"So saying, he arose and gave me a bow and arrow. I took it, and while trying it I left the house; but how I do not know.

"The next thing that I remember was being seated on the top of the cliffs of Eagle's Nest, below Lake Pepin. I heard a sound, and soon distinguished my mother's voice; she was weeping. I knew that she was bending over my body. I could see her as she cut off her hair, and I felt sad when I heard her cry, 'My son! my son!' Then I recollect being on the top of the half-side mountain on Lake Pepin. Afterwards I was on the Mountain near Red Wing's village, and again I stood on a rock, on a point of land near where the waters of the Mississippi and St. Peter's meet, on the 'Maiden's Jumping Rock;'* here I recovered my right mind."

The daughter of Ahaktah says that her father retained the "wahkun" bow and arrow that was given him by his uncle, and that he was always successful in hunting or in war; that he enjoyed fine health, and lived to be a very old man; and she is living now to tell the story.

———

* Near Fort Snelling is a high rock call the Maiden's Jumping Rock; where formerly the Dahcotah girls used to jump for amusement, a distance of many feet from the top to the ground.

Oeche-Monesah;

The Wanderer

View below St. Anthony [on Mississippi River] near Ft. Snelling, watercolor on paper, 1846-1848.

CHASKÈ WAS tired of living in the village, where the young men, finding plenty of small game to support life, and yielding to the languor and indolence produced by a summer's sun, played at checkers, or drank, or slept, from morn till night, and seemed to forget that they were the greatest warriors and hunters in the world. This did very well for a time; but, as I said, Chaskè got tired of it. So he determined to go on a long journey, where he might meet with some adventures.

Early one morning he shouldered his quiver of arrows, and drawing out one arrow from the quiver, he shot it in the direction he intended to go.

"Now," said he, "I will follow my arrow." But it seemed as if he were destined never to find it, for morning and noon had passed away, and the setting sun warned him, not only of the approach of night, but of musquitoes too. He thought he would build a fire to drive the musquitoes away; besides, he was both hungry and tired, though he had not yet found his arrow, and had nothing to eat.

When he was hesitating as to what he should do, he saw in the bushes a dead elk, and behold! his arrow was sticking in its side. He drew the arrow out, then cut out the tongue, and after making a fire, he put the tongue upon a stick to roast. But while the tongue was roasting, Chaskè fell asleep and slept many hours.

At day-break a woman came up to him and shook him, as if to awake him. Chaskè started and rubbed his eyes, and the woman pointed to the path which led across the prairies. Was he dreaming? No, he felt sure he was awake. So he got up and followed the woman.

He thought it very strange that the woman did not speak to him. "I will ask her who she is," said he; but as he turned to address her she raised her arms in the air, and changing her form to that of a beautiful bird, blue as the sky that hangs over the morning's mist, she flew away. Chaskè was surprised and delighted too. He loved adventures; had he not left home to seek them? so he pursued his journey, quite forgetting his supper, which was cooking when he fell asleep.

He shot his arrow off again and followed it. It was late in the evening when he found it, and then it was in the heart of a moose. "I will not be cheated out of my supper to-night," said he; so he cut the tongue out of the moose and placed it before the fire to roast. Hardly had he seated himself to smoke, when sleep overcame him, and he knew nothing until morning, when a woman approached and shook him as before, pointing to the path.

He arose quickly and followed her; and as he touched her arm, determined to find out who she was, she, turning upon him a brow black as night, was suddenly changed into a crow.

The Dahcotah was completely puzzled. He had never cared for women; on the contrary, had avoided them. He never wasted his time telling them they were beautiful, or playing on the flute to charm their senses. He thought he had left all such things behind him, but already had he been twice baffled by a woman. Still he continued his journey. He had this consolation, the Dahcotah girls did not turn into birds and fly away. At least there was the charm of novelty in the incidents. The next day he killed a bear, but as usual he fell asleep while the tongue was roasting, and this time he was waked by a porcupine. The fourth day he found his arrow in a buffalo. "Now," said he, "I will eat at last, and I will find out, too, who and what it is that wakes me."

But he fell asleep as usual, and was waked in the morning by a female who touched him lightly and pointed to the path. Her back was turned towards him, and instead of rising to follow her, he caught her in his arms, determined to see and talk with her.

Finding herself a prisoner, the girl turned her face to him, and Chaskè had never seen anything so beautiful.

Her skin was white as the fairest flower that droops its head over the banks of the "Lac qui parle." Her hair was not plaited, neither was it black like Dahcotah maidens', but it hung in golden ringlets about her face and neck. The warm blood tinted her cheeks as she met the ardent gaze of the Dahcotah, and Chaské could not ask her who she was. How could he speak when his heart was throbbing, and every pulse beating wildly?

"Let me go," said the girl; "why do you seek to detain me? I am a beaver-woman,* and you are a Dahcotah warrior. Turn from me and find a wife among the dark-faced maidens of your tribe."

"I have always despised them," said the Dahcotah, "but you are more beautiful than the Spirits of the water. I love you, and will make you my wife."

"Then you must give up your people," replied the girl, "for I cannot live as the Dahcotah women. Come with me to my white lodge, and we will be happy; for see the bright water as it falls on the rocks. We will sit by its banks during the heat of the day, and when we are tired, the music of its waves will lull us to sleep."

So she took Chaskè by the hand, and they walked on till they came to an empty white lodge, and there they lived and were very happy. They were still happier when their little boy began to play about the lodge; for although they

---

*According to the wise men of the Dahcotahs, beavers and bears have souls. They have many traditions about bear and beaver-women.

loved each other very much, still it was lonely where they lived, and the child was company for them both.

There was one thing, however, that troubled the Dahcotah; he could not turn his mind from it, and day after day passed without relieving him from his perplexity.

His beautiful wife never ate with him. When he returned in the evening from hunting, she was always glad to see him, and while he rested himself and smoked, she would cook his meat for him, and seem anxious to make him comfortable. But he had never seen her eat; and when he would tell her that he did not like to eat alone, and beg her to sit down and eat with him, she would say she was not hungry; and then employ herself about her wigwam, as if she did not wish him to say any more about it.

Chaskè made up his mind that he would find out what his wife lived upon. So the next morning he took his bow and arrows, as if he were going out on a day's hunt. After going a short distance from the lodge, he hid himself in the trees, where he could watch the motions of his wife.

She left the lodge after a while, and with an axe in her hand she approached a grove of poplar trees. After carefully looking round to satisfy herself that there was no one near, she cut down a number of the small and tender poplars, and, carrying them home, ate them as if she enjoyed them very much. Chaskè was infinitely relieved when he saw that his wife did eat; for it frightened him to think that she lived on nothing but air. But it was so droll to think she should eat young trees! surely venison was a great deal better.

But, like a good husband, he thought it was his duty to humor his wife's fancies. And then he loved her tenderly—he had given up country and home for her. She was so good and kind, and her beautiful hair! Chaskè called her "The Mocassin Flower," for her golden ringlets reminded him of that beautiful flower. "She shall not have to cut the trees down herself," said Chaskè, "I will bring her food while she prepares mine." So he went out to hunt, and returned in the evening; and while his wife was cooking his supper, he went to the poplar grove and cut a number of young trees; he then brought them to the lodge, and, laying them down, he said to his wife, "I have found out at last what you like."

No one would suppose but that the beaver-woman would have been grateful to her husband for thinking of her. Instead of that, she was very angry; and, taking her child in her arms, she left the lodge. Chaskè was astonished to see his gentle wife angry, but he concluded he would eat his supper, and then follow her, hoping that in the meantime she would recover her good temper.

When he went out, she was nowhere to be seen. He called her—he thought at first that she had hid herself. But, as night came on, and neither she nor the child returned, the deserted husband grew desperate; he could not stay in his lodge, and the only thing that he could do was to start in search of her.

He walked all night, but saw no trace of her. About sunrise he came to a stream, and following it up a little way he came to a beaver dam, and on it sat his wife with her child in her arms. And beautiful she looked, with her long tresses falling into the water.

Chaskè was delighted to find her. "Why did you leave me?" called he. "I should have died of grief if I had not found you."

"Did I not tell you that I could not live like the Dahcotah women?" replied Mocassin Flower. "You need not have watched me to find out what I eat. Return to your own people; you will find there women enough who eat venison."

The little boy clapped his hands with delight when he saw his father, and wanted to go to him; but his mother would not let him. She tied a string to his leg and told him to go, and the child would plunge into the water, and when he had nearly reached the shore where his father sat, then would the beaver-woman draw him back.

In the meantime the Dahcotah had been trying to persuade his wife to come to him, and return to the lodge; but she refused to do so, and sat combing her long hair. The child had cried itself to sleep; and the Dahcotah, worn out with fatigue and grief, thought he would go to sleep too.

After a while a woman came and touched him on the shoulder, and awaked him as of old. He started and looked at her, and perceiving it was not his wife, felt inclined to take little notice of her.

"Why," said she, "does a Dahcotah warrior still love a woman who hates him?"

"Mocassin Flower loves me well," replied the Dahcotah; "she has been a good wife."

"Yes," replied the woman, "she was for a time; but she sighs to return home—her heart yearns towards the lover of her youth."

Chaskè was very angry. "Can this be true?" he said; and he looked towards the beaver dam where his wife still sat. In the meantime the woman who had waked him, brought him some food in bark dishes worked with porcupine.

"Eat," she said to the Dahcotah; "you are hungry."

But who can tell the fury that Mocassin Flower was in when she saw that strange woman bringing her husband food. "Who are you," she cried, "that are troubling yourself about my husband? I know you well; you are the 'Bear-Woman.'"

"And if I am," said the Bear woman, "do not the souls of the bears enjoy forever the heaven of the Dahcotah?"

Poor Chaskè! he could not prevent their quarrelling, so, being very hungry, he soon disposed of what the Bear woman had brought him. When he had done eating, she took the bark dishes. "Come with me," she said; "you cannot live in the water, and I will take you to a beautiful lodge, and we will be happy."

The Dahcotah turned to his wife, but she gave him no encouragement to remain. "Well," said he, "I always loved adventures, and I will go and seek some more."

The new wife was not half as pretty as the old one. Then she was so wilful, and ordered him about—as if women were anything but dogs in comparison with a Dahcotah warrior. Yes, he who had scorned the Dahcotah girls, as they smiled upon him, was now the slave of a bear-woman; but there was one comfort—there were no warriors to laugh at him.

For a while they got on well enough. His wife had twin children—one was a fine young Dahcotah, and the other was a smart active little bear, and it was very amusing to see them play together. But in all their fights the young Dahcotah had the advantage; though the little bear would roll and tumble, and stick his claws into the Dahcotah, yet it always ended by the little bear's capering off and roaring after his mother. Perhaps this was the reason, but for some reason or other the mother did not seem contented and happy. One morning she woke up very early, and while telling her husband that she had a bad dream, the dog commenced barking outside the lodge.

"What can be the matter?" said Chaskè.

"Oh!" said the woman, "I know; there is a hunter out there who wants to kill me, but I am not afraid."

So saying, she put her head out of the door, which the hunter seeing, shot his arrow; but instead of hurting her, the arrow fell to the ground, and the bear-woman catching up her little child, ran away and was soon out of sight.

"Ha!" said Chaskè, "I had better have married a Dahcotah girl, for they do not run away from their husbands except when another wife comes to take their place. But I have been twice deserted." So saying, he took the little Dahcotah in his arms, and followed his wife. Towards evening he came up with her, but she did not seem glad to see him. He asked her why she left him; she replied, "I want to live with my own people." "Well," said the Dahcotah, "I will go with you." The woman consented, though it was plain she did not want him; for she hated her Dahcotah child, and would not look at him.

After travelling a few days, they approached a grove of trees, which grew in a large circle. "Do you see that nest of trees?" said the woman. "There is the great village of the bears. There are many young men there that loved me, and they will hate you because I preferred you to them. Take your boy, then, and return to your people." But the Dahcotah feared not, and they approached the village of the bears.

There was a great commotion among the bears as they discovered them. They were glad to see the young bear-woman back again, but they hated the Dahcotah, and determined on his death. However, they received him hospitably, conducted him and his wife to a large lodge, gave them food, and the tired travellers were soon asleep.

But the Dahcotah soon perceived he was among enemies, and he kept a careful look out upon them. The little Dahcotah was always quarrelling with the young bears; and on one occasion, being pretty hungry, a cub annoying him at the time very much, he deliberately shot the cub with his bow and arrow, and ate him up. This aroused the vengeance of the bears; they had a consultation among themselves, and swore they would kill both father and son.

It would be impossible to tell of the troubles of Chaskè. His wife, he could see, loved one of the bears, and was anxious for his own death; but whenever he contended with the bears he came off victor. Whether in running a foot race, or shooting with a bow and arrow, or whatever it might be, he always won the prize, and this made his enemies still more venomous.

Four years had now passed since Chaskè left his native village, and nothing had ever been heard of him. But at length the wanderer returned.

But who would have recognized, in the crest-fallen, melancholy-looking Indian, the gay warrior that had left home but a few years before? The little boy that held his hand was cheerful enough, and seemed to recognize acquaintances, instead of looking for the first time on the faces of his father's friends.

How did the young girls laugh when he told of the desertion of his first wife; but when he continued his story, and told them of the faithlessness of the bear woman also, you heard nothing but shouts of derision. Was it not a triumph for the Dahcotah women? How had he scorned them before he went away! Did he not say that women were only dogs, or worse than dogs?

But there was one among his old acquaintances who would not join in the laughter. As she looked on the care-worn countenance of the warrior, she would fain have offered to put new mocassins upon his feet, and bring him food. But she dared not subject herself to the ridicule of her companions— though as night came on, she sought him when there was no one to heed her.

"Chaskè," she called—and the Dahcotah turned hastily towards her, attracted by the kindness of her voice—"there are no women who love as the Dahctoah women. I would have gone to the ends of the earth with you, but you despised me. You have come back, and are laughed at. Care has broken your spirit, or you would not submit to the sneers of your old friends, and the contempt of those who once feared you. I will be your wife, and, mingling again in the feasts and customs of your race, you will soon be the bold and fearless warrior that you were when you left us."

And her words were true; for the Indians soon learned that they were not at liberty to talk to Chaskè of his wanderings. He never spoke of his former wives, except to compare them with his present, who was as faithful and obedient as they were false and troublesome. "And he found," says, Chequered Cloud, "that there was no land like the Dahcotah's, no river like the Father of waters, and no happiness like that of following the deer across the open prairies, or of listening, in the long summer days, to the wisdom of the medicine men."

And she who had loved him in his youth, and wept for him in his absence, now lies by his side—for Chaskè has taken another long journey.

Death has touched him, but not lightly, and pointed to the path which leads to the Land of Spirits—and he did not go alone; for her life closed with his, and together their spirits watch over the mortal frames that they once tenanted.

"Look at the white woman's life," said Chequered Cloud, as she concluded the story of Chaskè, "and then at the Dahcotah's. You sleep on a soft bed, while the Dahcotah woman lays her head upon the ground, with only her blanket for a covering; when you are hungry you eat, but for days has the Dahcotah woman wanted for food, and there was none to give it. Your children are happy, and fear nothing; ours have crouched in the earth at night, when the whoop and yell of the Chippways sent terror to their young hearts, and trembling to their tender limbs.

"And when the fire-water of the white man has maddened the senses of the Dahcotah, so that the blow of his war club falls upon his wife instead of his enemy, even then the Dahcotah woman must live and suffer on." "But Chequered Cloud, the spirit of the Dahcotah watches over the body which remains on earth. Did you not say the soul went to the house of spirits?"

"The Dahcotah has four souls," replied the old woman; "one wanders about the earth, and requires food; another protects the body; the third goes to the Land of Spirits, while the fourth forever hovers around his native village."

"I wish," said I, "that you would believe in the God of the white people. You would then learn that there is but one soul, and that that soul will be rewarded for the good it has done in life, or punished for the evil."

"The Great Spirit," she replied, "is the God of the Dahcotah. He made all things but thunder and wild rice. When we do wrong we are punished in this world. If we do not live up to the laws of our forefathers, the spirits of the dead will punish us. We must keep up the customs of our tribe. If we are afraid that the thunder will strike us, we dance in honor of it, and destroy its power. Our great medicine feasts are given in honor of our sacred medicine, which will not only heal the sick, but will preserve us in danger; and we make feasts for the dead.

"Our children are taught to do right. They are not to injure one who has not harmed them; but where is the Dahcotah who will not rejoice as he takes the life of his enemy?"

"But," said I, "you honor the thunder, and yet it strikes you. What is the thunder, and where does it come from?"

"Thunder is a large bird, flying through the air; its bright tracks are seen in the heavens, before you hear the clapping of its wings. But it is the young ones who do the mischief. The parent bird would not hurt a Dahcotah. Long ago a thunder bird fell dead from the heavens; and our fathers saw it as it lay not far from Little Crow's village.

"It had a face like a Dahcotah warrior, with a nose like an eagle's bill. Its body was long and slender, its wings were large, and on them was painted the lightning. Our warriors were once out hunting in the winter, when a terrible storm came on, and a large thunder bird descended to the earth, wearing snow-shoes; he took but a few steps and then rose up, leaving his tracks in the snow. That winter our hunters killed many bears."

TAH-WE-CHU-KIN;

THE WIFE

Fort Snelling from 2 miles below, watercolor on paper, 1846-1848.

IN FEBRUARY, 1837, a party of Dahcotahs (Warpetonian) fell in with
Hole-in-the-Day, and his band. When Chippeways and Dahcotahs meet there
is generally bloodshed; and, however highly Hole-in-the-Day may be esteemed
as a warrior, it is certain that he showed great treachery towards the Dahcotahs
on many occasions.

Now they meet for peaceable purposes. Hole-in-the-Day wished permission
to hunt on the Dahcotah lands without danger from the tomahawk of his
enemies. He proposed to pay them certain articles, which he should receive
from the United States Government when he drew his annuities, as a return

for the privilege he demanded.

The Dahcotahs and Chippeways were seated together. They had smoked the pipe of peace. The snow had drifted, and lay piled in masses behind them, contrasting its whiteness with their dark countenances and their gay ornaments and clothing. For some years there had been peace between these two tribes; hating each other, as they did, they had managed to live without shedding each other's blood.

Hole-in-the-Day was the master spirit among the Chippeways. He was the greatest hunter and warrior in the nation; he had won the admiration of his people, and they had made him chief. His word was law to them; he stood firmly on the height to which he had elevated himself.

He laid aside his pipe and arose. His iron frame seemed not to feel the keen wind that was shaking the feathers in the heads of the many warriors who fixed their eyes upon him.

He addressed the Dahcotah warriors. "All nations," said he, "as yet continue the practice of war, but as for me, I now abandon it. I hold firmly the hand of the Americans. If you, in future, strike me twice or even three times, I will pass over and not revenge it. If wars should continue, you and I will not take part in them. You shall not fight, neither will I. There shall be no more war in that part of the country lying between Pine Island and the place called Hanwi catintipi (They shot them in the night). Over this extent of country we will hold the pipe firmly. You shall hold it by the bowl, and we will hold it by the stem. The pipe shall be in your keeping."
So saying, Hole-in-the Day advanced and presented the Dahcotahs with a pipe.

After a moment he continued his speech. "On account of your misconduct, we did desire your death, and if you had met us last winter to treat of peace, however great your numbers, we should have killed you all. White men had ordered us to do so, and we should have done it; because the Mendewakantonwans had informed us that you intended by treachery to kill us."

The Dahcotah chief then replied to him saying, that the Dahcotahs were willing that the Chippeways should hunt on their lands to the borders of the prairie, but that they should not enter the prairie. The Chippeways then agreed to pay them a large quantity of sugar, a keg of powder, and a quantity of lead and tobacco.

After their engagement was concluded, Hole-in-the-Day rose again, and said, "In the name of the Great Spirit, this peace shall be forever," and, turning to Wandiokiya (the Man that talks to the Eagle), a Dahcotah who had been taught by the missionaries to read and write, requested him to commit to writing the agreement which had just been made.

Wandiokiya did so, and has since forwarded the writing to the Rev. Mr. P_____, who resides near Fort Snelling. The Dahcotah adds, "We have now learned that the object of Hole-in-the-Day was to deceive and kill us; and he and his people have done so, showing that they neither fear God nor the chief of the American people.

"In this manner, they deceived us, deceived us in the name of the Gods.

"Hole-in-the-Day led the band of murderers."

"WANDIOKIYA."

CHAPTER II

WE SHALL SEE how faithfully the Chippeway chief kept the treaty that he had called upon the Great Spirit to witness. There has been great diversity of opinion concerning Hole-in-the-Day. The Chippeways and Dahcotahs all feared him. Some of the white people who knew him admired, while others detested his character.

He was certainly, what all the Chippeways have been, a friend of the white people, and equally an enemy to the Dahcotahs. He encouraged all attempts that were made towards the civilization of his people; he tried to induce them to cultivate the ground; indeed, he sometimes assumed the duties which among savages are supposed to belong exclusively to females, and has been frequently seen to work in his garden. Had it been possible, he would even have forced the Chippeways to civilization.

He had three wives—all sisters. He was fond of them, but if they irritated him, by disputing among themselves, or neglecting any thing which he found necessary to his comfort, he was very violent. Blows were the only arguments he used on such occasions.

The present chief is one of his children; several of them died young, and their father felt their loss most keenly. Grave and stoical as was his deportment, his feelings were very strong, and not easily controlled.

He was a man of deep thought, and of great ambition. The latter passion was gratified to as great a degree as was possible. Loved by his tribe, feared by his enemies, respected and well treated by the white people, what more could a savage ask? Among the Indians he was a great man, but he was truly great in cunning and deceit.

On this occasion, however, the Dahcotahs had perfect confidence in him, and it was on the first day of April, in the same year, that they arrived at the place appointed to meet the Chippeways, near the east branch of the Chippeway river, about thirty miles northeast of Lac qui parle. The women raised the teepees, six in number, and prepared the scanty portion of food for their families. Here they remained, until their patience was almost exhausted, constantly expecting Hole-in-the-Day to appear; but day after day passed, and they were still disappointed. Now and then the reports of fire-arms were heard near them, but still the Chippeways did not visit the camp of the Dahcotahs.

Famine now showed itself among them. They had neither corn nor flour. Had the wild ducks flown over their heads in clouds, there was but little powder and shot to kill them—but there were few to be seen. Some of the Indians proposed moving their camp where game was more plenty— where they might see deer, and use their bows and arrows to some purpose. But others said, if they were not at the appointed place of meeting, they would violate the contract, and lose their claim to the articles that Hole-in-the-Day has promised to deliver to them.

It was finally concluded that the party should divide, one half moving off in search of food, the other half remaining where they were, in hopes that Hole-in-the-Day would make his appearance.

Three teepees then remained, and they were occupied by seventeen persons, all women and children excepting four.

It was drawing on towards evening, when the Dahcotahs heard the sound of footsteps, and their satisfaction was very great, when they perceived the Chippeway chief approach, accompanied by ten of his men. These men had been present at the council of peace in February.

One of the Dahcotahs, named Red Face, had left his family in the morning, to attend to the traps he had set for beaver. He had not returned when the Chippeways arrived. His two wives were with the Dahcotahs who received the Chippeways. One of these women had two children; the other was quite young, and, according to Indian ideas, beautiful too. She was the favorite wife.

The Dahcotahs received the Chippeways with real pleasure, in full faith and confidence. "Hole-in-the-Day has been long in coming," said one of the Dahcotahs; "his friends have wished to smoke the pipe of peace with him, but some of them have left us to seek for food. We welcome you, and will eat together, and our friendship shall last forever." Hole-in-the-Day met his advances with every appearance of cordiality. One thing, however, the Dahcotahs observed, that the Chippeways did not fire their guns off when they arrived, which is done by Indians when they make a visit of friendship.

The party passed the evening in conversation. All the provisions of the Dahcotahs were called in requisition to feast the Chippeways. After eating, the pipe went round again, and at a late hour they laid down to sleep, the Chippeways dividing their party, several in each teepee.

Hole-in-the-Day lay down by the side of his host, so motionless you would have thought that sleep had paralyzed his limbs and senses; his regular breathing intimates a heart at peace with himself and his foes; but that heart was beating fast, for in a moment he raises himself cautiously, gazes and smiles too upon the sleeping Dahcotah beside him. He gives the appointed signal, and instantaneously plunges the knife into the heart of the trusting Dahcotah. It was child's play afterwards to quiet the shrill shrieks of the terrified wife. A moment more, and she and her child lay side by side, never to awake again.

For a short time broken and shrill cries were heard from the other teepees, but they were soon over. The two wives of Red Face had laid down without a fear, though their protector was absent. The elder of the two clasped her children to her heart, consoled, in a measure, while listening to their calm breathing, for the loss of the love of her husband. She knew that the affections of a husband might vary, but the tie between mother and child is indissoluble.

The young wife wondered that Red Face was not by her side. But he would return to-morrow, and her welcome would be all the greeting that he would wish for. While her thoughts are assuming the form of dreams, she sees the fatal weapon pointed at the mother and child. The bullet that kills the sleeping infant on its mother's breast, wounds the mother also; but she flies in horror, though not soon enough to escape the sight of her other pleading child, her warrior son, vainly clasping his hands in entreaty to the savage, who, with another blow from his tomahawk, puts an end to his sufferings. The wretched mother escapes, for Hole-in-the-Day enters the teepee, and takes prisoner the younger wife. She escapes a present death— what will be her future fate?

CHAPTER III

THE ELDER of the two wives escaped from the murderous Chippeways. Again and again, in the darkness of the night, she turns back to flee from her deadly foe, but far more from the picture of her children, murdered before her eyes. She knew the direction in which the Dahcotahs who had left the party had encamped, and she directed her steps to find them. One would think she would have asked death from her enemies—her husband loved her no more, her children were dead—but she clung to life.

She reached the teepees at last, and hastened to tell of her sorrows, and of the treachery of Hole-in-the-Day. For a moment the utmost consternation prevailed among the Indians, but revenge was the second thought, and rapidly were their preparations made to seek the scene of the murder. The distance was accomplished in a short time, and the desolation lay before their eyes.

The fires in the teepees were not gone out; the smoke was ascending to the heavens; while the voices of the murdered Dahcotahs seemed to call upon their relatives for revenge. There lay the warriors, who, brave as Hole-in-the-Day, had laid aside their weapons, and reposed on the faith of their enemies, their strong limbs powerless, their faces turned towards the light, which fell upon their glassy eyes. See the mother, as she bends over the bodies of her innocent children!—her boy, who walked so proudly, and said he would kill deer for his mother; her infant, whose life had been taken, as it were, from her very heart. She strains them to her bosom, but the head leans not towards her, and the arms are stiff in death.

Red Face has asked for his young wife. She is alive, but, far worse than death, she is a prisoner to the Chippeways. His children are dead before his eyes, and their mother, always obedient and attentive, does not hear him when he speaks to her. The remains of the feast are scattered on the ground; the pipe of peace lies broken among them.

In the course of the morning the Rev. Mr._____, missionary among the Dahcotahs, with the assistance of an Indian named Round Wind, collected the bodies and buried them.

Of the fourteen persons who were in the three teepees, no more than four escaped; two young men and two women.

The Chippeways fled as quickly as possible from the country of the Dahcotahs, with their prisoner—sad change for her. A favorite wife finds herself in the power of ten warriors, the enemies of her people. The cries of her murdered friends are yet sounding in her ears; and she knows not how soon their fate may be hers. Every step of the weary journey she pursues, takes her farther from her country. She dares not weep, she cannot understand the language of her enemies, but she understands their looks, and knows she must obey them. She wishes they would take her life; she would take it herself, but she is watched, and it is impossible.

She sees by their angry gestures and their occasional looks towards her, that she is the subject of their dispute, until the chief raises his eyes and speaks to the Chippeways—and the difference ceases.

At length her journey is at an end. They arrive at the village, and Hole-in-the-Day and his warriors are received with manifestations of delight. They welcomed him as if he had performed a deed of valor instead of one of cowardice.

The women gaze alternately upon the scalps and upon the prisoner. She, poor girl, is calm now; there is but one thought that makes her tired limbs shake with terror. She sees with a woman's quickness that there is no female among those who are looking at her as beautiful as she is. It may be that she may be required to light the household fires for one of her enemies. She sees the admiring countenance of one of the young Chippeway warriors fixed upon her; worn out with fatigue, she cannot support the wretched thought. For a while she is insensible even to her sorrows.

On recovering, food is given her, and she tries to eat. Nothing but death can relieve her. Where are the spirits of the rocks and rivers of her land? Have they forgotten her too?

Hole-in-the-Day took her to his teepee. She was his prisoner, he chose to adopt her, and treated her with every kindness. He ordered his men not to take her life; she was to be as safe in his teepee as if she were his wife or child.

For a few days she is allowed to remain quiet; but at length she is brought out to be present at a council where her fate was to be decided.

Hole-in-the-Day took his place in the council, and ordered the prisoner to be placed near him. Her pale and resigned countenance was a contrast to the angry and excited faces that lowered upon her; but the chief looked unconcerned as to the event. However his warriors might contend, the result of the council would depend upon him; his unbounded influence always prevailed.

After several speeches had been made, Stormy Wind rose and addressed the chief. His opinion was that the prisoner should suffer death. The Dahcotahs had always been enemies, and it was the glory of the Chippeways to take the lives of those they hated. His chief had taken the prisoner to his teepee; she was safe; she was a member of his family—who would harm her there? But now they were in council to decide upon her fate. He was an old man, had seen many winters—he had often travelled far and suffered much to take the life of an enemy; and here, where there is one in their power, should they lose the opportunity of revenge? She was but a woman, but the Dahcotah blood flowed in her veins. She was not fit to live. The Eagle spoke next. He was glad that the chief had taken the prisoner to his teepee—it had been always customary occasionally to adopt a prisoner, and the chief did well to keep up the customs of their tribe. The prisoner was young, she could be taught to love the Chippeway nation; the white people did not murder their prisoners; the Chippeways were the friends of the white people; let them do as they did, be kind to the prisoner and spare her life. The Eagle would marry the Dahcotah girl; he would teach her to speak the language of her adopted tribe; she should make his mocassins, and her children would be Chippeways. Let the chief tell the Eagle to take the girl home to his teepee.

The Eagle's speech created an excitement. The Indians rose one after the other, insisting upon the death of their prisoner. One or two seconded the Eagle's motion to keep her among them, but the voices of the others prevailed. The prisoner saw by the faces of the savages what their words portended.

When the Eagle rose to speak, she recognized the warrior whose looks had frightened her; she knew he was pleading for her life too; but the memory of her husband took away the fear of death. Death with a thousand terrors, rather than live a wife, a slave to the Chippeways! The angry Chippeways are silenced, for their chief addresses them in a voice of thunder; every voice is hushed, every countenance is respectfully turned towards the leader, whose words are to decide the fate of the unhappy woman before them.

"Where is the warrior that will not listen to the words of his chief? my voice is loud and you shall hear. I have taken a Dahcotah woman prisoner; I have chosen to spare her life; she has lived in my teepee; she is one of my family; you have assembled in council to-day to decide her fate—I have decided it. When I took her to my teepee, she became as my child or as the child of my friend. *You* shall not take her life, nor shall *you* marry her. She is my prisoner—she shall remain in my teepee."

Seeing some motion of discontent among those who wished to take her life, he continued, while his eyes shot fire and his broad chest heaved with anger:

"Come then and take her life. Let me see the brave warrior who will take the life of my prisoner? Come! She is here; why do you not raise your tomahawks? It is easy to take a woman's scalp."

Not a warrior moves. The prisoner looks at the chief and at his warriors. Hole-in-the-Day leads her from the council and points to his teepee, which is again her home, and where she is as safe as she would be in her husband's teepee, by the banks of the Mine So-to.

CHAPTER IV

WHILE THE WIFE of Red Face lived from day to day in suspense as to her fate, her husband made every effort for her recovery. Knowing that she was still alive, he could not give up hope of seeing her again. Accordingly, the facts were made known at Fort Snelling, and the Chippeway interpreter was sent up to Hole-in-the-Day's village, with an order from the government to bring her down.

She had been expected for some time, when an excitement among a number of old squaws, who were standing outside the gate of the fort, showed that something unusual was occasioning expressions of pleasure; and as the wife of Red Face advanced towards the house of the interpreter, their gratification was raised to the utmost.

Red Face and some of the Dahcotah warriors were soon there too—and the long separated husband and wife were again united.

But whatever they might have felt on the occasion of meeting again, they showed but little joy. Red Face entered the room where were assembled the Indians and the officers of the garrison. He shook hands with the officers and with the interpreter, and, without looking at his wife, took his seat with the other Dahcotahs.

But her composure soon left her. When she saw him enter, the blood mantled in her pale cheek—pale with long anxiety and recent fatigue. She listened while the Dahcotahs talked with the agent and the commanding officer; and at last, as if her feelings could not longer be restrained, she arose, crossed the room, and took her seat at his feet!

THE CHIEF Hole-in-the-Day has been dead some years, and, in one of the public prints, it was stated that he was thrown from his carriage and killed. This was a genteel mode of dying, which cannot, with truth, be attributed to him.

He always deplored the habit of drinking, to which the Indians are so much addicted. In his latter years, however, he could not withstand the temptation; and, on one occasion, being exceedingly drunk, he was put into an oxcart, and being rather restive, was thrown out, and the cart wheel went over him.

Thus died Hole-in-the-Day—one of the most noted Indians of the present day; and his eldest son reigns in his stead.

Wah-Zee-Yah;

another of the

Giant Gods of the Dahcotahs

Pilot's Knob [overlooking the] Mouth of the St. Peters River, watercolor on paper, 1846-1848.

WAH-ZEE-YAH HAD a son who was killed by Etokah Wachastah, Man of the South. Wah-zee-yah is the god of the winter, and Etokah Wachastah is the god of the summer. When there is a cold spell early in the warm weather, the Dahcotahs say Wah-zee-yah is looking back. When the son of Wah-zee-yah was killed, there were six on each side; the Beings of the south were too strong for those of the north, and conquered them. When the battle was over, a fox was seen running off with one of the Beings of the north.

These gods of the Dahcotahs are said to be inferior to the Great Spirit; but if an Indian wants to perform a deed of valor, he prays to Haokah the

Giant. When they are in trouble, or in fear of anything, they pray to the Great Spirit. You frequently see a pole with a deer-skin, or a blanket hung to it; these are offerings made to the Great Spirit, to propitiate him. White Dog, who lives near Fort Snelling, says he has often prayed to the Great Spirit to keep him from sin, and to enable him and his family to do right. When he wishes to make an offering to the Great Spirit, he takes a scarlet blanket, and paints a circle of blue in the centre (blue is an emblem of peace) and puts ten bells, or silver brooches to it. This offering costs him $20. Christians are too apt to give less liberally to the true God. When White Dog goes to war, he makes this offering.

White Dog says he never saw the giant, but that "Iron Members," who died last summer, saw one of the giants several years ago.

Iron Members was going hunting, and when he was near Shah-co-pee's village, he met the Giant. He wore a three-cornered hat, and one side was bright as the sun; so bright one could not look upon it; and he had a crooked thing upon his shoulder.

Iron Members was on a hill; near which was a deep ravine, when suddenly his eye rested upon something so bright that it pained him to look at it. He looked down the ravine and there stood the Giant. Notwithstanding his position, his head reached to the top of the trees. The Giant was going northwards, and did not notice the Indian or stop; he says he watched the Giant; and, as he went forward, the trees and bushes seemed to make way for him. The visit was one of good luck, the Indians say, for there was excellent hunting that season.

The Dahcotahs believe firmly the story of Iron Members. He was one of their wisest men. He was a great warrior and knew how to kill his enemies. White Dog says that at night, when they were on a war party, Iron Members would extinguish all the fires of the Dahcotahs, and then direct his men where to find the Chippeways. He would take a spoonful of sugar, and the same quantity of whiskey, and make an offering to the spirits of their enemies; he would sing to them, and charm them so that they would come up so close to him that he would knock them on the head with his rattle, and kill them. These spirits approach in the form of a bear. After this is done, they soon find their enemies and conquer them.

The Dahcotahs think their medicine possesses supernatural powers; they burn incense, leaves of the white cedar tree, in order to destroy the supernatural powers of a person who dislikes them. They consider the burning of incense a preventive of evil, and believe it wards off danger from lightning. They say that the cedar tree is wahkun (spiritual) and on that account they burn its leaves to ward off danger. The temple of Solomon was built of cedar.

Unktahe, the god of the waters, is much reverenced by the Dahcotahs. Morgan's bluff, near Fort Snelling, is called "God's house" by the Dahcotahs; they say it is the residence of Unktahe, and under the hill is a subterranean passage, through which they say the water-god passes when he enters the St. Peter's. He is said to be as large as a white man's house.

Near Lac qui parle is a hill called "the Giant's house." On one occasion the Rev. Mr. _____, was walking with a Dahcotah, and as they approached this hill the Dahcotah exclaimed, "Do you not see him, there he is." And although no one else saw the Giant, he persisted in watching him for a few moments as he passed over the hill.

Near Lac qui parle, is living an old Dahcotah woman of a singular appearance. Her face is very black, and her hair singed and faded-looking. She was asked by a stranger to account for her singular appearance. "I dreamed of the Giant," she said; "and I was frightened when I woke; and I told my husband that I would give a dance to the Giant to propitiate him; but my husband said that I was not able to go through the Giant's dance; that I would only fail, and bring disgrace upon him and all my family. The Giant was very angry with me, and punished me by burning my face black, and my hair as you see it." Her husband might well fear that she would not be able to perform this dance.

It would be impossible to give any idea of the number of the gods of the Dahcotahs. All nature is animated with them; every mountain, every tree, is worshipped, as among the Greeks of old, and again, like the Egyptians, the commonest animals are the objects of their adoration.

May the time soon come when they will acknowledge but one God, the Creator of the Earth and Heaven, the Sovereign of the universe!

Storms in Life and Nature;

OR,

Unktahe and the Thunder Bird

Wabasha Prairie, Curious bluffs, watercolor on paper, 1846-1848.

"EVER," SAYS Checkered Cloud, "will Unktahe, the god of the waters, and Wahkeon (Thunder) do battle against each other. Sometimes the thunder birds are conquerors—often the god of the waters chases his enemies back to the distant clouds."

Many times, too, will the daughters of the nation go into the pathless prairies to weep; it is their custom; and while there is sickness, and want, and death, so long will they leave the haunts of men to weep where none but the Great Spirit may witness their tears. It is only, they believe, in the City of spirits, that the sorrows of Dahcotah women will cease—there, will their tears be dried forever.

Many winters have passed away since Harpenstah brought the dead body of her husband to his native village to be buried; my authority is the "medicine woman," whose lodge, for many years, was to be seen on the banks of Lake Calhoun.

This village is now deserted. The remains of a few houses are to be seen, and the broken ground in which were planted the poles of their teepees. Silence reigns where the merry laugh of the villagers often met in chorus. The scene of the feast and dance is now covered with long grass, but "desolation saddens all its green."

CHAPTER I

DARK AND HEAVY clouds hung over the village of "Sleepy Eyes," one of the chiefs of the Sioux. The thunder birds flapped their wings angrily as they flew along, and where they hovered over the "Father of many waters," the waves rose up, and heaved to and fro. Unktahe was eager to fight against his ancient enemies; for as the storm spirits shrieked wildly, the waters tossed above each other; the large forest tress were uptorn from their roots, and fell over into the turbid waters, where they lay powerless amid the scene of strife; and while the vivid lightning pierced the darkness, peal after peal was echoed by the neighboring hills.

One human figure was seen outside the many teepees that rose side by side in the village. Sleepy Eyes alone dared to stand and gaze upon the tempest which was triumphing over all the powers of nature. As the lightning fell upon the tall form of the chief, he turned his keen glance from the swift-flying clouds to the waters, where dwelt the god whose anger he had ever been taught to fear. He longed, though trembling, to see the countenance of the being whose appearance is the sure warning of calamity. His superstitious fears told him to turn, lest the deity should rise before him; while his native courage, and love of the marvellous, chained him to the spot.

The storm raged wilder and louder—the driving wind scattered the hail around him, and at length the chief raised the door of his teepee, and joined his frightened household.

Trembling and crouching to the ground were the mothers and children, as the teepee shook from the force of the wind. The young children hid their faces close against their mothers' breasts. Every head was covered, to avoid the streaked lightning as it glanced over the bent and terrified forms, that seemed to cling to the earth for protection.

At the end of the village, almost on the edge of the high bluff that towered above the river, rose a teepee, smaller than the rest. The open door revealed the wasted form of Harpstenah, an aged woman.

Aged, but not with years! Evil had been the days of her pilgrimage.

The fire that had burned in the wigwam was all gone out, the dead ashes lay in the centre, ever and anon scattered by the wind over the wretched household articles that lay around. Gone out, too, were the flames that once lighted with happiness the heart of Harpstenah.

The sorrows of earth, more pitiless than the winds of heaven, had scattered forever the hopes that had made her a being of light and life. The head that lies on the earth was once pillowed on the breast of the lover of her youth. The arm that is heavily thrown from her once clasped his children to her heart.

What if the rain pours in upon her, or the driving wind and hail scatter her wild locks? She feels it not. Life is there, but the consciousness of life is gone forever.

A heavier cloud hangs about her heart than that which darkens nature. She fears not the thunder, nor sees the angry lightning. She has laid upon the scaffold her youngest son, the last of the many ties that bound her to earth.

One week before, her son entered the wigwam. He was not alone; his comrade, "The Hail that Strikes," accompanied him.

Harpstenah had been tanning deer-skin near her door. She had planted two poles firmly in the ground, and on them she had stretched the deer-skin. With an iron instrument she constantly scraped the skin, throwing water upon it. She had smoked it too, and now it was ready to make into mocassins or leggins. She had determined, while she was tanning the deer-skin, how she would embroider them. They should be richer and handsomer even than those of their chief's son; nay, gayer than those worn by the chief himself. She had beads and stained porcupine quills; all were ready for her to sew.

The venison for the evening meal was cooked and placed in a wooden bowl before the fire, when the two young men entered.

The son hardly noticed his mother's greeting, as he invited his friend to partake of the venison. After eating, he filled his pipe, smoked, and offered it to the other. They seemed inclined to waste but little time in talking, for the pipe was put by, and they were about to leave the teepee, when the son's steps were arrested by his mother's asking him if he were going out again on a hunt. "There is food enough," she added, "and I thought you would remain at home and prepare to join in the dance of the sun, which will be celebrated tomorrow. You promised me to do so, and a Dahcotah values his word."

The young man hesitated, for he loved his mother, and he knew it would grieve her to be told the expedition upon which he was going.

The eyes of his comrade flashed fire, and his lip curled scornfully, as he turned towards the son of Harpstenah. "Are you afraid to tell your mother the truth," he said, "or do you fear the 'long knives'* will carry you a prisoner to their fort? *I* will tell you where we are going," he added. "The Dahcotahs have bought us whiskey, and we are going to meet them and help bring it up. And now cry—you are a woman—but it is time for us to be gone."

The son lingered—he could not bear to see his mother's tears. He knew the sorrows she had endured, he knew too (for she had often assured him) that should harm come to him she would not survive it. The knife she carried in her belt was ready to do its deadly work. She implored him to stay, calling to his mind the deaths of his father and of his murdered brothers; she bade him remember the tears they had shed together, and the promises he had often made, never to add to the trials she had endured.

It was all in vain; for his friend, impatient to be gone, laughed at him for listening to the words of his mother. "Is not a woman a dog?" he said. "Do you intend to stay all night to hear your mother talk? If so, tell me, that I may seek another comrade—one who fears neither a white man nor a woman."

This appeal had its effect, for the young men left the teepee together. They were soon out of sight, while Harpstenah sat weeping, and swaying her body to and fro, lamenting the hour she was born. "There is no sorrow in the land of spirits," she cried; "oh! that I were dead!"

_____

* Officers and soldiers are called long knives among the Sioux, from their wearing swords.

The party left the village that night to procure the whiskey. They were careful to keep watch for the Chippeways, so easy would it be for their enemies to spring up from behind a tree, or to be concealed among the bushes and long grass that skirted the open prairies. Day and night they were on their guard; the chirping of the small bird by day, as well as the hooting of an owl by night—either might be the feigned voice of a tomahawked enemy. And as they approached St. Anthony's Falls, they had still another cause for caution. Here their friends were to meet them with the fire water. Here, too, they might see the soldiers from Fort Snelling, who would snatch the untasted prize from their lips, and carry them prisoners to the fort—a disgrace that would cling to them forever.

Concealed under a rock, they found the kegs of liquor, and, while placing them in their canoes, they were joined by the Indians who had been keeping guard over it, and at the same time watching for the soldiers.

In a few hours they were relieved of their fears. The flag that waved from the tower at Fort Snelling, had been long out of sight. They kept their canoes side by side, passing away the time in conversation.

The women who were paddling felt no fatigue. They knew that at night they were to have a feast. Already the fires of the maddening drink had made the blood in their dull veins course quickly. They anticipated the excitement that would make them forget they had ever been cold or hungry; and bring to them bright dreams of that world where sorrow is unknown.

"We must be far on our journey to-night," said the Rattler; "the long knives are ever on the watch for Dahcotahs with whiskey."

"The laws of the white people are very just," said an old man of the party; "they let their people live near us and sell us whiskey, they take our furs from us, and get much money. *They* have the right to bring their liquor near us, and sell it, but if *we* buy it we are punished. When I was young," he added, bitterly, "the Dahcotahs were free; they went and came as they chose. There were no soldiers sent to our villages to frighten our women and children, and to take our young men prisoners. The Dahcotahs are all women now—there are no warriors among them, or they would not submit to the power of the long knives."

"We must submit to them," said the Rattler; "it would be in vain to attempt to contend with them. We have learned that the long knives *can work in the night.* A few nights ago, some young men belonging to the village of Marpuah Wechastah, had been drinking. They knew that the Chippeway interpreter was away, and that his wife was alone. They went, like cowards as they were, to frighten a woman. They yelled and sung, they beat against her door, shouting and laughing when they found she was afraid to come out. When they returned home it was just day; they drank and slept till night, and then they assembled, four young men in one teepee, to pass the night in drinking.

"The father of White Deer came to the teepee. 'My son,' said he, 'it is better for you to stop drinking and go away. You have an uncle among the Tetons, go and visit him. You brought the fire water here, you frightened the wife of the Interpreter, and for this trouble you will be punished. Your father is old, save him the disgrace of seeing his son a prisoner at the Fort.'

"'Fear not, my father,' said the young man, 'your son will never be a prisoner. I wear a charm over my heart, which will ever make me free as the wind. The *white men cannot work in the night;* they are sleeping even now. We will have a merry night, and when the sun is high, and the long knives come to seek me, you may laugh at them, and tell them to follow me to the country of the Tetons.' The father left the teepee, and White Deer struck the keg with his tomahawk. The fire water dulled their senses, for they heard not their enemies until they were upon them.

"It was in the dead of night—all but the revellers slept—when the soldiers from the fort surrounded the village.

"The mother of White Deer heard the barking of her dog. She looked out of the door of her teepee. She saw nothing, for it was dark; but she knew there was danger near.

"Our warriors, roused from their sleep, determined to find out the cause of the alarm; they were thrust back into their teepees by the bayonets of the long knives, and the voice of the Interpreter was heard, crying, 'The first Dahcotah that leaves his lodge shall be shot.'

"The soldiers found out from the old chief the teepee of the revellers. The young men did not hear them as they approached; they were drinking and shouting. White Deer had raised the cup to his lips, when the soldier's grasp was upon him. It was too late for him to fly.

"There was an unopened keg of liquor in the teepee. The soldiers struck it to pieces, and the fire water covered the ground.

"The hands of White Deer were bound with an iron chain; he threw from him his clothes and his blanket. He was a prisoner, and needed not the clothing of a Dahcotah, born free.

"The grey morning dawned as they entered the large door of the fort. His old father soon followed him; he offered to stay, himself, as a prisoner, if his young son could be set free.

"It is in vain, then, that we would contend with the white man; they keep a watch over all our actions. They *work in the night.*"

"The long knives will ever triumph, when the medicine men of our nation speak as you do," said Two Stars. "I have lived near them always, and have never been their prisoner. I have suffered from cold in the winter, and have never asked clothing, and from hunger, and have never asked food. My wife has never stood at the gate to ask bread, nor have my daughters adorned themselves to attract the eyes of their young men. I will live and die on the land of my forefathers, without asking a favor of an enemy. They call themselves the friends of the Dahcotahs. They are our friends when they want our lands or our furs.

"They are our worst enemies; they have trampled us under foot. We do not chase the deer on the prairies as eagerly as they have hunted us down. They steal from us our rights, and then gain us over by fair words. I hate them; and had not our warriors turned women, and learned to fear them, I would gladly climb their walls, and shout the war cry in their ears. The Great Spirit has indeed forsaken his children, when their warriors and wise men talk of submission to their foes."

CHAPTER II

WELL MIGHT Harpstenah sit in her lodge and weep. The sorrows of her life passed in review before her. Yet she was once the belle of an Indian village; no step so light, no laugh so merry as hers. She possessed too, a spirit and a firmness not often found among women.

She was by birth the third daughter, who is always called Harpstenah among the Sioux. Her sisters were married, and she had seen but fourteen summers when old Cloudy Sky, the medicine man, came to her parents to buy her for his wife.

They dared not refuse him, for they were afraid to offend a medicine man, and a war chief besides. Cloudy Sky was willing to pay them well for their child. So she was told that her fate for life was determined upon. Her promised bridegroom had seen the snows of eighty winters.

It was a bright night in the "moon for strawberries."* Harpstenah had wept herself to sleep, and she had reason too, for her young companions had laughed at her, and told her that she was to have for a husband an old man without a nose. And it was true, though Cloudy Sky could once have boasted of a fine aquiline. He had been drinking freely, and picked a quarrel with one of his sworn friends. After some preliminary blows, Cloudy Sky seized his antagonist and cut his ear sadly, but in return he had his nose bitten off.

She had wept the more when her mother told her than in four days she was to go to the teepee of her husband. It was in vain to contend. She lay down beside the fire; deep sleep came upon her; she forgot the events of the past day; for a time she ceased to think of the young man she loved, and the old one she hated. In her dreams she had travelled a long journey, and was seated on the river shore, to rest her tired limbs. The red light of the dying sun illuminated the prairies, she could not have endured its scorching rays, were it not for the sheltering branches of the tree under which she had found a resting place.

The waters of the river beat against her feet. She would fain move, but something chained her to the spot. She tried to call her mother, but her lips were sealed, and her voice powerless. She would have turned her face from the waters, but even this was impossible. Stronger and stronger beat the waves, and then parted, revealing the dreaded form of the fairy of the waters.

Harpenstah looked upon death as inevitable; she had ever feared that terrible race of beings whose home was in the waters. And now the fairy stood before her!

"Why do you tremble maiden? Only the wicked need fear the anger of the gods. You have never offended us, nor the spirits of the dead. You have danced in the scalp-dance, and have reverenced the customs of the Sioux. You have shed many tears. You loved Red Deer, and your father has sold you to Cloudy Sky, the medicine man. It is with you to marry the man you love, or the one you hate."

---

* The month of June

"If you know everything," sighed the girl, "then you must know that in four days I am to take my seat beside Cloudy Sky in his wigwam. He has twice brought calico and cloth, and laid them at the door of my father's teepee."

"You shall not marry Cloudy Sky, if you have a strong heart, and fear nothing," replied the fairy. The spirits of the water have determined on the death of Cloudy Sky. He has already lived three times on earth. For many years he wandered through the air with the sons of the thunder bird; like them he was ever fighting against the friends of Unktahe.

"With his own hand he killed the son of that god, and for that was he sent to earth to be a medicine man. But long ago we have said that the time should come, when we would destroy him from the earth. It is for you to take his life when he sleeps. Can a Dahcotah woman want courage when she is to be forced to marry a man she hates?"

The waters closed over the fairy as he disappeared, and the waves beat harder against Harpstenah's feet. She awoke with the words echoing in her heart, "Can a Sioux woman want courage when she is to be forced to marry a man she hates?" "The words of the fairy were wise and true," thought the maiden. "Our medicine men say that the fairies of the water are all wicked; that they are ever seeking to do harm to the Dahcotahs. My dream has made my heart light. I will take the life of the war chief. At the worst they can but take mine."

As she looked round the teepee, her eye rested upon the faces of her parents. The bright moonlight had found its way into the teepee. There lay her father, his haughty countenance calm and subdued, for the "image of death" had chased away the impression left on his features of a fierce struggle with a hard life. How often had he warned her of the danger of offending Cloudy Sky, that sickness, famine, death itself, might be the result. Her mother too, had wearied her with warnings. But she remembered her dream, and with all a Sioux woman's faith in revelations, she determined to let it influence her course.

Red Deer had often vowed to take the life of his rival, though he knew it would have assuredly cost him his own. The family of Cloudy Sky was a large one; there were many who would esteem it a sacred duty to avenge his death. Besides he would gain nothing by it, for the parents of Harpstenah would never consent to her marriage with the murderer of the war chief.

How often had Red Deer tried to induce the young girl to leave the village, and return with him as his wife. "Have we not always loved each other," he said. "When we were children, you made me mocassins, and paddled the canoe for me, and I brought the wild duck, which I shot while it was flying, to you. You promised me to be my wife, when I should be a great hunter, and had brought to you the scalp of an enemy. I have kept my promise, but you have broken yours."

"I know it," she replied; "but I fear to keep my word. They would kill you, and the spirits of my dead brothers would haunt me for disobeying my parents. Cloudy Sky says that if I do not marry him he will cast a spell upon me; he says that the brightness would leave my eye, and the color my cheek; that my step should be slow and weary, and soon would I be laid in the earth beside my brothers. The spirit that should watch beside my body would be offended for my sin in disobeying the counsel of the aged. You, too, should die, he says, not by the tomahawk, as a warrior should die, but by a lingering disease—fever should enter your veins, your strength would soon be gone, you would no longer be able to defend yourself from your enemies. Let me die, rather than bring such trouble upon you."

Red Deer could not reply, for he believed that Cloudy Sky could do all that he threatened. Nerved, then, by her devotion to her lover, her hatred of Cloudy Sky, and her faith in her dream, Harpstenah determined her heart should not fail her; she would obey the mandate of the water god; she would bury her knife in the heart of the medicine man.

CHAPTER III

IN THEIR HOURS for eating, the Sioux accommodate themselves to circumstances. If food be plenty, they eat three or four times a day; if scarce, they eat but once. Sometimes they go without food for several days, and often they are obliged to live for weeks on the bark of trees, skins, or anything that will save them from dying of famine.

When game and corn are plenty, the kettle is always boiling, and they are invariably hospitable and generous, always offering to a visitor such as they have it in their power to give.

The stars were still keeping watch, when Harpstenah was called by her mother to assist her. The father's morning meal was prepared early, for he was going out to hunt. Wild duck, pigeons, and snipe, could be had in abundance; the timid grouse, too, could be roused up on the prairies. Larger game was there, too, for the deer flew swiftly past, and had even stopped to drink on the opposite shore of the "Spirit Lake."

When they assembled to eat, the old man lifted up his hands—"May the Great Spirit have mercy upon us, and give me good luck in hunting."

Meat and boiled corn were eaten from wooden bowls, and the father went his way, leaving his wife and daughter to attend to their domestic cares.

Harpstenah was cutting wood near the lodge, when Cloudy Sky presented himself. He went into the teepee and lighted his pipe, and then, seating himself outside, began to smoke. He was, in truth, a sorry figure for a bridegroom. Always repulsive in his looks, his present dress was not calculated to improve him. He wore mourning for his enemy, whom he had killed.

His face was painted perfectly black; nothing but the whites of his eyes relieved the universal darkness. His blanket was torn and old—his hair unbraided, and on the top of his head he wore a knot of swan's down.

Every mark of grief or respect he could have shown a dead brother, he now assumed in honor of the man whom he had hated—whose life he had destroyed—who had belonged to the hateful tribe which had never been the enemy of his nation.

He looked very important as he puffed away, now watching Harpstenah, who appeared to be unconscious of his presence, now fixing his eyes on her mother, who was busily employed mending mocassins.

Having finished smoking, he used a fan which was attached to the other end of his pipe-stem. It was a very warm day, and the perspiration that was bursting from his forehead mingled with the black paint and slowly found its way down his face.

"Where is your husband?" at length he asked of the mother.

"He saw a deer fly past this morning," she replied, "and he has gone to seek it, that I may dry it."

"Does he come back to-night?"

"He does; he said you were to give a medicine feast to-morrow, and that he would be here."

Harpstenah knew well why the medicine feast was to be given. Cloudy Sky could not, according to the laws of the Sioux, throw off his mourning, until he had killed an enemy or given a medicine dance. She knew that he wanted to wear a new blanket, and plait his hair, and paint his face a more becoming color. But she knew his looks could not be improved, and she went on cutting wood, as unconcernedly as if the old war chief were her grandfather, instead of her affianced husband. He might gain the good will of her parents, he might even propitiate the spirits of the dead: She would take his life, surely as the senseless wood yielded to the strength of the arm that was cleaving it.

"You will be at the feast too," said Cloudy Sky to the mother; "you have always foretold truly. There is not a woman in the band who can tell what is going to happen as well as you. There is no nation so great as the Dahcotah," continued the medicine man, as he saw several idlers approach, and stretch themselves on the grass to listen to him. "There is no nation so great as the Dahcotah—but our people are not so great now as they were formerly. When our forefathers killed buffaloes on these prairies, that the white people now ride across as if they were their own, mighty giants lived among them; they strode over the widest rivers, and the tallest trees; they could lay their hands upon the highest hills, as they walked the earth. But they were not men of war. They did not fight great battles, as do the Thunder Bird and his warriors.

There were large animals, too, in those days; so large that the stoutest of our warriors were but as children beside them. Their bones have been preserved through many generations. They are sacred to us, and we keep them because they will cure us when we are sick, and will save us from danger.

I have lived three times on earth. When my body was first laid upon the scaffold, my spirit wandered through the air. I followed the Thunder Birds as they darted among the clouds. When the heavens were black, and the rain fell in big drops, and the streaked lightning frightened our women and children, I was a warrior, fighting beside the sons of the Thunder Bird.

Unktahe rose up before us; sixty of his friends were with him; the waters heaved and pitched, as the spirits left them to seek vengeance against the Thunder Birds. They showed us their terrible horns, but they tried to frighten us in vain. We were but forty; we flew towards them, holding our shields before our breasts; the wind tore up the trees, and threw down the teepees, as we passed along.

All day we fought; when we were tired we rested awhile, and then the winds were still, and the sun showed himself from behind the dark clouds. But soon our anger rose. The winds flew along swifter than the eagle, as the Thunder Birds clapped their wings, and again we fought against our foes.

The son of Unktahe came towards me; his eyes shone like fire, but I was not afraid. I remembered I had been a Sioux warrior. He held his shield before him, as he tried to strike me with his spear. I turned his shield aside, and struck him to the heart.

He fell, and the waters whirled round as they received his body. The sons of Unktahe shouted fearful cries of rage, but our yells of triumph drowned them.

The water spirits shrank to their home, while we returned to the clouds. The large rain drops fell slowly, and the bow of bright colors rested between the heavens and the earth. The strife was over, and we were conquerors. I know that Unktahe hates me—that he would kill me if he could—but the Thunder bird has greater power than he; the friend of the 'Man of the West'* is safe from harm."

Harpstenah had ceased her work, and was listening to the boaster. "It was all true," she said to herself; "the fairy of the water told me that he had offended her race. I will do their bidding. Cloudy Sky may boast of his power, but ere two nights have passed away, he will find he cannot despise the anger of the water spirits, nor the courage of a Dahcotah woman."

CHAPTER IV

THE APPROACH of night brought with it but little inclination to sleep to the excited girl. Her father slept, tired with the day's hunt; and her mother dreamed of seeing her daughter the wife of a war chief and a medicine man.

The village was built on the shores of the lake now known as Lake Calhoun. By the light of the moon the teepees were reflected in its waters.

———

* Thunder is sometimes called the Man of the West.

It was bright as day; so clear was the lake, that the agates near the shore sparkled in its waters. The cry of the whippoorwill alone disturbed the repose of nature, except when the wild scream of the loon was heard as she gracefully swept the waters.

Seated on the shore, Harpstenah waited to hear the low whistle of her lover. The villagers were almost all asleep, now and then the laugh of some rioters was heard breaking in upon the stillness of night. She had not seen her lover for many days; from the time that her marriage was determined upon, the young warrior had kept aloof from her. She had seized her opportunity to tell him that he must meet her where they had often met, where none should know of their meeting. She told him to come when the moon rose, as her father would be tired, and her mother wished to sleep well before the medicine feast.

Many fears oppressed her heart, for he had not answered her when she spoke to him, and he might not intend to come. Long she waited in vain, and she now arose to return to the teepee, when the low signal met her ear.

She did not wait to hear it a second time, but made her way along the shore: now her steps were printed in the wet sand, now planted on the rocks near the shore; not a sound followed her movements until she stood on the appointed place. The bright moonlight fell upon her features, and her rich dress, as she waited with folded arms for her lover to address her. Her okendokenda of bright colors was slightly open at the neck, and revealed brooches of brass and silver that covered her bosom; a heavy necklace of crimson beads hung around her throat; bracelets of brass clasped her wrists, and her long plaited hair was ornamented at the end of the braids with trinkets of silver.

Her cloth petticoat was richly decorated with ribbons, and her leggins and mocassins proved that she had spent much time and labor on the adorning of a person naturally well formed, and graceful.

"Why have you wished to meet me, Harpstenah?" said the young man, gloomily. "Have you come to tell me of the presents Cloudy Sky has made you, or do you wish to say that you are ashamed to break the promise you made me to be my wife?"

"I have come to say again that I will be your wife," she replied: "and for the presents Cloudy Sky left for me, I have trampled them under my feet.

See, I wear near my heart the brooches you have given me."

"Women are ever dogs and liars," said Red Deer, "but why do you speak such words to me, when you know you have agreed to marry Cloudy Sky? Your cousin told me your father had chosen him to carry you into the teepee of the old man. Your father beat you, and you agreed to marry him. You are a coward to mind a little pain. Go, marry the old medicine man; he will beat you as he has his other wives; he may strike you with his tomahawk and kill you, as he did his first wife; or he will sell you to the traders, as he did the other; he will tell you to steal pork and whiskey for him, and then when it is found out, he will take you and say you are a thief, and that he has beaten you for it. Go, the young should ever mate with the young, but you will soon lie on the scaffold, and by his hand too."

"The proud eagle seeks to frighten the timid bird that follows it," said the maiden; "but Red Deer should not speak such angry words to the woman that will venture her life for him. Cloudy Sky boasts that he is the friend of the thunder bird; in my dreams, I have seen the fairy of the waters, and he told me that Cloudy Sky should die by my hand. My words are true. Cloudy Sky was once with the sons of the thunder birds when they fought against Unktahe. He killed a son of the water god, and the spirits of the water have determined on his death.

"Red Deer, my heart is strong. I do not fear the medicine man, for the power of Unktahe is greater than his. But you must go far away and visit the Tetons; if you are here, they will accuse you of his death, and will kill you. But as I have promised to marry him, no one will think that I have murdered him. It will be long ere I see you again, but in the moon that we gather wild rice,* return, and I will be your wife. Go, now," she added, "say to your mother that you are going to visit your friends, and before the day comes be far away. To-morrow Cloudy Sky gives a medicine feast, and to-morrow night Haokah will make my heart strong, and I will kill the medicine man. His Soul will travel a long journey to the land of spirits. There let him drink, and boast, and frighten women."

Red Deer heard her, mute with astonishment. The color mantled in her cheek, and her determined countenance assured him that she was in earnest.

———

* September

He charged her to remember the secret spells of the medicine man. If she loved him it was far better to go with him now; they would soon be out of the reach of her family. To this she would not listen, and repeating to him her intention of executing all she had told him of, she left him.

He watched her as she returned to her teepee; sometimes her form was lost in the thick bushes, he could see her again as she made her way along the pebbled shore, and when she had entered her teepee he returned home.

He collected his implements of war and hunting, and, telling his mother he was going on a long journey, he left the village.

CHAPTER V

THE FEAST given in honor of their medicine was celebrated the next day, and Cloudy Sky was thus relieved of the necessity of wearing mourning for his enemy.

His face was carefully washed of the black paint that disfigured it; his hair, plentifully greased, was braided and ornamented. His leggins were new, and his white blanket was marked according to Indian custom. On it was painted a black hand, that all might know that he had killed his enemy. But for all he did not look either young or handsome, and Harpstenah's young friends were astonished that she witnessed the preparations for her marriage with so much indifference.

But she was unconscious alike of their sympathy and ridicule; her soul was occupied with the reflection that upon her energy depended her future fate. Never did her spirit shrink from its appointed task. Nor was she entirely governed by selfish motives; she believed herself an instrument in the hand of the gods.

Mechanically she performed her ordinary duties. The wood was cut and the evening meal was cooked; afterwards she cut down branches of trees, and swept the wigwam. In the evening, the villagers had assembled on the shores of the lake to enjoy the cool air after the heat of the day.

Hours passed away as gossiping and amusement engaged them all. At length they entered their teepees to seek rest, and Harpstenah and her mother were the last at the door of their teepee, where a group had been seated on the ground, discussing their own and others' affairs. "No harm can come to you, my daughter, when you are the wife of so great a medicine man.

If any one hate you and wish to do you an injury, Cloudy Sky will destroy their power. Has he not lived with the Thunder Birds, did he not learn from them to cure the sick, and to destroy his enemies? He is a great warrior too."

"I know it, my mother," replied the girl, "but we have sat long in the moonlight, the wind that stirred the waters of the spirit lake is gone. I must sleep, that I may be ready to dress myself when you call me. My hair must be braided in many braids, and the strings are not yet sewed to my mocassins. You too are tired; let us go in and sleep."

Sleep came to the mother—to the daughter courage and energy. Not in vain had she prayed to Haokah the Giant, to give her power to perform a great deed. Assured that her parents were sleeping heavily, she rose and sought the lodge of the medicine man.

When she reached the teepee, she stopped involuntarily before the door, near which hung, on a pole, the medicine bag of the old man. The medicine known only to the clan had been preserved for ages. Sacred had it ever been from the touch of woman. It was placed there to guard the medicine man from evil, and to bring punishment on those who sought to do him harm. Harpstenah's strength failed her. What was she about to do?

Could she provoke with impunity the anger of the spirits of the dead? Would not the Great Spirit bring terrible vengeance upon her head. Ready to sink to the earth with terror, the words of the fairy of the waters reassured her. "Can a Dahcotah woman want courage when she is to be forced to marry a man she hates?"

The tumult within is stilled—the strong beating of her heart has ceased—her hand is upon the handle of her knife, as the moonlight falls upon its glittering blade.

Too glorious a night for so dark a deed! See! They are confronted, the old man and the maiden! The tyrant and his victim; the slave dealer and the noble soul he had trafficked for!

Pale, but firm with high resolve, the girl looked for one moment at the man she had feared—whose looks had checked her childish mirth, whose anger she had been taught to dread, even to the sacrificing of her heart's best hopes.

Restlessly the old man slept; perchance he saw the piercing eyes that were fixed upon him, for he muttered of the road to the land of spirits. Listen to him, as he boasts of the warrior's work.

"Many brave men have made this road. The friend of the Thunder Birds was worthy. Strike the woman who would dare assist a warrior. Strike—"

"Deep in his heart she plunged the ready steel," and as she drew it out, the life blood came quickly. She alone heard his dying groan.

She left the teepee—her work was done. It was easy to wash the stains of her knife in the waters of the lake.

When her mother arose, she looked at the pale countenance of her daughter. In vain she sought to understand her muttered words. Harpstenah, as she tried to sleep, fancied she heard the wild laugh of the water spirits. Clouds had obscured the moon, and distant thunder rolled along the sky; and, roused by the clamorous grief of the many women assembled in the lodge, she heard from them of the dark tragedy in which she had been the principal actor.

The murderer was not to be found. Red Deer was known to be far away. It only remained to bury Cloudy Sky, with all the honors due to a medicine man.

Harpstenah joined in the weeping of the mourners—the fountains of a Sioux woman's tears are easily unlocked. She threw her blanket upon the dead body.

Many were the rich presents made to the inanimate clay which yesterday influenced those who still trembled lest the spirit of the dead war-chief would haunt them. The richest cloth enrobed his body, and, a short distance from the village, he was placed upon a scaffold.

Food was placed beside him; it would be long before his soul would reach the city of spirits; his strength would fail him, were it not for the refreshment of the tender flesh of the wild deer he had loved to chase, and the cooling waters he had drank on earth, for many, many winters.

But after the death of Cloudy Sky, the heart of Harpstenah grew light. She joined again in the ball plays on the prairies. It needed no vermilion on her cheek to show the brightness of her eye, for the flush of hope and happiness was there.

The dark deed was forgotten; and when, in the time that the leaves began to fall, they prepared the wild rice for winter's use, Red Deer was at her side.

He was a good hunter, and the parents were old. Red Deer ever kept them supplied with game—and winter found her a wife, and a happy one too; for Red Deer loved her in very truth—and the secret of the death of the medicine man was buried in their hearts.

CHAPTER VI

TEN YEARS HAD passed away since their marriage, and Red Deer had never brought another wife to his teepee. Harpstenah was without a rival in his affections, if we except the three strong boys who were growing up beside them.

Chaskè (the oldest son) could hunt for his mother, and it was well that he could, for his father's strength was gone. Consumption wasted his limbs, and the once powerful arm could not now support his drooping head.

The father and mother had followed Cloudy Sky to the world of spirits; they were both anxious to depart from earth, for age had made them feeble, and the hardships of ninety years made them eager to have their strength renewed, in the country where their ancestors were still in the vigor of early youth. The band at Lake Calhoun were going on a hunt for porcupines; a long hunt, and Harpstenah tried to deter her husband from attempting the journey; but he thought the animating exercise of the chase would be a restorative to his feeble frame, and they set out with the rest.

When the hunters had obtained a large number of those valued animals, the women struck their teepees and prepared for their return. Harpstenah's lodge alone remained, for in it lay the dying man—by his side his patient wife. The play of the children had ceased—they watched with silent awe the pale face and bright eye of their father—they heard him charge their mother to place food that his soul might be refreshed on its long journey. Not a tear dimmed her eye as she promised all he asked.

"There is one thing, my wife," he said, "which still keeps my spirit on earth. My soul cannot travel the road to the city of spirits—that long road made by the bravest of our warriors—while it remembers the body which it has so long inhabited shall be buried far from its native village. Your words were wise when you told me I had not the strength to travel so far, and now my body must lie far from my home—far from the place of my birth—from the village where I have danced the dog feast, and from the shores of the 'spirit lakes' where my father taught me to use my bow and arrow."

"Your body shall lie on the scaffold near your native village," his wife replied. "When I turn from this place, I will take with me my husband; and my young children shall walk by my side. My heart is as brave now as it was when I took the life of the medicine man. The love that gave me courage then, will give me strength now. Fear not for me; my limbs will not be weary, and when the Great Spirit calls me, I will hear his voice, and follow you to the land of spirits, where there will be no more sickness nor trouble."

Many stars shone out that night; they assisted in the solemn and the sacred watch. The mother looked at the faces of her sleeping sons, and listened to their heavy breathing; they had but started on the journey of life.

She turned to her husband: it was but the wreck of a deserted house, the tenant had departed.

The warrior was already far on his journey; ere this, he had reached the lodge where the freed spirit adorns itself ere entering upon its new abode.

Some days after, Harpstenah entered her native village, bearing a precious burden. Strapped to her back was the body of her husband. By day, she had borne it all the weary way; at night, she had stopped to rest and to weep. Nor did her strength fail her, until she reached her home; then, insensible to sorrow and fatigue, she sunk to the earth.

The women relieved her from the burden, and afterwards helped her to bury her dead.

Many waters could not quench her love, nor could the floods drown it. It was strong as death.

Well might she sit in her lodge and weep! The village where she passed her childhood and youth was deserted. Her husband forgotten by all but herself. Her two sons were murdered by the Chippeways while defending their mother and their young brother.

Well might she weep! And tremble too, for death among the Dahcotahs comes as often by the fire water purchased from the white people, as from the murderous tomahawk and scalping-knife of the Chippeways.

Nor were her fears useless; she never again saw her son, until his body was brought to her, his dark features stiff in death. The death blow was given, too, by the friend who had shamed him from listening to his mother's voice.

△△△△△

WHAT WONDER that she should not heed the noise of the tempest! The storms of her life had been fiercer than the warring of the elements. But while the fountains of heaven were unsealed, those of her heart were closed forever. Never more should tears relieve her, who had shed so many. Often had she gone into the prairies to weep, far from the sight of her companions. Her voice was heard from a distance. The wind would waft the melancholy sound back to the village.

"It is only Harpstenah," said the women. "She has gone to the prairies to weep for her husband and her children."

The storm raged during the night, but ceased with the coming of day. The widowed wife and childless mother was found dead under the scaffold where lay the body of her son.

The Thunder Bird was avenged for the death of his friend. The strength of Red Deer had wasted under a lingering disease; his children were dead; their mother lay beside her youngest son.

The spirit of the waters had not appeared in vain. When the countenance of Unktahe rests upon a Dahcotah, it is the sure prognostic of coming evil. The fury of the storm spirits was spent when the soul of Harpstenah followed her lost ones.

⋀⋀⋀⋀⋀

DIMLY, AS THE lengthened shadows of evening fall around them, are seen the outstretched arms of the suffering Dahcotah women, as they appeal to us for assistance—and not to proud man!

He, in the halls of legislation, decides when the lands of the red man are needed—one party makes a bargain which the other is forced to accept.

But in a woman's heart God has placed sympathies to which the sorrows of the Dahcotah women appeal. Listen! for they tell you they would fain know of a balm for the many griefs they endure; they would be taught to avoid the many sins they commit; and, oh! how gladly would many of them have their young children accustomed to shudder at the sight of a fellow creature's blood. Like us, they pour out the best affections of early youth on a beloved object. Like us, they have clasped their children to their hearts in devoted love. Like us, too, they have wept as they laid them in the quiet earth.

But they must fiercely grapple with trials which we have never conceived. Winter after winter passes, and they perish from disease, and murder, and famine.

There is a way to relieve them—would you know it? Assist the missionaries who are giving their lives to them and God. Send them money, that they may clothe the feeble infant, and feed its starving mother.

Send them money, that they may supply the wants of those who are sent to school, and thus encourage others to attend.

As the day of these forgotten ones is passing away, so is ours. They were born to suffer, we to relieve. Let their deathless souls be taught the way of life, that they and we, after the harsh discords of earth shall have ceased, may listen together to the "harmonies of Heaven."

Haokah Ozape;

the

Dance to the Giant

View on the Mississippi 70 miles below the Falls of St. Anthony, watercolor on paper, 1846-1848.

CHAPTER I

THE DANCE to the Giant is now rarely celebrated among the Dahcotahs. So severe is the sacrifice to this deity, that there are few who have courage to attempt it; and yet Haokah is universally reverenced and feared among the Sioux.

They believe in the existence of many Giants, but Haokah is one of the principal. He is styled the antinatural god. In summer he feels cold, in winter he suffers from the heat; hot water is cold to him, and the contrary.

The Dahcotah warrior, however brave he may be, believes that when he dreams of Haokah, calamity is impending and can only be avoided by some sort of sacrifice to this god.

The incident on which this story is founded, occurred while I resided among the Sioux. I allude to the desertion of Wenona by her lover. It serves to show the blind and ignorant devotion of the Dahcotah to his religion.

And as man is ever alike in every country, and under every circumstance of life—as he often from selfish motives tramples upon the heart that trusts him—so does woman utterly condemn a sister, feeling no sympathy for her sorrow, but only hatred of her fault.

Jealous for the honor of the long-reverenced feasts of the Dahcotahs—the "Deer Killer" thought not for a moment of the sorrow and disgrace he would bring upon Wenona, while Wanska loved the warrior more than ever, triumphing in his preference of her, above her companion. And Wenona—

> A cloud came o'er the prospect of her life,
> And evening did set in
> Early, and dark and deadly.

But she loved too truly to be jealous, and departed without the revenge that most Indian women would have sought, and accomplished too. Her silence on the subject of her early trial induced her friends to believe that her mind was affected, a situation caused by long and intense suffering, and followed by neglect; in such cases the invalid is said to *have no heart.*

The girl from whom I have attempted to draw the character of Wanska, I knew well.

Good looking, with teeth like pearls, her laugh was perfect music. Often have I been roused from my sewing or reading, by hearing the ringing notes, as they were answered by the children. She generally announced herself by a laugh, and was welcomed by one in return.

She was pettish withal, and easily offended, and if refused calico for an okendokenda, or beads, or ribbon to ornament some part of her dress, she would sullenly rest her chin on her hand, until pacified with a present, or the promise of one.

It is in Indian life as in ours—youth believes and trusts, and advancing years bring the consciousness of the trials of life; the necessity of enduring, and in some cases the power to overcome them. Who but she who suffers it, can conceive the Sioux woman's greatest trial—to feel that the love that is her right, is gone! To see another take the place by the household fire, that was hers; to be last where she was first.

It may require some apology that Wanska should have vowed destruction upon herself if the Deer Killer took another wife, and yet should have lived on and become that most unromantic of all characters—a virago. She was reconciled in time to what was inevitable, and as there are many wives among the Sioux, there must be the proportion of scolding ones. So I plead guilty to the charge of wanting sentiment, choosing rather to be true to nature. And there is this consideration: if there be among the Dahcotahs some Catharines, there are many Petruchios.

A GROUP OF Indian girls were seated on the grass, Wanska in the centre, her merry musical laugh echoed back by all but Wenona. The leaves of the large forest tree under which they were sheltered seemed to vibrate to the joyous sounds, stirred as they were by a light breeze that blew from St. Peter's. Hark! they laugh again, and "old John" wakes up from his noon-day nap and turns a curious, reproving look to the noisy party, and Shah-co-pee, the orator of the Sioux, moves towards them, anxious to find out the cause of their mirth.

"Old John," after a hearty stretch, joins them too, and now the fumes of the pipe ascend, and mix with the odor of the sweet-scented prairie grass that the young girls are braiding.

But neither Shah-co-pee the chief, nor old John the medicine man, could find out the secret; they coaxed and threatened in turns—but all in vain, for their curiosity was not gratified. They might have noticed, however, that Wenona's face was pale, and her eyes red with weeping. She was idle too, while the others plaited busily, and there was a subdued look of sadness about her countenance, contrasting strangely with the merry faces of the others.

"Why did you not tell Shah-co-pee what we were laughing at, Wenona?" said Wanska. "Your secret is known now. The Deer-killer told all at the Virgin's feast. Why did you not make him promise not to come? If I had been you, I would have lain sick the day of the feast, I would have struck my foot, so that I could not walk, or, I would have died before I entered the ring.

"The Deer-killer promised to marry me," replied Wenona. "He said that when he returned from his hunt I should be his wife. But I know well why he has disgraced me; you have tried to make him love you, and now he is waiting to take you to his lodge. He is not a great warrior, or he would have kept his word."

"Wenona!" said Wanska, interrupting her, "you have not minded the advice of your grandmother. She told you never to trust the promises of the bravest warriors. You should not have believed his words, until he took you to his wigwam. But do not be afraid that I will marry the Deer-killer. There was never but one woman among the Dahcotahs who did not marry, and I am going to be the second."

"You had better hush, Wanska," said the Bright Star. "You know she had her nose cut off because she refused to be a wife, and somebody may cut yours off , too. It is better to be the mother of warriors than to have every one laughing at you."

"Enah! then I will be married, rather than have my nose cut off, but I will not be the Deer-killer's wife. So Wenona may stop crying."

"He says he will never marry me," said Wenona; "and it will do me no good for you to refuse to be his wife. But you are a liar, like him; for you know you love him. I am going far away, and the man who has broken his faith to the maiden who trusted him, will never be a good husband."

"If I were Wenona, and you married the Deer-killer," said the Bright Star to Wanska, "you should not live long after it. She is a coward or she would not let you laugh at her as you did. I believe *she has no heart* since the Virgin's feast; sometimes she laughs so loud that we can hear her from our teepee, and then she bends her head and weeps. When her mother places food before her she says, 'Will he bring the meat of the young deer for me to dress for him, and will my lodge be ever full of food, that I may offer it to the hungry and weary stranger who stops to rest himself?' If I were in her place, Wanksa," added the Bright Star, "I would try and be a medicine woman, and I would throw a spell upon the Deer-killer, and upon you too, if you married him."

"The Deer-killer is coming," said another of the girls. "He has been watching us; and now that he sees Wenona has gone away, he is coming to talk to Wanska. He wears many eagle feathers: Wenona may well weep that she cannot be his wife, for there is not a warrior in the village who steps so proudly as he."

But he advanced and passed them indifferently. By and by they separated, when he followed Wanska to her father's teepee.

Her mother and father had gone to dispose of game in exchange for bread and flour, and the Deer-killer seated himself uninvited on the floor of the lodge.

"The teepee of the warrior is lonely when he returns from hunting," said he to the maiden. "Wanska must come to the lodge of the Deer-killer. She shall ever have the tender flesh of the deer and buffalo to refresh her, and no other wife shall be there to make her unhappy."

"Wanska is very happy now," she replied. "Her father is a good hunter. He has gone to-day to carry ducks and pigeons to the Fort. The promises of the Deer-killer are like the branch that breaks in my hand. Wenona's face is pale, and her eyes are red like blood from weeping. The Deer-killer promised to make her his wife, and now that he has broken his word to her, he tells Wanska that he will never take another wife, but she cannot trust him."

"Wanska was well named the Merry Heart," the warrior replied; "she laughs at Wenona and calls her a fool, and then she wishes me to marry her. Who would listen to a woman's words? And yet the voice of the Merry Heart is sweeter than a bird's—her laugh makes my spirit glad. When she sits in my lodge and sings to the children who will call me father, I shall be happy. Many women have loved the Deer-killer, but never has he cared to sit beside one, till he heard the voice of Wanska as she sang in the scalp-dance, and saw her bear the scalp of her enemy upon her shoulders."

Wanska's face was pale while she listened to him. She approached him, and laid her small hand upon his arm—"I have heard your words, and my heart says they are good. I have loved you ever since we were children. When I was told that you were always by the side of Wenona, the laugh of my companions was hateful to me—the light of the sun was darkness to my eyes. When Wenona returned to her village with her parents, I said in the presence of the Great Spirit that she should not live after you had made her your wife. But her looks told me that there was sadness in her heart, and then I knew you could not love her.

"You promise me you will never bring another wife to your wigwam. Deer-killer! the wife of the white man is happy, for her husband loves her alone. The children of the second wife do not mock the woman who is no longer beloved, nor strike her children before her eyes. When I am your wife

I shall be happy while you love me; there will be no night in my teepee while I know your heart is faithful and true; but should you break your word to me, and bring to your lodge another wife, you shall see me no more, and the voice whose sound is music to your ears you will never hear again."

Promises come as readily to the lips of an Indian lover as trustfulness does to the heart of the woman who listens to them; and the Deer-killer was believed.

Wanska had been often at the Fort, and she had seen the difference between the life of a white and that of an Indian woman. She had thought that the Great Spirit was unmindful of the cares of his children.

And who would have thought that care was known to Wanska, with her merry laugh, and her never-ceasing jokes, whether played upon her young companions, or on the old medicine man who kept everybody but her in awe of him.

She seemed to be everywhere too, at the same time. Her canoe dances lightly over the St. Peter's, and her companions try in vain to keep up with her. Soon her clear voice is heard as she sings, keeping time with the strokes of the axe she uses so skillfully. A peal of laughter rouses the old woman, her mother, who goes to bring the truant home, but she is gone, and when she returns, in time to see the red sun fade away in the bright horizon, she tells her mother that she went out with two or three other girls, to assist the hunters in bringing in the deer they had killed. And her mother for once does not scold, for she remembers how she used to love to wander on the prairies, when her heart was as light and happy as her child's.

When Wanska was told that the Deer-killer loved Wenona, no one heard her sighs, and for tears, she was too proud to shed any. Wenona's fault had met with ridicule and contempt; there was neither sympathy nor excuse found for her. And now that the Deer-killer had slighted Wenona, and had promised to love her alone, there was nothing wanting to her happiness.

Bright tears of joy fell from her eyes when her lover said there was a spell over him when he loved Wenona, but now his spirit was free; that he would ever love her truly, and that when her parents returned he would bring rich presents and lay them at the door of the lodge.

Wanska was indeed "the Merry Heart," for she loved the Deer-killer more than life itself, and life was to her a long perspective of brightness. She would lightly tread the journey of existence by his side, and when wearied with the joys of this world, they would together travel the road that leads to the Heaven of the Dahcotahs.

She sat dreaming of the future after the Deer-killer had left her, nor knew of her parents' return until she heard her mother's sharp voice as she asked her "if the corn would boil when the fire was out, and where was the bread that she was told to have ready on their return?"

Bread and corn! When Wanska had forgot all but that she was beloved. She arose quickly, and her light laugh drowned her mother's scolding. Soon her good humor was infectious, for her mother told her that she had needles and thread in plenty, besides more flour and sugar, and that her father was going out early in the morning to kill more game for the Long Knives who loved it so well.

CHAPTER II

A FEW MONTHS ago, the Deer-killer had told Wenona that Wanska was noisy and tiresome, and that her soft dark eyes were far more beautiful than Wanska's laughing ones. They were not at home then, for Wenona had accompanied her parents on a visit to some relations who lived far above the village of Shah-co-pee.

While there the Deer-killer came in with some warriors who had been on a war party; there Wenona was assured that her rival, the Merry Heart, was forgotten.

And well might the Deer-killer and Wenona have loved each other. "Youth turns to youth as the flower to the sun," and he was brave and noble in his pride and power; and she, gentle and loving, though an Indian woman; so quiet too, and all unlike Wanska, who was the noisiest little gossip in the village.

Often they had wandered together through the "solemn temples of the earth," nor did she ever fear, with the warrior child for a protector. She had followed him when he ascended the cliffs where the tracks of the eagle were seen; and with him she felt safe when the wind was tossing their canoe on the Mississippi, when the storm spirits had arisen in their power. They were still children when Wenona would know his step among many others, but they were no longer children when Wenona left Shah-co-pee's village, for she loved with a woman's devotion—and more than loved. She had trembled when she saw the Deer-killer watch Wanska as she tripped merrily about the village. Sleeping or waking, his image was ever before her; he was the idol to which her spirit bowed, the sun of her little world.

The dance to the giant was to be celebrated at the village where they were visiting; the father of Wenona and "Old John" the medicine man, were to join in it. The maiden had been nothing loth to undertake the journey, for the Deer-killer had gone on a war party against the Chippeways, and she thought that in the course of their journey they might meet him—and when away from Wanska, he would return to her side. He could not despise the love she had given him. Hope, that bright star of youth, hovered over her, and its light was reflected on her heart.

When they arrived at the village of the chief Markeda, or "Burning Earth," the haughty brow of the chief was subdued with care. He had dreamed of Haokah the giant, and he knew there was sorrow or danger threatening him. He had sinned against the giant, and what might be the consequence of offending him? Was his powerful arm to be laid low, and the strong pulse to cease its beatings? Did his dream portend the loss of his young wife? She was almost as dear to him as the fleet hunter that bore him to the chase.

It might be that the angry god would send their enemies among them, and his tall sons would gladden his sight no more. Sickness and hunger, phantom-like, haunted his waking and sleeping hours.

There was one hope; he might yet ward off the danger, for the uplifted arm of the god had not fallen. He hoped to appease the anger of the giant by dancing in his honor.

"We have travelled far," said old John the medicine man, to Markeda, "and are tired. When we have slept we will dance with you, for we are of the giant's party."

"Great is Haokah, the giant of the Dahcotahs," the chief replied; "it is a long time since we have danced to him."

"I had been hunting with my warriors, we chased the buffalo, and our arrows pierced their sides; they turned upon us, bellowing, their heads beating the ground; their terrible eyes glared upon us even in death; they rolled in the dust, for their strength was gone. We brought them to the village for our women to prepare for us when we should need them. I had eaten and was refreshed; and, tired as my limbs were, I could not sleep at first, but at last the fire grew dim before my eyes, and I slept.

"I stood on the prairie alone, in my dream, and the giant appeared before me. So tall was he that the clouds seemed to float about his head. I trembled at the sound of his voice, it was as if the angry winds were loosed upon the earth.

"'The warriors of the Dahcotahs are turned women,' said he; 'that they no longer dance in honor of the giant, nor sing his songs. Markeda is not a coward, but let him tremble; he is not a child, but he may shed tears if the anger of the giant comes upon him.'

"Glad was I when I woke from my dream—and now, lest I am punished for my sins, I will make a sacrifice to the giant. Should I not fear him who is so powerful? Can he not take the thunder in his hand and cast it to the earth?

"The heart of the warrior should be brave when he dances to the giant. My wigwam is ready, and the friends of the giant are ready also."

"Give me your mocassins," said the young wife of Markeda to old John; "they are torn, and I will mend them. You have come from afar, and are welcome. Sleep, and when you awake, you will find them beside you." As she assisted him to take them off, the medicine man looked admiringly into her face. "The young wife of Markeda is as beautiful as the white flowers that spring up on the prairies. Her husband would mourn for her if the giant should close her eyes. They are bright now, as the stars, but death would dim them, should not the anger of the giant be appeased."

The "Bounding Fawn" turned pale at the mention of the angry giant; she sat down, without replying, to her work; wondering the while, if the soul of her early love thought of her, now that it wandered in the Spirit's land. It might be that he would love her again when they should meet there. The sound of her child's voice awakening out of sleep, aroused her, and called to her mind who was its father.

"They tore me away from my lover, and made me come to the teepee of the chief," was her bitter reflection. "Enah! that I cannot love the father of my child."

She rose and left the teepee. "Where is the heaven of the Dahcotahs," she murmured, as she looked up to the silent stars. "It may be that I shall see him again. He will love my child too, and I will forget the many tears I have shed."

CHAPTER III

THE DANCE to the Giant is always performed inside the wigwam. Early in the morning the dancers were assembled in the chief's lodge. Their dress was such as is appointed for the occasion. Their hats were made of the bark of trees, such as tradition says the Giant wears. They were large, and made forked like the lightning. Their leggins were made of skins. Their ear-rings were of the bark of trees, and were about one foot long.

The chief rose ere the dawn of day, and stood before the fire. As the flames flickered, and the shadows of the dancers played fantastically about the wigwam, they looked more like Lucifer and a party of attendant spirits, than like human beings worshipping their God.

Markeda stood by the fire without noticing his guests, who awaited his motions in silence. At last, moving slowly, he placed a kettle of water on the fire, and then threw into it a large piece of buffalo meat.

Lighting his pipe, he seated himself, and then the dancers advanced to the fire and lit theirs; and soon they were enveloped in a cloud of smoke.

When the water began to boil, the Indians arose, and, dancing round the fire, imitated the voice of the Giant.

"Hah-hah! hah hah!" they sung, and each endeavored to drown the voice of the other. Now they crouch as they dance, looking diminutive and contemptible, as those who are degrading themselves in their most sacred duties. Then they rise up, and show their full height. Stalwart warriors as they are, their keen eyes flash as they glance from the fire to each other's faces, distorted with the effort of uttering such discordant sounds. Now their broad chests heave with the exertion, and their breath comes quickly.

They seat themselves, to rest and smoke. Again the hellish sounds are heard, and the wife of the chief trembles for fear of the Giant, and her child clings closer to her breast. The water boils, and, hissing, falls over into the fire, the flames are darkened for a moment, and then burst up brighter than before.

Markeda addresses the dancers—"Warriors! the Giant is powerful—the water which boils before us will be cold when touched by a friend of the Giant. Haokah will not that his friends should suffer when offering him a sacrifice."

The warriors then advanced together, and each one puts his hand into the kettle and takes the meat from the boiling water; and although suffering from the scalds produced, yet their calmness in enduring the pain, would induce the belief that the water really felt to them cool and pleasant.

The meat is then taken out, and put into a wooden dish, and the water left boiling on the fire. The dancers eat the meat while hot, and again they arrange themselves to dance. And now, the mighty power of the Giant is shown, for Markeda advances to the kettle, and taking some water out of it he throws it upon his bare back, singing all the while, "The water is cold."

"Old John" advances and does the same, followed by the next in turn, until the water is exhausted from the kettle, and then the warriors exclaim, "How great is the power of Haokah! We have thrown boiling water upon ourselves and we have not been scalded."

The dance is over—the sacrifice is made. Markeda seeks his young wife and fears not. He had fancied that her cheeks were pale of late, but now they are flushed brilliantly, his heart is at rest.

The warriors disperse, all but the medicine man, and the chief's store of buffalo meat diminishes rapidly under the magic touch of the epicure.

Yes! and epicure thou wert old John! For I mind me well when thou camest at dinner time, and how thou saidst thou couldst eat the food of the Indian when thou wert hungry, but the food of the white man was better far. And thou! A Dahcotah warrior, a famous hunter, and a medicine man. Shame! That thou shouldst have loved venison dressed with wine more than when the tender meat was cooked according to the taste of the women of thy nation. I have forgotten thy Indian name, renegade as thou wert! but thou answerest as well to "old John!"

Thou art now forgotten clay, though strong and vigorous when in wisdom the Sioux were punished for a fault they did not commit. Their money was not paid them—their provisions were withheld. Many were laid low, and thou hast found before now that God is the Great Spirit, and the Giant Haokah is not.

And it may be that thou wouldst fain have those thou has left on earth know of His power, who is above all spirits, and of His goodness who would have all come unto Him.

CHAPTER IV

WENONA HAD not hoped in vain, for her lover was with her, and Wanska seemed to be forgotten. The warrior's flute would draw her out from her uncle's lodge while the moon rose o'er the cold waters. Wrapped in her blanket, she would hasten to meet him, and listen to his assurances of affection, wondering the while that she had ever feared he loved another.

She had been some months at the village of Markeda, and she went to meet her lover with a heavy heart. Her mother had noticed that her looks were sad and heavy, and Wenona knew that it would not be long ere she should be a happy wife, or a mark for the bitter scorn of her companions.

The Deer-killer had promised, day after day, that he would make her his wife, but he ever found a ready excuse; and now he was going on a long hunt, and she and her parents were to return to their village. His quiver was full of arrows, and his leggins were tightly girded upon him. Wenona's full heart was nigh bursting as she heard that the party were to leave to-morrow. Should he desert her, her parents would kill her for disgracing them; and her rival, Wanska, how would she triumph over her fall?

"You say that you love me," said she to the Deer-killer, "and yet you treat me cruelly. Why should you leave me without saying that I am your wife? Who would watch for your coming as I would? and you will disgrace me when I have loved you so truly. Stay—tell them you have made me your wife, and then will I wait for you at the door of my teepee."

The warrior could not stay from the chase, but he promised her that he would soon return to their village, and then she would be his wife.

Wenona wept when he left her; shadows had fallen upon her heart, and yet she hoped on. Turning her weary steps homeward, she arrived when the maidens of the village were preparing to celebrate the Virgin's Feast.

There was no time to deliberate—should she absent herself, she would be suspected, and yet a little while ere the Deer-killer would return, and her anxious heart would be at rest.

The feast was prepared, and the crier called for all virgins to enter the sacred ring.

Wenona went forward with a beating heart; she was not a wife, and soon must be a mother. Wanska, the Merry Heart, was there, and many others who wondered at the pale looks of Wenona—she who had been on a journey, and who ought to have returned with color bright as the dying sun, whose light illuminated earth, sky and water.

As they entered the ring a party of warriors approached the circle. Wenona does not look towards them, and yet the throbbings of her heart were not to be endured. Her trembling limbs refused to sustain her, as the Deer-killer, stalking towards the ring, calls aloud—"Take her from the sacred feast; should she eat with the maidens?—she, under whose bosom lies a warrior's child? She is unworthy."

And as the unhappy girl, with features of stone and glaring eyes, gazed upon him bewildered, he rudely led her from the ring.

Wenona bowed her head and went—even as night came on when the sun went down. Nor did the heart of the Deer-killer reproach him, for how dare she offend the Great Spirit! Were not the customs of his race holy and sacred?

Little to Wenona were her father's reproaches, or her mother's curse; that she was no more beloved was all she remembered.

Again was the Deer-killer by the side of Wanska, and she paid the penalty. Her husband brought other wives to his wigwam, though Wanska was ever the favorite one.

With her own hand would she put the others out of the wigwam, laughing when they threatened to tell their lord when he returned, for Wanska managed to tell her own story first, and, termagant as she was, she always had her own way.

Wenona has ceased to weep, and far away in the country of the Sissetons she toils and watches as all Indian women toil and watch. Her young son follows her as she seeks the suffering Dahcotah, and charms the disease to leave his feeble frame.

She tells to the child and the aged woman her dreams; she warns the warrior what he shall meet with when he goes to battle; and ever, as the young girls assemble to pass away the idle hours, she stops and whispers to them.

In vain do they ask of her husband: she only points to her son and says, "My hair, which is now like snow, was once black and braided like his, and my eyes as bright. They have wept until tears come no more. Listen not to the warrior who says he loves." And she passes from their sight as the morning mists.

U-MI-NE-WAH-CHIPPE;

OR,

TO DANCE AROUND

Medicine Dance of the Sioux, watercolor on paper, 1847.

I HAVE NOTICED the many singular notions of the Sioux concerning thunder, and especially the fact that they believe it to be a large bird. This figure is often seen worked with porcupine quills on their ornaments. Ke-on means to fly. Thunder is called Wah-ke-on or All-flier. U-mi-ne-wah-chippe is a dance given by some one who fears thunder and thus endeavors to propitiate the god and save his own life.

A ring is made, of about sixty feet in circumference, by sticking saplings in the ground, and bending their tops down, fastening them together. In the centre of this ring a pole is placed. The pole is about fifteen feet in height and painted red. From this swings a piece of birch bark, cut so as to represent thunder. At the foot of the pole stand two boys and two girls.

The two boys represent war: they are painted red, and hold war-clubs in their hands. The girls have their faces painted with blue clay: they represent peace.

On one side of the circle a kind of booth is erected, and about twenty feet from it a wigwam. There are four entrances to this circle.

When all the arrangements for the dance are concluded, the man who gives the dance emerges from his wigwam dressed up as hideously as possible, crawling on all fours towards the booth. He must sing four tunes before reaching it.

In the meantime the medicine men, who are seated in the wigwam, beat time on the drum, and the young men and squaws keep time to the music by first hopping on one foot, and then on the other—moving around inside the ring as fast as they can. This is continued for about five minutes, until the music stops. After resting a few moments, the second tune commences, and lasts the same length of time, then the third, and the fourth; the Indian meanwhile making his way towards the booth. At the end of each tune, a whoop is raised by the men dancers.

After the Indian has reached his booth inside the ring, he must sing four more tunes as before. At the end of the fourth tune the squaws all run out of the ring as fast as possible, and must leave by the same way that they entered, the other three entrances being reserved for the men, who, carrying their war implements, might be accidentally touched by one of the squaws—and the war implements of the Sioux warrior have from time immemorial been held sacred from the touch of woman. For the same reason the men form the inner ring in dancing round the pole, their war implements being placed at the foot of the pole.

When the last tune is ended, the young men shoot at the image of thunder which is hanging to the pole, and when it falls a general rush is made by the warriors to get hold of it. There is placed at the foot of the pole a bowl of water colored with blue clay. While the men are trying to seize the parts of the bark representation of their god, they at the same time are eagerly endeavoring to drink the water in the bowl, every drop of which must be drank.

The warriors then seize on the two boys and girls—the representations of war and peace—and use them as roughly as possible—taking their pipes and war-clubs from them, and rolling them in the dirt until the paint is entirely rubbed off from their faces. Much as they dislike this part of the dance, they submit to it through fear, believing that after this performance the power of thunder is destroyed.

Now that the water is drank up and the guardians of the Thunder bird are deprived of their war-clubs and pipes, a terrible wailing commences. No description could convey an idea of the noise made by their crying and lamentation. All join in, exerting to the utmost the strength of their lungs.

Before the men shoot at thunder, the squaws must leave the ring. No one sings at this dance but the warrior who gives it; and while the visitors, the dancers, and the medicine men, women and children, all are arrayed in their gayest clothing, the host must be dressed in his meanest.

In the dance Ahahkah Koyah, or to make the Elk a figure of thunder, is also made and fought against. The Sioux have a great deference for the majesty of thunder, and, consequently for their own skill in prevailing or seeming to prevail against it.

A Sioux is always alarmed after dreaming of an elk, and soon prevails upon some of his friends to assist him in dancing, to prevent any evil consequences resulting from his dream. Those willing to join in must lay aside all clothing, painting their bodies with a reddish gray color, like the elk's. Each Indian must procure two long saplings, leaving the boughs upon them. These are to aid the Indians in running. The saplings must be about twelve feet in length. With them they tear down the bark image of thunder, which is hung with a string to the top of the pole.

All being ready, the elks run off at a gallop, assisted by their saplings, to within about two hundred yards of the pole, when they stop for a while, and then start again for the pole, to which is attached the figure of thunder.

They continue running round and round this pole, constantly striking the figure of thunder with their saplings, endeavoring to knock it down, which after a while they succeed in accomplishing.

The ceremony is now ended, and the dreamer has nothing to fear from elks until he dreams again.

There is no end to the superstitions and fancies entertained by the Sioux concerning thunder. On the cradle of the Indian child we frequently see the figure of thunder represented. It is generally carved on the wood by the father of the child, with representations of the Elk, accompanied with hieroglyphic looking figures, but thunder is regarded as the type of all animals that fly.

There are many medicine feasts—and I saw one celebrated near the Oak Grove mission, and near, also, to the villages of Good Road, and the chief Man in the Clouds. It was on a dark cold day about the first of March. We left the fort at about nine o'clock and followed the road on the St. Peter's river, which had been used for many months, but which, though still strong, was beginning to look unsafe. As we advanced towards the scene of the feast, many Indians from every direction were collecting, and hurrying forward, either to join in the ceremony about to be celebrated, or to be spectators. We ascended quite a high hill, and were then at the spot where all the arrangements were made to celebrate one of the most sacred forms of their religion. Many of the Indians to be engaged in the performance were entirely without protection from the severe cold—their bodies being painted and their heads adorned with their choicest ornaments, but throwing aside even their blankets, according to the laws of the ceremony. The Indians continued to assemble. At eleven o'clock, the dance commenced. Although I could not faithfully describe, yet I never can forget the scene. The dark lowering sky—the mantle of snow and ice thrown over all the objects that surrounded us, except the fierce human beings who were thus, under Heaven's arch for a roof, about to offer to their deities a solemn worship.

Then the music commenced, and the horrid sounds increased the wildness of the scene; and the contortions of the medicine man, as he went round and round, made his countenance horrible beyond expression. The devoted attention of the savages, given to every part of the ceremony, made it in a measure interesting. There were hundreds of human beings believing in a Great Spirit, and anxious to offer him acceptable service; but how degraded in that service! How fallen from its high estate was the soul that God had made, when it stooped to worship the bones of animals, the senseless rock, the very earth that we stood upon! The aged man, trembling with feebleness, ready to depart to the spirit's land, weary with the weight of his infirmities—

the warrior treading the earth with the pride of middle age—the young with nothing to regret and everything to look forward to,—all uniting in a worship which they ignorantly believe to be religion, but which we know to be idolatry.

I was glad to leave the scene, and turn towards the house of the Rev. Mr. Pond, who lives near the spot where the feast was celebrated. Here, pursuing his duties and studies, does this excellent man improve every moment of his time to the advantage of the Sioux. Always ready to converse kindly with them in order to gain their confidence—giving medicine to the sick, and food to the hungry; doing all that lies in his power to administer to their temporal comfort, he labors to improve their condition as a people. How can it better be done than by introducing the Christian religion among them? This the missionaries are gradually doing; and did they receive proper assistance from government, and from religious societies, they would indeed go on their way rejoicing.

Placed under the government of the United States, these helpless, unhappy beings are dependent upon us for the means of subsistence, in a measure, and how much more for the knowledge of the true God? Churches will soon rise where the odious feast and medicine dance are celebrated, but will the Indians worship there? When the foundations of these churches are laid, the bones of the original owners of the country will be thrown out—but where will be the souls of those who were thrust out of their country and their rights to make way for us?

I have seen where literally two or three were met together—where in a distant country the few who celebrated the death of the Redeemer were assembled—where the beautiful service of our church was read, and the hearts that heard it responded to its animating truths. We rejoiced that the religion which was our comfort was not confined to places; here were no altars, nor marble tablets—but here in this humble house we knew God would meet and be with us.

An Indian silently opened the church door and entered. As strange to him was the solemn decorum of this scene, as to us were the useless ceremonies we every day witnessed. He watched the countenance of the clergyman, but he knew not that he was preaching the doctrine of a universal religion. He saw the sacred book upon the desk, but he could not read the glorious doctrine of a world redeemed by a Saviour's blood. He heard the